DOMITILA BARRIOS DE CHUNGARA (1937–2013) is the daughter of a mine worker and lived most of her life in a tin mining camp in the Bolivian highlands. In 1975 Domitila was invited to testify at the first United Nations Conference on Women, Development, and Peace, where she met Moema Viezzer, who helped her to write and publish her life story. *Let Me Speak!* has been translated into fourteen languages.

MOEMA VIEZZER is a Brazilian sociologist and popular educator who has dedicated her life to women's causes and environmental issues. Viezzer continues to fight for the international recognition and application of the Declaration of the Rights of the Mother Earth—*Pachamama*—with an emphasis on the rights of water. She is the author of eight books.

Let Me Speak!

Testimony of Domitila,
A Woman of the Bolivian Mines

DOMITILA BARRIOS DE CHUNGARA
with MOEMA VIEZZER

Translated by Victoria Ortiz

MONTHLY REVIEW PRESS
New York

Library of Congress Cataloging-in-Publication Data
available from the publisher

ISBN (paper) 978-168590-050-2
ISBN (cloth) 978-168590-051-9

Typeset in Minion Pro

MONTHLY REVIEW PRESS, NEW YORK
monthlyreview.org

5 4 3 2 1

Contents

Foreword to the Argentine Edition

By Álvaro García Linera

Let Me Speak! (Si me permiten hablar) is Bolivia's most ubiquitous and well-known book. It has been translated into more than fourteen languages, and thousands of copies can be found all around the country. For many people, Domitila and *Let Me Speak!* were even better known than Bolivia itself. Curiously, despite being the best-known Bolivian text, until now no one had published the book in Bolivia. There were, of course, photocopies and pirated editions, but never a Bolivian edition per se. Now, for the first time, CIS[1] is publishing a Bolivian edition of *Let Me Speak!*, in recognition of its being one of the most universally acclaimed texts on the struggles of the Bolivian people.

There are various ways of studying a country's history. One is the classic method from the nineteenth century, which some still employ, of studying the country based on the presidents and their names, with their photos and medals, and their biographies. This method reduces the country to the will of one person. A second way to relate a country's history is through its institutions: its laws, ministries, and the decisions of its government. This is more of a twentieth-century method, often associated with liberal perspectives. Yet there is another, alternative way of studying history that is based on the people: on what simple, poor, and hardworking people think and do. In effect, *Let Me Speak!* is that type of history. It is not just Domitila's story: it is the story of Bolivia. It is the history of Bolivia told by a woman of the people, the daughter of a worker, a mine worker's wife, who is herself a worker. Domitila's story embodies the story of thousands or rather millions of Bolivians who built Bolivia between the 1950s and the 2000s.

Do you want to know about Bolivia's history? Then read Domitila. The history of Bolivia cannot be known by recalling its presidents. That's a paltry view of history. A country is known through its people: those who generate its wealth, those who care for the children, those who produce food, those who struggle and die, and those no one even remembers. They may not appear on the front pages of the newspapers, but they form the real fabric of our society. *Let Me Speak!* is the history of the Bolivian people, of the working class, of the labor movement.

You can read union organizer Guillermo Lora's books about the history of the labor movement, which is an amazing story.[2] In those books, you can read the documents that were debated among the political parties. But what about the lives of the workers? How did they cook, come together, raise children, struggle, take care of their wounded, and bury their dead? How was all that done? It's not to be found in those texts. Nor is it to be found in the Central Obrera Boliviana's socialist thesis[3] or the documents of the Miners' Federation. Rather, it is to be found here, in this alternative kind of story. So, this is a different way of approaching a country's history, based on the daily lives of ordinary people.

People who want to know what Bolivia was like in the '50s, '60s, '70s, up through the '80s, should read *Let Me Speak!* If you want to investigate what the working class was like, the working class that shaped Bolivia's history during those years and functioned as a vanguard that united the country, then you can find that story in those political documents. However, the *daily life* of the working class is to be found here in this testimony by Domitila Barrios de Chungara.

And what about the very interesting relationship between class and gender. Does one belong to a class or a gender? Is class struggle different from struggle from the standpoint of gender identity? In Domitila, you can see both things simultaneously: gender identity as a form in which class struggle takes place and also see social classes, their existence and the way they are constructed, occurring through practices and languages of gender. Here you see how women come together in self-defense against the government, repression, and injustice. But you also see how there is a struggle within the struggle: women organizing themselves so that men do not subordinate them, and their voices are taken into account. It is not something simple. Men do not accept this change easily. In Domitila's story, one can see how the labor struggle is beginning to learn from, draw on, and gradually incorporate the demands of women's struggles which, although complementary, are not always the same as men's demands. Their demands were slowly brought into the trade unions, which had an eminently masculine composition at that time. Today, the composition of the working class has changed remarkably: 48 percent of the Bolivian working class are women. In Domitila's time, it was not that way. Those in the role of being a worker, laborers, were 80 to 90 percent men and only 20 percent women, who were highly marginalized and underrecognized. Inside this working class, however, there were other kinds of organizations that were being organized and led by women, organizations such as the Housewives' Committee.

In addition to telling the history of the working class, the history of nation-building, and the history of Bolivia, *Let Me Speak!* is also a story about the construction of democracy. Today there are terrible people who might constantly talk about democracy but were delighted when miners died or when Alteños were killed.[4] These people were happily drinking their coffee, while they watched on television how Indigenous people and workers were killed. Now, however, these people like to babble about democracy and the rule of law, despite their never having done anything in the fight for the rule of law or democracy. Domitila's book serves as an example, a living testimony, of what it means to fight for democracy; that is, democracy not only as the right to vote every five years, but also the right to associate, to think, to organize, and discuss fundamental issues, such as salary, rights, constitutional guarantees, and party politics, in one's community. This is democracy as a continuous and daily affair, an everyday practice that, much more than the law, much more than the constitutional order, much more than elections, is the ability to intervene in public matters.

Let Me Speak! is also a text of political theory, because you learn here how the miners and workers built democracy, how they were able to fight so that the right to assemble, think, participate, and make decisions would extend to all Bolivians universally. This includes the democracy we enjoy today that allows us to meet here knowing that at the exit to COMIBOL,[5] there are no armored cars waiting to take us somewhere where they'll beat us up. That freedom, which we take for granted today, like breathing air, was not easy to build. It was the workers, hardworking workers, and wives of workers like Domitila who did it. The new generations enjoy all this, but there was a high price paid for it. And it's important to come back to that. It is important to return to the organizational and social wellsprings of democracy and how democracy is constructed.

Today people are talking about dictatorship. So, to illustrate what the term means, I will read a paragraph of Let Me Speak! It is the year 1967. . . at the Siglo XX mine. . . . Che's guerrillas are in Bolivia. The Siglo XX mine was the Leningrad of Latin America. . . . The miners lived there, in their little houses made of corrugated tin, with one room or at most two rooms . . . and ten, twelve people per house. Whoever has been to the Siglo XX-Catavi mining complex or to the Caracoles or Central Sud mines knows what the wind and the cold are, the houses there being made of corrugated tin so that the cold doesn't creep inside. That's where the miners lived.

At this point in the book, Domitila is accused of having ties to the guerrillas—which she would later have, in the 1970s, but not in the 1960s. The San Juan Massacre has taken place, dozens of miners have been arrested, men and children murdered. They arrest Domitila. She is pregnant, and they want to make her talk. Look at what Moema Viezzer—who redacted the text but keeps herself in the background—recounts with her skillful pen.

You also deserve to be learned from, Moema, with your ability to write, collect, and organize material; not to speak for others, but so that others can speak for themselves. For the younger generation who wants to work with the people, there is a lesson to be learned in how your talent as an intellectual connects with the creative and intellectual capacity of workers. You also have the humility and commitment to place yourself behind and not in front of these workers, so that for example it is Domitila who speaks, not you.

I will read another section of the text to encourage you to read *Let Me Speak!* Here Domitila has been arrested, and they are interrogating her:

"Where did you put the money? God dammit! Where did you put it?" the guy shouted [he was an officer]. And he hit me. He hit me very hard, and me in my eighth month. . . .

The young soldier who was next to me with his submachine gun looked shocked at how bad that guy was hitting me. And the guy said to him that one shouldn't have pity on these heretics, these communists who have no morals, who are worse than beasts. . . . And he went on hitting me without letup.

I defended myself as much as I could. And the more I defended myself, the more the guy got infuriated, because he was also a little drunk, see, and he hit me all the harder.

At one point, he put his knee here, on my stomach. He pressed on my throat and was about to strangle me. I shouted and shouted. . . . It was like he wanted to make my stomach burst open. . . . I realized that he was pressing more and more, I was having trouble breathing. So then, with both my hands, with all my strength, I pulled his hands down. And I don't remember how, but I grabbed him by his wrist, and I bit him over and over again. . . . I was so furious and so nervous that I didn't realize I'd been biting his hand, see. Really, I didn't realize it. I was so desperate!

Then suddenly I tasted a warm and salty liquid in my mouth.... I let go of his hand and I saw it: there was flesh hanging from his hand, ripped off, like that. I felt a terrible nausea on tasting his blood in my mouth. . . . Then, with all my anger . . . tcha! . . . I spat his blood all over his face.

Well, that was the end of me. The end!

"Huah!" shouted the guy. A terrible screeching began. He began kicking me . . . he shouted. . . . He called the soldiers and made four of them grab me. He had on one of those big, square rings. I don't know what he did with his hand, but he tightened and tightened it, making me really scream loud. And as I screamed, he punched all over my face. And I don't remember anything else. . . . The only thing I do remember is that I felt as if something in my head had burst open.... I saw something like fire falling all around me. Nothing else.

When I woke up like from a dream, I'd been swallowing a piece of my tooth. I felt it stick here in my throat. Then I noticed that the guy had broken six of my teeth. Blood was gushing out of me and I couldn't open my eyes or breath through my nose. My eyes were swollen closed.

The story continues two pages later. The man exits the prison cell, leaving Domitila alone in the room.

And, as if fate had a hand in it, I began to go into labor. I began feeling pains, pains, and more pains. And at times the baby to be born got the better of me. I was so nervous. . . . I heard the young soldier's footsteps . . . and I tried to hold back. I didn't want it to be born! And I said to myself: "If it's born, let it be born dead. I

don't want the colonel to kill it! Don't let my baby be born alive!"
Really, I lived through a terrible odyssey. The head was about to
come out and I pushed it back in. It was a terrible moment.

Finally, I couldn't stand any more. And I went to kneel in a
corner. I leaned against a wall and covered my face, because I
couldn't even make the slightest effort. My face hurt so much it
seemed like it would burst. And in one of those moments, I gave
in. I don't remember if my baby was born alive or if it was born
dead . . . I don't know anything. The only thing I remember is
that I knelt there and covered my face because I couldn't stand
anymore. It got the better of me, it really did. I noticed that the
head was already coming out . . . and right at that moment I
fainted.

After who knows how long, I seemed to be waking up from
a dream and seemed to be in bed. And I tried to cover myself.
I wanted to feel my feet, move them, but I couldn't feel them. It
seemed like I didn't have feet . . . it seemed like I only had one
arm, because I couldn't feel the other one. And I tried to cover
myself . . . and there weren't any blankets.

"Where am I, where am I?"

I tried to think clearly and I heard the soldier's footsteps,
click, click, click. Then I realized: "Oh, yes, I'm in jail. What's
happened? What's happened?

I remembered a few things and I thought:

"Where is the baby?"

I tried to sit up. But my whole body was numb, I was freezing
right there on the floor. I was soaking wet. It was blood and the
liquid you lose during childbirth that had wet me all over. Even
my hair was wet with water and blood.

Then I made an effort and found the baby's cord. And along
the cord, stretching it out, I found the little baby . . . completely
cold, freezing, there on the floor.

I don't know now. Did the baby die inside of me? Did it die
after being born, because no one helped it? I don't know.

It's very painful to lose a child that way.

This is Domitila's story. It's the story of hundreds of women who experienced similar situations.

That's what a dictatorship is like. That you get beat up when you're pregnant. That your child is made to die. That you want your child to die so that the person who is torturing you does not kill them.

It is important that the youth be aware of this. I am referring to the new generation that doesn't know what the dictatorship was like, that doesn't know about the Bolivian working class, and doesn't know what other generations did so that today one can enjoy freedom, and so that today they can have Internet and WhatsApp.

That's all to be found in Domitila. That's why reading Domitila is reading about who we are. It is not reading the history of a distant country or of some far away moment in time. No, it is the story of what led to our present moment. It's also a story we don't have to repeat. We should remember that, thanks to women like Domitila, we can live and go forward in peace today. Thanks to women like Domitila and the social class she represents, today we can read and write without being afraid of being beaten up, disappeared, exiled, killed, or buried.

So this is the history of Bolivia, the real one, the true one, the authentic one—history as it was made by its peoples. It is a story that we have to continue to defend as our own, because what the future brings for Bolivia cannot be the return of the privileged elites, or the story of a few saviors. It has to continue being the story of the people—of ordinary and working people—like Domitila.

Moema, I want to thank you for being with us. I want to thank you for creating this work of art, that is also a work of history, literature, knowledge, and political engagement. I wish there were more Moemas in the world, because I am sure that if there were more writers like her, capable of interacting with the people and telling their true history, the world would be very different.

Please read the book.

Notes

These comments were made in El Alto on November 24, 2018, by Álvaro García Linera, then Vice President of Bolivia, at the headquarters of the state-owned mining company COMIBOL, at an event with Moema Viezzer in which the Bolivian edition of Let Me Speak! *was launched as one of the titles in the Biblioteca Bicentenaria de Bolivia-BBB.*

1. The Centro de Investigaciones Sociales (Center for Social Research, CIS) is a department of the Vice Presidency of the Bolivian State. It is dedicated to research in the social and human sciences that contributes to the strengthening of the Bolivian state. CIS edits and publishes the Bicentennial Library of Bolivia (BBB, for its Spanish-language initials), the largest and most important editorial project in Bolivian history. The second Bolivian edition of *Let Me Speak!* is part of this collection.

2. Guillermo Lora Escobar wrote the *Historia del movimiento obrero boliviano* (History of the Bolivian Labor Movement), which is generally divided into six volumes, and began to be published in 1966 by Los Amigos del Libro. It is the most important work of Lora (1921–2009), a renowned Bolivian historian and Trotskyist leader of the Partido Obrero Revolucionario (Revolutionary Workers' Party). In 1946, the miners approved his *Thesis of Pulacayo* during a special congress in the mining town of that name which brought together representatives from the forty-four most important miners' unions in Bolivia. The *Thesis of Pulacayo* is considered the main ideological document of the Bolivian labor movement, a kind of "bible" of Bolivian trade unionism, and it constitutes the political and programmatic manifesto of the Federation of Mining Workers of Bolivia (FSTMB). Lora never claimed to be its author, always stating that he merely transcribed what the workers had dictated to him.

3. The Central Obrera Boliviana (Bolivian Workers' Union, COB) was founded on April 17, 1952, in the midst of the National Revolution that began on April 9 of that year. It is Bolivia's chief trade union federation, with a long tradition of struggle. The COB's *Socialist Thesis*, approved in May of 1973, follows on the *Thesis of Pulacayo* (see note 2), updating it both in relation to the political moment and based on the lessons learned since the National Revolution. Section 1.7 reads: "Our goal is socialism, and our method to achieve this historical project is the social revolution that will allow us to transform the nationalist process into a socialist one."

4. Alteños are people from the largely Indigenous city of El Alto. The Bolivian Gas War occurred in September and October of 2003. It consisted of a series of conflicts about the potential export of Bolivian natural gas to the United States and Mexico through Chile. President

Gonzalo Sánchez de Lozada deployed the armed forces, who were already prepared to intervene according to his "Plan República." El Alto was one of the cities occupied by the military, leading to over 60 deaths in what was called the October Massacre. The October Massacre precipitated Sánchez de Lozada's resignation and flight from the country, and it initiated a process that culminated in the election of the Movement for Socialism's candidates Evo Morales and Álvaro García Linera in December 2005. The slogan "El Alto de pie, nunca de rodillas" (El Alto upright, never on its knees) was born in this conflict.

5.   The Bolivian State Mining Corporation COMIBOL was set up on Octuber 2, 1952, during the National Revolution, to manage the mines that had formerly belonged to the "Tin Barons," Patiño, Hochschild, and Aramayo. As indicated by Supreme Decree No. 31196, COMIBOL oversees the state mining industry and does the "exploration, prospecting, exploiting, use, and sale of the major mineral deposits under that nation's subsoil, in accordance with a rational overall technical plan."

Preface to the 15th Brazilian Edition

By Moema Viezzer

Domitila Barrios de Chungara's testimony *Let Me Speak!* was published for the first time in 1977. The book spread rapidly throughout the world and had an impact on millions of people from different classes and social strata. The narration's spontaneity and its depth, along with the protagonist's commitment, has allowed her message to go beyond the narrow confines of any particular time or space.

Domitila is known internationally for her tireless promotion of human rights in the course of Bolivia's recent history, and she is one of the most celebrated working-class women worldwide. Twenty-five years after her story was first published, it continues to generate interest in the reading public and has led many readers to wonder: Where is Domitila? How is she? What is she doing? These questions, together with the book's success—as published in 15 languages and 70 editions—and above all the fact that Domitila continues to be active, inspired my decision to amplify *Let Me Speak!*, republishing what has become a Latin American classic.

In 2002, I returned to Bolivia to interview Domitila. The country was in the midst of an electoral process, and its streets were full of political propaganda. Domitila had just participated in a press conference about the significance of the elections in the context of Bolivia's twenty-year-old formal democracy.

The hours I spent with her, in the modest house she now lives in on Derechos Humanos Street in the Wayra Q'asa neighborhood of Cochabamba, were intense. The time involved exchanging information and feelings; recording new personal interviews and public talks; and my taking part in an *ayni,* a community meeting with new leaders in training, which usually takes place on Sundays in the courtyard of her house.

Additionally, we went through the copious documentation stored in the classroom of the Domitila Mobile School: photographs, video documentaries, tapes, awards, and books. There were also newspaper and magazine articles in Spanish, English, French, German, and Swedish that Domitila had collected in the countries she traveled in, and which served to complement the contents of her travel notebooks. Finally, I acquired the additional information I needed by going to various places in Cochabamba and La Paz, visiting institutions, talking to people who knew Domitila at some point in her career, and looking for texts dealing with her life in the years since the book's original publication.

The two encounters between us occurred in very different contexts. In 1975, Bolivia was internationally known as a tin producer due to its mining operations, located mainly in the Altiplano region. At that time, Bolivia's working class was also nationally and internationally recognized for its strength, cohesion, and impact on society and politics. The Federation of Bolivian Mine Workers (FSTMB) was the backbone of the Bolivian Workers Union (COB). At that time, Domitila was a woman from the Bolivian mines, a miner's wife, and the mother of seven children who were still minors and living with her in the Siglo XX-Catavi mining camp. She was a strong forty-year-old who shone as a representative of her organization, the Housewives' Committee, and her reflections and analyses centered on the lifeworld of a miner's wife at a state-owned mine.

In 2002, Bolivia was expanding into the Amazon area in the Beni and Santa Cruz departments and the Chapare region, where natural resources, notably gas and oil, had newly been discovered. This period also saw increases in coca cultivation, soybean monoculture on large tracts of arable land, and commerce in timber from the tropical rainforests, together with the privatization of various state-owned companies. This led to significant changes in the national economy. Domitila, in her new testimony, continually refers to the neoliberal model applied to Bolivia. She mostly reflects on the consequences of that model, such as large-scale agricultural production for export; the problem of coca cultivation that is linked to drug trafficking; the deforestation of the Amazon region by logging companies; and the privatization of state enterprises, to mention just a few of those issues.

Today the mine workers and their families are no longer found at the mines, since they have been "relocated" as a consequence of the state-owned company COMIBOL's denationalization. Now, those former miners and their families are scattered in coca, soybean, sugarcane, and other plantations, when they are not looking for employment or inventing new jobs, or wandering the streets because they cannot find work.

Domitila is one of those thousands of "relocated" people. She now has thirteen grandchildren. Two of her children live in the neighborhood, while the other five are in Sweden, where they settled after their mother's exile there. Domitila shows some signs of her advancing years and has health problems that make it difficult for her body to keep up with her mind, which is still lucid, and with her heart, which still beats for the cause of her people. Without the support structure that was formerly her arena of action—the Housewives' Committee of the Siglo XX-Catavi Mine Trade Union, the FSTMB, and the COB—she is now developing her own life project as a social and political educator through the Domitila Mobile School.

In the midst of the countless changes Domitila has gone through—and in spite of them—her objective remains the same. It is like a compass that guides and orients her thought: "I'm loyal to the COB's political thesis, which is that we need to replace the current society with a new one and that has to be a socialist society." Now, after going through the adjustments and making so many decisions, Domitila tirelessly repeats her new leitmotif for the context in which she lives: the need for a "popular organization at all levels that extends throughout the country, along with a broad 'Continent-wide Anti-Neoliberal Front for a Just Society.'"

That is to say, Domitila carries forward the same dreams, the same yearnings, the same desires, and the same commitments, but now in a very different context and in changed conditions. It's truly extraordinary to see this in a person who has been struggling for economic and social change in her country for forty years and is now sixty-five [in 2002], an age when people are generally retired in Bolivia.

Part 4 of this book takes up Domitila's story a quarter of a century [2003] after the original publication of *Let Me Speak!* In this preface, I deal with "Domitila the Person" and "Domitila's Testimony" during the course of those twenty-five years, along with a brief explanation of "Why I Undertook the Project."

DOMITILA THE PERSON

It was in 1975 that Domitila packed her bags to leave the Siglo XX mining camp in Bolivia and head to Mexico to participate in the NGO Tribune of the World Conference on Women in Denmark. At that time, she had no idea what would happen after she said "Let me speak . . ." in the conference's plenary session and began to raise global awareness about the situation of the women and men she knew in the mines.

Today, it's completely normal for women from the grassroots to participate in international events. From a local to global level, organizations bringing together women from diverse social groups and strata are numerous and increasingly important. However, that was not the case in 1975. Then, the participation of women from the working class and popular sectors in the upper echelons of organizations or in international events was an unusual occurrence, especially in Latin American countries, where social and political organizations were banned under the military dictatorships. The majority of women involved in underground activism did little more than assist the men leading these organizations.

It is worth remembering some of the specifics of Domitila's life: the isolation of the mining camps on the Bolivian Altiplano where she lived; the novelty of being a housewife from a mining center representing her sector of the working class abroad; the political situation in Bolivia, crushed by a military regime, which made communication difficult for those defending popular causes; the unprecedented occurrence in Bolivia's history, that an invitation from the United Nations reached the hands of a woman from a tin-mining camp.

Domitila arrived at the plenary with a clear sense of her mission and ready to seize an opportunity to explain her reasons for going there. Her remarks—all based on her experiences—had a profound impact on the organizers and participants. That was because she cogently described the exploitation and oppression of the women and men in the mining centers. Moreover, her speeches stirred up the polemic between the two principal currents present at the tribune: the debate for many being between "what unites women by the fact of being women" versus "what separates women because of their social conditions." In this context, Domitila became a central figure in one of the opposing currents. At that time, there was no developed analysis of the social relations of gender: how societies define, organize, maintain, and reorganize the social roles attributed to men and women and how this intersects with class, race, skin color, ethnicity, and age. Those theoretical developments mostly came after the Mexico Conference.[1]

In this general milieu, the Women's Conference in Mexico was a watershed moment, and it represented a milestone with regard to public policies for women and for the various women's movements operating in the world. The conference also signaled the beginning of a new era: the entry of women into the international arena, with a vision of politics that comes from women, but is for all humanity.

Domitila's testimony *Let Me Speak!* came out of the context of that event. The original version deals with her life from her birth up to her 1975 visit to Mexico, plus the events that occurred in 1976, when she was already back at the Siglo XX-Catavi mine in Bolivia.

In 2002, Domitila's narrative picks up the thread of the conversation. It relates the most important things she had experienced during the twenty-five years following the original publication of *Let Me Speak!* in Mexico in 1977.

The event that would undoubtedly leave the deepest mark on Domitila in the 1970s was the hunger strike she initiated with four other *compañeras*. That hunger strike proved decisive in sparking the series of events that led to the defeat of the dictator General Hugo Banzer. The epic story of those five women, whose victory depended on the movement's internal unity and on international solidarity, became well known through textual accounts and a video documentary.

Domitila recalls with excitement the hunger strike and other historical events in which she actively participated, events that contributed to overthrowing the ruthless military dictatorships in her country. However, she never ceases to express bewilderment at the election results in Bolivia and in other Latin American countries. These sometimes brought back former military dictators who were responsible for massacres of the people in earlier years, or introduced new figures who had sold out to the neoliberal model and were thus "unable" to respond to people's real aspirations and needs. Domitila repeatedly discusses the fragile and clouded nature of any "real democracy" in Bolivia. At the same time, she highlights the enormous difficulties the poor face in the context of a "formal democracy," which is far from the New Democratic Bolivia that she and so many others risked their lives for.

The year 1980 was a turning point in Domitila's life. Once again, she was invited by the United Nations, this time to Copenhagen to participate in the UN's five-year follow up to the original 1975 Conference on Women. She accepted the invitation. However, on the very day that the Conference began, General García Meza's military coup took place, one of the bloodiest coups in Bolivia. Domitila was then forced to alter her plans. Now she became the Bolivian people's spokesperson to the world, denouncing the coup before world public opinion, and asking for solidarity with her country and a coherent position from democratic governments around the world toward the usurping government in Bolivia.

The solidarity of thousands of women who attended and organized the conference, foremost among them Latin American women, was key to this project's success. Bolivian exiles from various countries also joined in to help. However, as a result of Domitila's work, the dictatorial government of Bolivia declared her a "traitor to the homeland," and she was unable to return to the country. With the help of Bolivian exiles, she was granted political asylum in Sweden, where she lived for two years with her family, who joined her in exile.

Domitila's political exile in Sweden between 1980 and 1982 led her to forge new directions in her personal and family life, as well as in her social and political work. Separated from her family during the first few months of exile, she continued her political activism, despite being unable to communicate easily with the COB, for which she had become an international spokesperson. She was invited to speak at numerous events organized by trade unions and solidarity organizations from different countries, and she began to travel intensely, covering thousands of kilometers.

The awards, honorable mentions, and invitations to committees and boards that Domitila has received speak for the international recognition of her Human Rights work. Notably, she received the Bruno Kreisky Award (Austria, 1981) and the Women's World Summit Foundation's prize for Women's Creativity in Rural Life (Geneva, 2000). In 1983, she was appointed as a member of the Honorary Committee of the World Council of Churches "Patria Grande" Commission, together with Eduardo Galeano, Adolfo

Pérez Esquivel, and Noam Chomsky. In 1984, she became a member of the board of directors of the Casa de la Amistad Boliviano-Nicaragüense (Bolivia-Nicaragua Friendship House). She was featured in *Notable Twentieth-Century Latin American Women: A Biographical Dictionary*[2] and in the 1999 *Agenda Latinamerica*, published in Uruguay. Dozens of diplomas and certificates testify to the many honors conferred on her.

The long list of international events to which Domitila was invited is also indicative of the power of her testimony and how it was received. These journeys of Domitila's are documented in hundreds of interviews in the written press, in radio and television programs, as well as in some documentary films. When asked about what she said at these events, Domitila explains:

> I was trying to dissiminate the untold story . . . to explain why, Bolivia being such a rich country, the Bolivian people are so poor . . . why military dictatorships are so harmful to the people . . . why it is so important to create conditions for organizing and changing the course of things . . . and why information and international solidarity are so important.

At the end of 1982, Domitila returned from exile to Bolivia. Five of her children stayed on in Sweden and took up residence there. Domitila went back to her small house at the Siglo XX mining camp, incorporating herself once again into the Siglo XX Union and the Miners' Federation, while her husband resumed work in the mine. However, nothing was the same anymore: the country had changed, the mining centers had changed, the Housewives' Committee had changed, her family had changed, and she herself had changed.

By 1984, Bolivia's economic and political situation had become extremely fragile. Inflation was out of control. Alliances between political parties came and went, and the so-called "Tin Era" began to collapse. The elected president, Hernán Siles Zuazo, brought to power by the Unidad Democrática Popular (UDP), completely lost control of the situation and was forced to resign and call new elections. The winner of those elections was Víctor Paz Estenssoro of the Movimiento Nacionalista Revolucionario (MNR) which, under the tutelage of the United States, implemented drastic changes.

The year 1985 marked the end of one historical era and the beginning of another. The government issued Supreme Decree 21060, which Domitila sees as heralding Bolivia's official embrace of the neoliberal model. The decree shut down the state-owned Corporación Minera de Bolivia (COMIBOL), and nearly 35,000 workers were laid off from one day to the next. Domitila was one of those thousands of people who were "relocated"—that is, fired. In this way, she lost her earlier lifeworld: a mining center linked to a state-owned company that, despite precarious conditions, provided workers with a minimum of stability. At the same time, she lost her institutional framework: the trade union organization where she had militated since 1963, participating directly in the Siglo XX-Catavi Mine Workers Union via the Housewives' Committee and, through these organizations, in the FSTMB and COB.

"Beginning again" literally became Domitila's mantra during this period. It's not hard to imagine the impact on her personal life caused by the avalanche of events she lived through in those years: exile, returning to the country without most of her family, separation and divorce from her husband René (who could not cope with the new context in Bolivia), and pressure from women and men, fellow mine workers, who had never left the country. The final blow was being forced to leave the mining center.

The changes that Domitila went through, in addition to causing her stress, with evident effects on her health, brought her face to face with new challenges. The first was the need to find a new home and start building new kinship and neighborly relationships. Another challenge was the need to support herself financially as a self-employed worker, paying for all the social services previously included as benefits in a mine worker's small salary. To make matters worse, Domitila could not find the market she expected in Cochabamba for the traditional *salteñas* she sold.

She also had to find a new arena for her social and political activism. The answer turned out to be the Domitila Mobile School, created in 1990 with comrades from both the city and countryside. This was another significant change for someone who was accustomed to volunteer work within the labor movement, since the new project meant seeking her own channels of action and communication and also her own means of support.

In the Mobile School, Domitila continues to tell "the unofficial story," which she doesn't want to be erased from people's memory and which never appears in the school curricula or in the mass media. This is her new way of contributing to the political education of women and men from the various social sectors to which she has access. The key themes guiding this educational work are: organization, education, and unity.

Although Domitila feels there has been significant progress regarding intersectional issues such as gender relations, race/ethnicity, and age, the central problem is still outstanding: the liberation "of the working class, of the poor, of the people." A revealing comment she made as a member of the Bolivian Women's Coordinator addressed the difficulty of analyzing and responding correctly to Bolivia's complex reality of social relations involving gender, class, race/ethnicity, and generational differences. She said: "In Bolivia, we still haven't achieved enough understanding among classist, feminist, and feminist-generalist perspectives."

Domitila describes the overarching purpose of her struggle over the past twenty-five years as follows: "I still believe that Bolivia will be a socialist country, a country without poverty, with its wealth in the hands of the Bolivian people, guaranteeing a hopeful future for its children."

DOMITILA'S TESTIMONY

In 1975, Mexico was thought to be the "paradise" of Latin American exiles. There were communists and socialists from diverse Bolivian parties, members of Colombia's National Liberation Army (ELN), mentors and militants of the Brazilian Peasant Leagues, Guevarists, Tupamaros, Montoneros, and many others, who all found much-cherished refuge there. I myself was exiled in Mexico and was a member of the Committee of Solidarity with Bolivia, along with my partner who was also exiled from Bolivia by the Banzer dictatorship. On the eve of the opening of the UN Conference's parallel NGO Tribune, various committees of exiles met to prepare a "Latin American stance" to present in the Tribune. The Bolivian committee also met and even drafted a document.

The following day, I listened to Domitila, first on the podium and then in her initial meeting with the Committee of Solidarity with Bolivia. I was quite impressed, mainly for two reasons. On the one hand, I was hearing firsthand a detailed picture of daily life in the Bolivian mining centers. This was information that hardly ever left the country, because communications were highly censored, and Bolivia was not in the international spotlight. On the other hand, I was also struck by how this housewife from a mining camp, with so little formal education, always provided a social and political analysis of every event she narrated.

I volunteered to serve as Domitila's translator when she spoke, translation being one of the various forms of solidarity that members of the Solidarity Committee offered to her. That's how I began to accompany Domitila every day, translating her interviews for the international press and for various groups and individuals.

It was while making the rounds with her that I had the idea of writing Domitila's testimony, including her life story. I communicated the idea to her in a gathering of the Solidarity Committee organized by Bolivians living in Mexico. That was on August 5, the eve of Bolivia's Independence Day. I said to Domitila: "After Mexico, you are going to return to the isolated mining camp of Siglo XX. There is no way of knowing if you'll have another chance to share your experiences with an international audience again or if all this will be forgotten."

We talked about what she herself had already observed: that people in North America, Europe, Africa and even in other Latin American countries did not know much about Bolivia and especially its mine workers. We talked about the impact of her testimony at the podium, where she was given only a few minutes, and how it could be potentially even greater if the account were elaborated to include the testimony of her whole life. We discussed the importance that a testimony like hers could have for her country's new generation, who had not lived through the same historical processes as she had. The new generation also lacked the information that people like her father had conveyed about the Chaco War or the National Revolution of 1952, in which he had participated. Nor did they know about the massacres of miners and peasants in Bolivia, the organization of women in the trade union movement, and so on, because the schoolbooks did not incorporate that version of history.

But what weighed most heavily in Domitila's decision was my commitment to work so that her testimony would reach women and men who lived in similar situations: in mining centers, in poor urban neighborhoods, or in the countryside. It was primarily with these people that she wanted to share her knowledge and experience.

We reached an agreement and started recording the next day. It was a beautiful way to commemorate Bolivia's Independence Day! I arrived early, with my recorder in hand. Domitila was already waiting for me with an opening statement that would set the tone for her life testimony: "I don't want this testimony to be seen as something that is only personal. I want to speak about my people, because I owe everything I have and am to my people."

Before beginning to work, we again discussed the agreement we had reached the previous night. Since this was all untraveled territory, we imagined various ways of publishing the text, even as a photocopied pamphlet or booklet in case we could not find other means. But we also talked about sharing the copyright, if it was possible to publish the work with a publishing house. I also ratified my commitment to look for ways of disseminating the work among people and groups in a way consonant with the mission Domitila had given me when sharing her story: her wish was that the testimony "return to the working class from which it had come."

It was not an easy decision for Domitila, who had received previous invitations to publish her testimony. In Mexico, she was far from home and separated from her usual context for making important decisions. Besides, she was a Bolivian and I was a Brazilian, and we had known each other for only a brief time. Those who have been exiled and lived in clandestinity know about the unique fears that haunt human relationships in such contexts. As Domitila revealed in interviews she did later on with the press, there were times when she was afraid that she was talking to a "CIA agent" or to someone who would not uphold the commitments we made on the basis of mutual trust.

That is how we began our collaboration, in which there was a synergy of interests between two Latin American women: a militant of the Bolivian trade union movement and a Brazilian educator. We took advantage of the three months Domitila stayed in Mexico—responding to numerous invitations to give talks in unions, associations, universities, artists' groups, as well as numerous interviews for the press, radio, and television in Mexico—to record material for the testimony. In addition to the tapes made on those occasions, we sat down for several days to make recordings about the story of her personal life. Some of the interviews lasted two, three, or even four hours. Others had to be reprised later on, because Domitila could not contain her feelings when talking about very emotional events, such as when she described the loss of her son, with whom she was pregnant, after being beaten and abused in prison by a colonel who wanted to extract information about Che's whereabouts in Bolivia.

Once all the recordings were finished, I began transcribing the tapes, categorizing the material by topics, and also did the initial "stitching together" of her words. I adopted a Freirean method of text assembly, the reflection-action approach, adding Domitila's analysis to the description of each topic we had discussed. Putting together paragraphs, eliminating repetitions, organizing sentences in a way so that they could be read and not just heard—I did all that very carefully, with a view to being faithful to her thinking and her interpretation of the facts at that time. I deliberately preserved the language of oral testimony and also the very different ways that Domitila had of expressing herself when she gave personal interviews or spoke to small groups versus when participating in assemblies. This explains the diversity of styles in the same book, making *Let Me Speak!* a unique literary construction.

I was helped by reading a range of books and biographies about Bolivia's contemporary history and engaging in conversations with various Bolivian exiles in Mexico and Lima. The latter helped me understand certain events that, because of the censorship and lack of communication imposed by the continent's dictatorships, had never come to light or had never been recorded. The constant support of my partner, who was knowledgeable about the Bolivian Altiplano and a specialist in Quechua, was key to my being able to faithfully represent the diction of a person whose thoughts are articulated in Quechua even when she expresses herself in Spanish.

After completing that initial phase of work, I traveled to Bolivia in 1976 to go over the manuscript with Domitila. General Banzer's dictatorship at that time was particularly severe. Like the other union leaders, Domitila was under close surveillance by government agents who hovered around the camp, and it was only in secrecy that she acted as a leader. For that reason, we relied on the solidarity of the Siglo XX-Catavi parish community. They took us in, along with the baby that Domitila was still breastfeeding. We spent more than a week there, revising the first manuscript and complementing her testimony with important facts that had been recalled by other people I had interviewed. We also developed a new chapter based on the events of 1976 and established the priorities to apply in reducing the size of the text, following the guidelines of the initial editor.

The joint review of the manuscript in that hideaway at Siglo XX was crucial because of the methodology we had adopted. According to that approach, it was important to verify that Domitila recognized herself in the redacted testimony. The written testimony resulted from transcribing the tapes and assembling almost a thousand pages, which were then organized and reduced to just 250 pages—as per the instructions of an editor who was trying to satisfy our wish for a book that could be widely disseminated.

The original version, published in Spanish by Siglo XXI Editores in Mexico, was later translated and published in fifteen languages. The book was the subject of numerous reviews and articles, and selections were included in anthologies. In addition to the book's being distributed through publishers and bookstores, *Let Me Speak!* had a parallel distribution to achieve the goal its protagonist and author had initially set of its being an instrument of communication "so that it returns to the working class, from which it came." Support from social movements and NGOs in various Latin American countries that I was in contact with proved important for the book's multilevel distribution.

For example, hundreds of popular organizations and trade unions in Mexico read from the book as a way of initiating their meetings, or held workshops on parts of the book. A group of women workers from the Mexico City Metro would hurry to finish their work before midnight to collectively read sections of the book. In Tanzania, at the University of Dar es Salaam, it was used by groups doing participatory-action-research. In Dakar the book was circulated among women's groups to encourage the development of leaders and, according to the then coordinator of the Association des Femmes Africaines, to encourage compiling the testimonies of "our African Domitilas." In Lima, Peru, the book was read by thousands of striking miners and their families from the La Oroya mine, who camped in the capital city for several weeks.

Let Me Speak! was received with open arms wherever the people's main goal was to oust the continent's remaining dictatorships: Argentina, Uruguay, Paraguay, etc. The same thing happened in

Nicaragua, El Salvador, and Guatemala, where thousands of women and men welcomed Domitila's testimony and found inspiration in it as they organized themselves according to their specific needs in wartime.

The Siglo XXI publishing house in Mexico facilitated the book's wide dissemination by granting special discounts to Mexican popular organizations. The same can be said of our Brazilian publisher, who allowed for the book's publication in an edition, coordinated by Pedro Jacob and Regina Festa, that circulated outside of commercial circuits.

On top of that, the book underwent several adaptations. It was the subject of a play in Costa Rica, a video production in Germany, a radio program in Quechua and Aymara in Bolivia and Peru, and recordings for use in cassette-forums among Black women's groups on the Colombian coast. At the University of Bielefeld, in Germany, a translator-interpreter used it as a reference text so that her students, while learning Spanish, would also learn something about Bolivia and Latin America.

As a tool for popular communication, the book was read and discussed in schools in the Dominican Republic, inspiring children to develop essays and poems. It was also presented in workshops with trade unionists, peasant organizations, and women's groups where the testimony itself was highly appreciated, but it mostly served as a mirror to reflect the social and political situation of those who read it. Group readings of the text would be interrupted to make room for new testimonies about the local situation, thus helping others to re-create their own histories. Each fact and event related by Domitila about Bolivia was taken up by readers to reflect on similar issues that had occurred in their own countries.

This wide distribution demonstrates the rich use of Domitila's testimony as an instrument of popular communication. In an interview she did in 1978, Domitila made the following comment about the book's distribution among the people:

I have been interviewed by hundreds of journalists, historians, and others who have come here from various parts of the world with television crews, cameras, and photographers. I also know how anthropologists, sociologists, and economists visit other parts of the country, to study Bolivia. They take a lot of material with them, but very few return it to the working class, to the people, you see? So, I would like to ask all those people who want to collaborate with us that, with regard to all the material they take away, that they should return it to us. I believe that films, papers, and studies about the Bolivian people should be returned to Bolivians to be read, analyzed, and criticized here. Because otherwise the situation in the country simply remains the same, and those investigations do not help us better understand our reality and solve our problems. There are very few works—they can easily be listed—that have actually done that.

Because of the adverse conditions in Bolivia when the book was published, it was one of the places where the work was least read in Latin America. Police at La Paz Airport retained the first copies sent there, which were to be distributed to the Housewives' Committees at the mines and to union leaders. Another batch of copies, specifically intended for distribution at the Siglo XX-Catavi mine, was sent to neighboring Peru upon arrival. Bookstores were reluctant to order the book. That's how things were at the time, under the dictatorship, with the censorship and lack of communication.

In the 1980s, the book was widely used in academic circles, entering the bibliographies of courses on history, anthropology, politics, sociology, literature, geography, and translation. Feminists in Tunisian universities used the French-language version to reflect on their country's dependent condition, which is so like that of Bolivia, despite the different ways that both countries experienced colonization. At the Autonomous University of Mexico (UNAM), the book was used in a study group on "the value of domestic work and the surplus value it produces," based on the thinking of Italian feminists such as Mariarosa Della Costa. Domitila, in calculating the value of the various domestic activities she performs that are not socially recognized, provides a simple and lively description of her "double shift" as the wife of a mine worker. In this way, she demonstrates why she considers herself a member of the working class in her role as a housewife, wife of a worker.

The book also led people to reflect on the traditional style of "studying poor populations" that characterized the world of the social sciences at that time. In 1977, the feminist anthropologist Lourdes Arizpe wrote to me: "I read the book in one sitting and spent the night without sleep, pacing back and forth in my apartment, having doubts about the point of so much research in which the data and statements of the interviewed populations are totally diluted in the investigators' interpretations, with no feedback to the people from which the information was collected."

At the annual meeting of the Brazilian Society for the Progress of Science (SBPC) in 1980, researchers highlighted the importance of testimonies such as this one. In this meeting, which occurred at the time Brazil was beginning to leave behind the military regime, Mauricio Tragtemberg said that such testimonies "show the flesh-and-blood working class."

Brazilian actors in the film *Para frente Brasil* (*Go Ahead Brazil*, 1982) remarked on how reading the book helped them understand the oppressiveness of their own country's military dictatorship, so similar to Bolivia's.

Let Me Speak! also played a role in the world of international cooperation; it was included in lists of recommended readings for people preparing to participate in cooperation programs in Latin America (for example, Germans and Canadians). In the Nordic countries, publishing houses and organizations dedicated to international cooperation took responsibility for translating and disseminating the book to encourage solidarity with Latin American peoples.

The universe of *Let Me Speak!*'s readers of was thus very broad. It reached people with very diverse interests and aroused the most varied opinions, as is usually the case with oral histories of individuals or groups.

WHY I UNDERTOOK THE PROJECT

There were various things about Domitila that caught my attention and led me to write her testimony. The first was the quality of the information she provided about the life of working-class people, combined with her message of hope when analyzing real situations. I was also struck by the way she did it, always interspersing examples that illustrated what she was saying and left no doubt about her commitments with regard to the theme of the conversation. "Domitila the Person" and "Domitila's Testimony" were unquestionably interconnected.

I was also surprised by the way that the Committee in Solidarity with the Bolivian People in Mexico received Domitila. There were a great many ideological divergences that separated the representatives of the various leftist parties exiled there. However, it was as if her words expressed what they had in common, including what was behind their all having to flee their country.

When I listened to Domitila in her public speeches or translated her interviews for the international press, I was reminded of the millions of women of her social class who did not have access to the information that she was presenting. Nor could they come together to deal with the issues presented in the book, benefiting from the work of a woman from their same social class. In a male-dominated world, the least likely thing to happen would be to pay attention to the wisdom acquired by a woman from the mines (when the testimony of the mine leaders had not been written either). All that made me realize how much the testimony of a woman like Domitila would contribute to the theory and practice of social and political organizations.

Domitila had exceptional class consciousness and was able to give voice to it. That became one of the strengths of *Let Me Speak!*, making it similar to but also distinct from other testimonies I had read, such as *Quarto de Despejo* (*Child of the Dark*) by Carolina Maria de Jesus, *Los hijos de Sánchez* (*The Children of Sánchez*) by Oscar Lewis, *He agotado mi vida en la mina* by Juan Rojas and June

Nash, among others. Mexican researcher Elena Urrutia aptly captured this aspect of the work: "What is most surprising is not this particular, difficult life; it is the lucid knowledge that the protagonist has of her situation, of the exploitation that she, her husband, her children and her class are all subjected to, of the causes and mechanisms that create and maintain the situation, and of the commitment she assumed alongside her people to change it."

As an educator, I saw Domitila's language as a powerful vehicle for transmitting her message, but one that needed a relay mechanism. That made it worth all the time and effort that such a project involves from the initial interviews to the final publication.

The process of developing *Let Me Speak!* was based on the general methodology of testimonial investigation, used to reconstruct social, economic, and cultural processes and to complement or correct previous analyses of events and figures in working-class history. According to the method, testimonies should be edited following self-determined guidelines and procedures. The role I assigned myself in making *Let Me Speak!* was that of an instrument of communication, who did not alter Domitila's way of expressing herself or include analyses other than those of the protagonist. This is the path I pursued, though there may have been other equally valid ones. In developing this never-before-written "alternative history," I also tried to assemble the testimony with a view to the book's becoming an instrument of popular communication, generating analysis, criticism, and dialogue.

Any testimony raises many more questions than it answers, but that's even more true of a testimony with a political character like *Let Me Speak!* The English sociologist and researcher Olivia Harris was inspired to ask such questions as:

What makes the life story of a woman from a Bolivian tin mine become internationally known, translated into multiple languages in a few years, and read with interest by people who had never heard of Bolivia before? Can that happen without distorting the reality to which it refers? What makes this book more

than just a tale of misery and exploitation, evoking both sym-
pathy and discomfort from us? The answer lies in the book's
title: it is a Testimony. Domitila is giving her testimony, not just
telling a story.

After the book's publication, some individuals and groups had
difficulty seeing it for what it was: a statement from a woman of the
people. They didn't see the testimony as a reflection of the protagonist's own work with women in leftist unions and political parties.
Instead, a few leaders wanted to see in it, at all costs, an account
of their own work, which she was not involved in, or of their own
interpretations of Bolivia at that time, which were not necessarily
her own. Some went so far as to write a text to be appended to the
original book, which had already been published in various languages. Domitila's response came after we met for a project review
in 1978. To publishers and the general public, she wrote:

> I think the book is a narrative, and it ought to be read as a whole.
> You shouldn't take out a particular paragraph, and mold it to
> your way of thinking or being. It is an integral whole, and should
> be read and understood that way from beginning to end. I also
> think that the text could be used for analysis and criticism, but
> one shouldn't look for an explicit theoretical line in it. It is an
> account of my experience. And I endorse it.

The issue of class struggle and its relationship with feminism
was another topic that generated various debates. Some women
associated with the traditional left seized on Domitila's account,
using it to defend their own claims about the exclusivity of the
general struggle against exploitation and dictatorships, without
any consideration of how social relations of class intersect with
gender relations, race, ethnicity, age, religion, and so on. Others,
like Norma Chinchilla, took the opposite position by locating
Domitila in the current of "proletarian feminism" along with
Clara Zetkin. Still others, such as Kate Young, raised some very

relevant and urgent issues: "Why does Domitila think that feminism is irrelevant to working women in the Third World? And why do people who consistently question the imperialist press's perspectives and analyses on themes such as development, political alliances, and workers' struggles, accept without question what the same press says about women?"

Questions such as these highlighted both the richness and limits of Domitila's testimony. They also point to the need for further research and analysis of, for example, the ideology and practice of the political parties, of the Bolivian trade union movement, and of the Bolivian women's movement at the time.

Today, we can say that *Let Me Speak!* went beyond our expectations. First of all, the book brought an end to the invisibility of women in the mining centers. In the process of writing it, we found publications written by men about the mines and the Siglo XX-Catavi Union, but we did not find any mention of women or women's participation. Nor was there any discussion of the role of the Housewives' Committee in the work of the labor movement, in the hunger strikes, or in the resistance to the army. Canadian writer Lynda Yanz has said:

> It is not uncommon for stories of working-class struggle, even those told by its participants, to leave women out of the picture, as if these accounts could only refer to the workplace. Because it's the story of a woman, this testimony reveals the full extent of working-class oppression.

Let Me Speak! also helped to put Bolivia more fully on the map as part of the universal struggle for human rights. The newspaper *Le Monde Diplomatique* referred to the book as "a kind of *Germinal* of the Third World," while Bolivian anthropologist Xavier Albó claimed that *Let Me Speak!* is the most widely read book on Bolivia in the world today.

Nobel Prize–winner Heinrich Böll included *Let Me Speak!* in his anthology *Mein Lesebuch (My Reading Book)*, which brought together texts by classic authors that had made a mark on his personal and professional life. He remarked: "Domitila's story complements and confirms what is said in a different way in intellectual analyses of the Latin American situation such as Eduardo Galeano's book *The Open Veins of Latin America* or the outstanding works of literature by [Gabriel] García Márquez, Alejo Carpentier, and Vargas Llosa."

Likewise, Eduardo Galeano wrote:

This book is the story of a person's life, a country, and a social class. The country is Bolivia, to which many other countries owe apologies, starting with Spain, which took all the silver from Potosí. The social class is the Bolivian working class, with its long tradition of struggle, undying courage, and abundant creativity. The testimony of this woman, who in an honest, straightforward way tells the story of her life, goes beyond the narrowness of statistics. It takes history out of the museum and into everyday life, while returning politics to the world of flesh and blood.

At the Book Fair held in Cochabamba in 2001 where, in homage to Domitila, the professor of literature Javier Sanjinés pointed out:

The hegemony of the written word is part of a system of domination dating back to the colonial period. By contrast, the spoken word offers an important counterbalance in a country like Bolivia, where there is not full literacy. New aspects of Bolivia, such as the women of the mines and the Indigenous people, were included in Domitila's testimony. Its greatest legacy, despite the different historical conjuncture that gave rise to *Let Me Speak!*, is how it focuses on *the real*, unearthing issues that society still does not want to recognize. It is important that we don't erase alternative forms of political representation and work to overcome the internal colonialism that still afflicts us."

The multifaceted nature of oral history becomes even more evident when the same person is interviewed again. This always brings to light realities and issues in a given country or region, as well as the value systems and beliefs operating in the speaker's context.

I collected the current testimony twenty-five years after the original one. Domitila has spent that time struggling for human rights and fighting against poverty in Bolivia. The current testimony shows how, during those years, she has gradually gained more awareness about how the exploitation and inhuman abuses suffered by her class and her people are not just due to specific circumstances—such as the dictatorships she helped overthrow. Instead, they result from a global system of exploitation, which today has the United States government at its epicenter. Domitila's new approach—though the concrete political proposal is still up for debate—means continuing to fight for her class and people at the local and national level. However, she has now broadened the focus of her reflections and analysis to include the neoliberal system that dominates the world, while urging Latin American peoples and those from other parts of the world to join together in challenging it. Undoubtedly, Domitila is still saying to the world: *Let Me Speak!*

The present book consists of four parts: in the first, Domitila talks about "Her People": the working and living conditions of men and women in the mines and their involvement in Bolivia's organized labor movement. In the second, she narrates "Her Life," which she always connects to developments in Bolivian popular history. In the third, she focuses on 1976 and key events that occurred during that year. The fourth part presents her current testimony, from the 1978 hunger strike to the year 2002. It also answers the question that so many people have asked: "Where is Domitila?"

Notes

1. After the World Conference on Women in Mexico, two additional conferences on Women, Development, and Peace were held in Nairobi (1985) and Beijing (1995), in addition to the midpoint evaluation meeting held in Copenhagen (1980). During this time period, many women's and gender studies programs and centers were established in academic contexts. However, it was only after the 1980s and 1990s that non-governmental organizations (NGOs) and social movements incorporated the perspective of gender analysis into their programs, along with the projects and actions that correspond to it.

2. *Notable Twentieth-Century Latin American Women* was a biographical dictionary published by Greenwood Press in the United States. Along with Domitila, it features mini-biographies of women that include Isabel Allende, Rigoberta Menchú, Alicia Alonso, Celia Cruz, Gioconda Belli, Carolina Maria de Jesus, Chiquinha Gonzaga, Clarice Lispector, Haydée Santamaría, Benedita da Silva, Mercedes Sosa, Virginia Vargas, Hebe de Bonafini, Ivone Gebara, Frida Kahlo, Julieta Kirkwood, the Mirabal sisters (María Teresa, Minerva, and Patria), Elena Poniatowska, and the Bolivian Teresa Gisbert.

LET ME SPEAK!

PLACES MENTIONED IN THE TEXT

To the Reader

The idea for this testimony arose out of the presence of Domitila Barrios de Chungara at the International Women's Year Tribunal, organized by the United Nations and held in Mexico in 1975.

It was there that I met this woman from the Bolivian Andes. She is the wife of a miner, the mother of seven children, and she had come to the Tribunal representing the "Housewives' Committee of Siglo XX," an organization of the wives of workers in that tin mining center.

Her years of struggle and the recognition of her commitment earned her an official invitation from the UN to be present at the event.

The only woman from the working class participating actively in the Tribunal as a representative of Bolivia, her contributions had a profound impact on all those present. In large part this was due to the fact that "Domitila lived what the other women spoke of," as a Swedish newspaperwoman put it.

This account, which Domitila considers the "culmination" of her work at the Tribunal, is the cry of a people who suffer because they are exploited. Furthermore, it shows how the liberation of women is fundamentally linked to the socioeconomic, political, and cultural liberation of the people and how women's participation in this process must be seen in that context.

What I present here is not Domitila's monologue with herself. It is the product of numerous interviews I had with her in Mexico and Bolivia, of her speeches at the Tribunal, as well as discussions, conversations, and dialogues she had with groups of workers, students, and university employees, people living in workers' neighborhoods, Latin American exiles living in Mexico, and representatives of the press, radio, and television. All of this taped material, as well as some written correspondence, was organized and then revised with Domitila, and resulted in the present volume of oral history.

Domitila adapts herself to the concrete circumstances she is in and to the public she is addressing. The way she expresses herself in personal conversations is quite different from the way she speaks in speeches and formal presentations in assemblies or in exchanges with small groups. This explains the variety of styles in this book, which might surprise some readers.

Domitila's language is that of a woman of the people, with her own expressions, her localisms, and her grammatical constructions, marked, at times, by the Quechua language which she has spoken since childhood. I have purposely kept this language, which is an intrinsic part of her testimony and which contributes to literature one more example of the richness of popular speech.

Written documentation concerning the experiences of ordinary and poor people is quite scarce. In this sense, this account can fill a gap and serve as an instrument for reflection and orientation, and as such it can be useful to other women and men who are committed to the cause of the people of Bolivia and other countries, especially in Latin America.

Therefore, this book is a working tool. Domitila agreed to give her testimony as a way to "contribute a little grain of sand, with the hope that our experience may serve in some way for the new generation." "Because," she says, "it's important to take experiences from our own history," as well as from "the experience of other peoples." And to this end, "there must be testimony" which will help us to "reflect on our actions and criticize them."

Domitila has been forged in the school of the people's life. In the monotonous and hard daily work of a housewife in the mining region she discovered that the worker is not the only one exploited, since the system affects and exploits the woman and her family also. This motivated her to participate actively in the organized struggle of the working class. Together with her sisters, she lives directly the defeats and the victories of her people. And from this experience she interprets reality. Everything she says is life and projection.

Domitila does not pretend to present a historical analysis of Bolivia, nor of the miners' union movement, nor of the "Housewives' Committee of Siglo XX." She simply narrates what she has lived, how she has lived it, and what she has learned in order to continue in the struggle through which the working class and the people's movement will come to control their own destiny.

Nevertheless, there are few testimonials by men or women from the mines, the factories, the slums, or the countryside in which the protagonist not only narrates the situation in which he or she lives but is also conscious of the causes and mechanisms that create and maintain such a situation and is committed to the struggle to change it. In this sense, it's true: Domitila's testimony contains the elements of a profoundly innovative historical analysis, because it is also an interpretation of the facts from the popular point of view.

So that the value of this account is not lessened, we must allow this woman of the people to speak; we must listen to her and try to understand how she lives, feels, and interprets events.

Nothing of what appears here is alien to Bolivia's reality, because Domitila's personal itinerary is a part of the great march of the Bolivian working class and people.

This is why I divided the book into three parts: the first, where Domitila describes her people, the living and working conditions of the men and women of the mines and their integration into the organized workers' movement; the second, where she narrates her life in relation to the historical events lived through by her people; the third, which presents the panorama of the mines in 1976, especially after the strike of the miners during June and July.

I should like to express my admiration of and my gratitude to the women of the Bolivian mines who, in the person of Domitila, give us the opportunity to gain greater knowledge and better understanding of the Bolivian working class and of the women who, since the days of Bartolina Sisa, Juana Azurduy de Padilla, Maria Barzola, have not ceased to struggle for the real freedom of their people.

I should also like to express my thanks to all the friends, sisters, and brothers who, in different ways, have collaborated so that this testimony might become a reality.

Let Domitila speak.

— MOEMA VIEZZER
DECEMBER 30, 1976

Domitila Speaks

I don't want anyone at any moment to interpret the story I'm about to tell as something that is only personal. Because I think that my life is related to my people. What happened to me could have happened to hundreds of people in my country. I want to make this clear, because I recognize that there have been people who have done much more than I for the people, but who have died or who haven't had the opportunity to be known.

That's why I say that I don't just want to tell a personal story. I want to talk about my people. I want to testify about all the experience we've acquired during so many years of struggle in Bolivia, and contribute a little grain of sand, with the hope that our experience may serve in some way for the new generation, for the new people.

I also want to say that I consider this book the culmination of my work in the International Women's Year Tribunal. There we had little time to talk and communicate all that we would have liked. And I have the opportunity to do that now.

Finally, I want to clarify that this account of my personal experience of my people, who are fighting for their liberation— and to whom I owe my existence—well, I want it to reach the poorest people, the people who don't have any money, but who need some orientation, some example which can serve them in their future life. It's for them that I agreed that what I am going to tell be written down. It doesn't matter what kind of paper it's put down on, but it does matter that it be useful for the working class and not only for intellectual people or for people who only make a business of this kind of thing.

Her People

THE MINE

I'll begin by saying that Bolivia is located in the Southern Cone, in the heart of South America. It only has about five million inhabitants. There are awfully few of us Bolivians.

Like almost all South American peoples, we speak Spanish. But our ancestors had their different languages. The two main ones were Quechua and Aymara. These two languages are also spoken today by a lot of people among the peasants and lots of miners. In the cities also they are somewhat preserved, especially in Cochabamba and Potosí, where a lot of people speak Quechua, and in La Paz, where a lot of people speak Aymara. Also, lots of the traditions of these cultures are maintained, like for example their art of weaving, the dances, and music, which even today draw a lot of attention abroad, no?

I'm proud to have Indian blood in my heart. And I'm also proud of being the wife of a miner. I'd like everyone to be proud of what they are and what they have, of their culture, their language, their music, their way of being, and not accept the influences from abroad so much, or try to imitate other people who, ultimately, have given little of worth to our society.

Our country is very rich, especially in minerals: tin, silver, gold, bismuth, zinc, iron. Oil and gas are also important sources of exploitation. In the eastern zone we also have large fields where livestock are raised, we have woods, fruit, and lots of agricultural products.

Apparently the Bolivian people own these riches. For example, the mines, especially the big ones, are state-owned. They were nationalized and taken away from their owners, who were Patiño, Hochschild, and Aramayo, whom we used to call the "tin barons," and who were famous everywhere for their immense fortunes. They even say that Patiño got to be one of the five richest millionaires in the world, don't they? Those gentlemen were Bolivian, but Bolivians with such evil hearts that they betrayed the people. They sold all our tin to other countries and left us in misery because they invested all their capital abroad, in banks, industries, hotels, and that kind of thing. And so, when those mines were nationalized, there was really very little left in Bolivia. And in spite of that, they indemnified them. And, as bad luck would have it, new rich people have been created and the people haven't enjoyed any benefits from the nationalization.

The majority of the inhabitants of Bolivia are peasants. About 70 percent of our population lives in the countryside. And they live in the most terrible poverty, even worse than us miners, despite the fact that we live like gypsies in our own land, because we don't have homes, just dwellings loaned to us by the company during the time that the worker is active.

Now, if it's true that Bolivia is a country that's so rich in raw materials, why is it a country with so many poor people? And why is its standard of living so low in comparison with other countries, even in Latin America?

Well, it's because of a currency drain. There are lots of people who've gotten rich, but they invest all their money abroad. And our wealth is handed over to the voracity of the capitalists, at the lowest possible prices, through agreements which don't benefit us. Bolivia is a country that's well favored by nature and we could be a very rich country in the world; however, even though we inhabitants are so few, that wealth doesn't belong to us. Someone said: "Bolivia is immensely rich, but its inhabitants are just beggars." And that's the truth, because Bolivia is dominated by the multinational corporations that control my country's economy. And a lot of Bolivians take advantage of this and let themselves be bought off for a few dollars and they make politics with the gringos and they back them up in their tricks. The problem, for them, is only how much more can they get for themselves. The more they can exploit the workers, the happier they are. Even if the worker collapses from hunger, from sickness, that doesn't bother them.

Well, maybe I could tell you about some experiences we've had in Bolivia. Since I live in a mining center, what I know most about is miners.

In Bolivia, about 60 percent of the income that enters the country comes from mining. The other income comes from oil and other sources of exploitation.

In the state mines, it seems that there are about thirty-five thousand workers. But in the private mines, there are another thirty-five thousand, so I think there are about seventy thousand miners in Bolivia.

The nationalized mines are administered by the Mining Corporation of Bolivia, which we call COMIBOL (Corporación Minera de Bolivia). There's a main office in La Paz and there are local offices in each mining center in the country. Where I live, for example, there's a manager who administers the mining center called Siglo X-Cataví-Socavón-Patiño-Miraflores. This is the biggest mining center in Bolivia, with the greatest amount of revolutionary experience, and it's where there've been the most massacres by the various governments.

On the outside the company technicians and employees work, in the warehouses, the foundry, the mill or mineral processing plant, the company stores.[1] Inside the mine work the miners. Every morning they have to go deep inside, as far as a very unhealthy place where there isn't enough air, lots of gas and fetidness produced by the copagira.[2] And they've got to stay there for eight hours, extracting the ore.

Before, when the mine was new, they only took out the good tin, following a vein. But for about the last twenty years things have been different. There isn't so much tin any more. So they began the system of block-caving. Inside they put dynamite, and that makes part of the hillside explode. The miners take out all that stone, they send it to the grinder and then to the mill so that the ore can be extracted. From many tons of stone very few tons of pure ore are extracted. This work in the block is very hard and dangerous, because everything explodes, everything flies around. And there's so much dust, so much that you can't even see a meter in front of you. And also there are lots of accidents, because sometimes the workers think all the dynamite has exploded and then they go on with their work and, suddenly, there's another explosion . . . and the people, see, they just stay there, blown to bits. That's why I don't want my husband to work in the block, even though the men who do work there earn a little more.

There are also other kinds of workers. For example, the *veneristas* or "veiners" are miners who work on their own and sell their ore to the company. There are about two thousand veneristas who work in groups of three or four with a group leader. They dig holes a meter or a meter and a half wide and fifteen meters deep, till they reach rock. Then they go down on the end of a rope and inside they make small tunnels into which they drag themselves. And they look for the tin that's deposited in the hollows of the rock.

---

1. These are known as "supply centers" and are administered by the company, and the company's department of social service. Food and other necessities are sold to the workers on a rationing system and discounted from the monthly wage.

2. Copagira comes from the word *copaquira*, meaning mineralized water, which has a yellowish or steely color and comes from the metal washings.

There's no protection, no kind of ventilation. It's the worst kind of job. Lots of miners who do that work are men the company retired because they have silicosis, the occupational disease of the mines. And since they don't have any other source of work, they have to find some way to survive. There are also peasants who come to Llallagua and start their lives as miners working with the veneristas, but they live in a terrible situation of exploitation, because the veneristas pay them ten pesos a day, or half a dollar.

Other workers are the *locatarios*, who also work on their own and sell the ore to the company. But the company doesn't even provide them with shovels or picks or dynamite or anything. They have to buy everything, everything. The company tells them the places that have already been mined, where there is always more ore—more or less, but there's always some left. The company pays the locatarios according to the high or low quality of the ore they find. But they always keep 40 percent of the right of use of the terrain, I think.

Others are the *lameros*, that is, the people who work panning the ore. In the plant, the company compresses the ore and from that comes a liquid, which as it flows leaves remnants of tin, and turns into a sort of river of turbid, thick water. The lameros collect the tin, wash it, concentrate it, and turn it over to the company. But the lameros are less favored than the locatarios, because the locatarios have assigned places, whereas the lameros look here and there, at random. And so lots of times they work hard and then don't find anything.

So there are various groups of people working in the mining centers.

WHERE THE MINERS LIVE

Siglo XX is a mining camp and all the houses belong to the company. A lot of miners also live in the village of Llallagua, next door, and in other non-company villages nearby.

The miners' houses in the camp, which from every point of view are on loan, are theirs after they complete some years of service.

The company doesn't lend us housing immediately, because there's a shortage. Most miners work as many as five or ten years without getting a house. So they have to rent rooms in one of the non-company villages.

Also, they can only use the house during the time they are with the company. Once a miner dies or retires because of occupational disease or miner's sickness, they throw the widow or the miner's wife out of the house and she has ninety days to go somewhere else.

Our houses are very small, that is, we have a little room measuring four by five or six meters. That little room has to be living room, dining room, pantry, and bedroom. In some houses there are two little rooms, and one of them is the kitchen; they also have a little corridor. This is what the company housing is like, only the four walls, without any water or sanitary installations. And that's how we have to live, with our children, all crowded together. In my case, we set up three beds in the room; that's all that will fit. That's where my seven children sleep, that's where they do their homework, that's where we eat, that's where the kids play. In the little back room I have a table and a bed where I sleep with my husband. The few things we have just have to be piled one on top of the other, or hung from the ceiling, in the corridor. And the babies, well, some of them have to sleep in the beds and some of them under the beds. Wherever.

It's very cold in the highlands. So on the beds we have to put straw *payasas*, or pallets, that are made in the region. A real mattress costs from 800 to 1,000 pesos. It's hard for us to buy one. The majority of the miners have those straw payasas. In my home, for example, we don't have a single real mattress. And the *payasas* don't last too long because they're made of jute, and they're pretty uncomfortable too. But what can you do? The *payasas* come apart on one side, come apart on the other side, and we have to find a way to make them last, mending them here and there.

For some hours during the day and all through the night we have electric light in the camp which the company gives us.

We also have drinking water. But not in the houses. In the

neighborhoods there are public water pumps. You have to line up to get water.

So you see, we don't have too many comforts. For example, we don't have a bath in the house. Of course, there are public baths, but there are ten to twelve showers for everyone, for so many people, and these showers are for the whole camp. So the showers are open on alternate days: one day for the women and one day for the men. The showers only work when there's oil. Because the water is heated by oil.

Not only that, but there are only sanitary facilities, latrines, in the houses of the company's technical personnel. There aren't any in the workers' houses. There are public latrines but only about ten of them, for a whole neighborhood. For a whole neighborhood! They get dirty very fast and there's no running water. In the mornings the company workers assigned to the job clean them; but afterward, all day long they're very dirty. And if there's no water, they're dirty for several days. Even so, we have to use them. Just like they are.

There are plenty of problems with water, especially in the non-company villages. They suffer there more than we do. They have to stand in long lines. They have to come from very far away to get their water. And in these villages they don't have electric light like us. Their life is really hard.

But despite the lack of comfort in the houses, it's not easy to get one, because of the shortage. In order to get one there's sort of a contest. For example, a compañero who's worked ten years gets ten points; if he has seven kids as well as a wife, they put down eight points; if he works inside the mine, he gets more points. So, to get a house, the worker has to earn a certain number of points: have seniority in the company, have a greater number of kids, and work inside the mine. There are compañeros who get mine sickness very soon and die without even having the benefit of a loaned house.

Naturally there are complaints. That problem always comes up in the mines. But the company tells us it's going bankrupt, that it can't build more housing. Yet the majority of the houses in the camp are the same ones that were built when the company was private [before 1952]. After nationalization, almost everything stayed the same and very few houses were built. Recently they're making some of them bigger. After so many complaints and strikes we got them to do a few repairs on the houses that were about to collapse. The construction companies have patched them up a bit but in some cases that didn't do much good. A little rain and they fall right down. That's the way it is.

Because of the housing shortage, other people go to live with the people who have the right to a house. They're called *agregados*, or additional tenants. In my case, for example, my three sisters came to live with me. So I put a bed in the kitchen and turned it into a room for them. And I fixed up the kitchen outside, under a little zinc lean-to roof. And we lived like that for years.

The agregados aren't always relatives. They can be friends. For example, when I had just come to Siglo XX, I lived as an agregada. But I didn't even know the people we went to live with. My husband had met the man at work. He was very old and my husband was new in the company. I told the man how bad the woman whose house we lived in was, how she'd lock the door on us and things like that. And the man said to my compañero: "Come to my house." And me and my husband went to live there. We lived with them for a year. We were newlyweds. They had three little kids and his little sisters lived there also. We got along well, we took turns cooking. And we cooked in a great big pot for everyone. That's how lots of people live for several years.

Of course, there are company laws on how they have to give housing to the workers. But those laws don't do any good. And the mine workers, who in large part support the country's economy, don't even have a little house in the end.

HOW THE MINERS WORK

In the mine there are two systems of work: one is for the technicians and the other for the miners.

The mine doesn't stop. It works day and night. And that's why they've divided the miners into three shifts. Some of them change shift every month, others every two weeks, and others every week. My compañero, for example, changes shifts every week.

There are three shifts a day. Counting the time needed to enter the mine on the convoy and to leave the mineshaft, the first shift goes in at six in the morning and leaves at three in the afternoon; the second goes in at two in the afternoon and leaves at eleven at night; the third goes in at ten at night and leaves at seven in the morning.

When the worker is on the first shift, we women have to get up at four in the morning to prepare our compañero's breakfast. At three in the afternoon he gets back from the mine and he hasn't eaten anything yet. There's no way to take any food into the mine. It's not allowed. And anyway, it would get spoiled passing through so many places inside the mine. There's so much dust, so much heat, apart from the exploding dynamite, that even if they were able to eat anything at all, they'd be eating something that was bad for them. Everything would have to be organized some other way. And the company says that's impossible. If the company wanted to, it could set up clean and healthy dining rooms inside. But they aren't interested. The company only gives this kind of preferential treatment to the technicians. For example, the engineers work shorter hours. At 10:30 their food is brought to them. They're entitled to that. By 11:30 they've had lunch inside the mine. If the company wanted the workers to have lunch, they could give them the same privilege. But no. With only breakfast in their stomachs, the workers go from five in the morning till three in the afternoon, when they get back home. And the ones who live farther away, like in Uncía, have to get up at three in the morning and go to Socavón, Patiño, Miraflores, and other mine entrances that are really far away.

So how do they stand the mine? By chewing coca mixed with lye. Coca is a leaf that has a sort of bitter flavor but that makes you forget your hunger. Lye is the ashes from quinoa stalks [grain from the highlands] mixed with rice and aniseed, that people chew with coca in order to get rid of its bitter taste. So that's what the miners chew to raise their spirits and so that their stomachs can stand it.

The work in the mine is exhausting. My compañero, for example, gets home and goes to sleep without undressing. He sleeps two or three hours and then he gets up to eat.

The worst, the hardest, is the night shift. The miner works all night long and comes home to sleep during the day. But since the house is small and the houses in the camp are right next to each other, there's no place for the kids to play; they have to stay right there making a racket. And the walls are so thin that when the neighbors talk it seems like they're right there beside us. So the worker can't sleep, and he gets fed up and leaves the house. He can't even rest. This is the shift that my husband hates the most and so do the workers in general. But they're forced to work that shift. They have to obey the company rules; if not, they're fired.

My compañero has worked this way for almost twenty years. All the miners work a full eight hours inside the mine. The shifts are all the same.

The average life expectancy of a miner is barely thirty-five years. By then he's totally sick with mine sickness. Since there are so many explosions in order to get the ore out, these dust particles are breathed into the lungs, through the mouth and nose. This dust consumes and finally destroys the lungs. Their mouths turn black, purple. In the end they vomit pieces of lung and then they die. This is the occupational disease of the mine, called silicosis.

The miners suffer another misfortune: despite the fact that they support the national economy with their sweat and blood, throughout their lives they're despised by everyone, because people are terrified of us and think that we'll give them our disease, even though it isn't true. But those beliefs exist in the countryside and in the city. And that's why a lot of people don't want to rent us houses; they think that the mine sickness of our compañeros is going to go through the walls and infect the neighbors. And also, since the miners chew coca to get them through the day's work, they say that the miners are drug addicts, are *khoya locos,* madmen of the mines. So you can see that our problem is serious.

Those who live in the mining camps are mostly peasants who left their places in the highlands because they didn't earn enough to be able to eat. The highlands produce only one crop once a year: potatoes. Other than that, very little is produced there. There are years when the weather's favorable, and good potatoes are produced, but there are years when they produce hardly anything and the peasants can't even gather up the seeds they've planted. So then the whole family goes to the city or comes to the mines. And once they're here, well, they find the situation I've described.

Of course, government propaganda makes it seem that we lead an easy life, and when they speak of the miners they even say that we get free housing, free drinking water, free electricity, free education, cheap groceries, and other things. But let anyone who wants come to Siglo XX and they'll be able to see reality for themselves: the housing is terrible, and in addition it isn't given, it's just loaned; we only have water in public pumps; the baths are public; we only have electricity during the hours the company chooses; education's very expensive for us because we have to buy uniforms, school supplies, and so many other things. And the cheap groceries are part of our compañero's wages, understand?

So to keep us in this miserable state, they pay the miners a pittance. For example, my husband, who works in a special section inside the mine, gets 28 pesos a day now, or about 740 pesos a month. Last year they paid him 17 pesos a day, that is, not even a dollar a day. We have a family subsidy of about 347 pesos, as well as a cost of living allowance the government set because of devaluation, which is a bit more than 135 pesos a month. There's also a wage increase for night work. Adding it all up, my compañero can earn about 1,500 to 1,600 pesos a month. But with what the company discounts for the social security fund, the groceries, school buildings, and other things, we never see all of that money. Sometimes my husband gets 700 pesos, sometimes 500, sometimes we end up owing the company money. And from that my family of nine has to live. But there are workers who are even worse off.

One of our leaders, a great man who was killed, once explained to us, in a very simple manner, the reasons for this situation. He told us: "Compañeros, the ten thousand workers of Siglo XX produce 300 or 400 tons of tin per month." And he took out a sheet of paper and continued: "This represents what we produce, this whole sheet. This is all the profits we have produced in a month. How is this distributed?"

Then he tore the sheet of paper into five equal parts. "Of these five parts," he said, "four go to the foreign capitalist. That's his profits. Bolivia only keeps one part.

"Now, this fifth part is also distributed according to the system in which we live, right? So from this the government takes almost a half for transportation, customs, and export expenses, which is another way to make the capitalist earn a profit, no? Because, in our case, using our own trucks, wearing them out, we have to take our ore to Guaqui, on the border with Peru. In Peru there's a port. So, from there the ore has to go by boat to England, to the Williams Harvey foundry. From there it has to be transported by boat to the United States, so that they can manufacture the things that later the other countries, even Bolivia, buy from the United States at tremendously high prices. With all of this, the capitalist once again gets almost half of this fifth of the profits that were ours.

"Then, of the half which remains, the government again grabs some, for its own benefit and for the following groups: for the armed forces, for the salaries of their ministers, and to pay for their trips abroad. And they invest this money in foreign cities so that when they fall from power then they can go to another country as new millionaires, with the money already guaranteed.

"And another part of that is used for representative measures, for the army, for the DIC [*Departamento de Investigaciónes Criminales*—Department of Criminal Investigation] for their stool pigeons.

"And of the little bit that's left over, the government takes another part for social security services, for health, for hospitals, to pay for the electricity used by the people. Then another little part goes for the cheap groceries, to keep the miners happy and contented. And they make us believe that we, by the 'goodness of the government,' have four price-frozen articles, bread, meat, rice, and sugar, and they say that 'through their goodness' the government gives us a gift. But the government grabs it from here, from what we produce, right?

"And from this other little part that's left over, they also take some out for materials for the workers, like shovels and picks.

"Furthermore, they take out for their wives and the wives of the ministers, so that they can give gifts on Mother's Day and Christmas.

"And so they take and they keep on taking. And, look, from all the money that tin brings in, after using it up on so many things, just a little bit remains, a little bit for the wages of the ten thousand workers who mined that tin. So that we end up with almost nothing, see?"

That's how the leader explained the situation to us.

Once I had the opportunity to explain this in a conference I was invited to. That was in 1974, I think. In Alto de la Paz they were giving some training courses for some compañeras who had formed the Federation of Mothers.

There were some young men there from the university, economists. And there was a very important speech made. They took a blackboard and talked to the women about the country's economic problems, how money was being taken out of the country and about how wealth was distributed in Bolivia.

But there were lots of women there who didn't know how to read and who didn't understand the problem. And a poor woman, carrying a baby, stood up and said: "Young man, you've put a lot of numbers down there, but we haven't understood them. And you haven't talked about El Mutún.[3] What's happening with El Mutún?

---

3. An unexploited iron deposit located in the department of Santa Cruz, on the border with Brazil.

What's the government doing with El Mutún? My son came back from the army and told me that there's iron in El Mutún and that with the iron they make trucks. So why doesn't the government put some factories there, instead of giving El Mutún away to foreigners, so that maybe our children could find work?"

Well, even with the little education I have, I was able to understand what those compañeros from the university were saying. I wanted to simplify what I understood from all those numbers they wrote up on the board. So I spoke to the compañeras and I explained things in our language, more or less in the same way that the leader had taught us.

The women got very angry. They said that their husbands didn't know that, but that they were going to tell them about how the economy is manipulated in Bolivia. And they asked: "Why do they do that?" So I told them: "Well, that's what you've got to ask the government: why do they do that?"

So now I think: if the people came into power and changed this system of life, with the measures we'd take that wouldn't happen. We would even live longer. Because the first thing we'd do would be to straighten things out in the mines, buy new machinery, for example, so that we could work better, make our system of nutrition suit the physical wear and tear our compañeros have to put up with. I especially think that our compañeros shouldn't have to die that way in the mine. You go in there until you literally can't lift a shovel or a pick, and only then do you have the right to retire and receive a little pension. Before that, they don't give you a penny.

On the other hand, if the state looked after its human capital, the first thing it would do—and when one day we're in power I think it will be done—would be to decree that each miner must not work more than five years inside the mine. And at the same time that he's working there, the company itself should have him learn some trade so that when he leaves the mine after five years, he can work at some other job, as a good carpenter, a good shoemaker, for example. But he should have some field where he can earn his living and not spend the rest of his life in the mine.

Because, after all, if we go on the way we are . . . when will we ever have a healthy society? And if we go on treating people only as human machines that have to produce, produce and then die; and when they die they're exchanged for another force, that is, another person, who is also to be wiped out. . . . Well, this way human capital is just being thrown away, and that's the most important thing a society has, don't you agree?

HOW A MINER'S WIFE SPENDS HER DAY

My day begins at four in the morning, especially when my compañero is on the first shift. I prepare his breakfast. Then I have to prepare the *salteña*,[4] because I make about one hundred salteñas every day and I sell them in the street. I do this in order to make up for what my husband's wage doesn't cover in terms of our necessities. The night before, we prepare the dough and at four in the morning I make the salteñas while I feed the kids. The kids help me: they peel potatoes and carrots and make the dough.

Then the ones that go to school in the morning have to get ready, while I wash the clothes I left soaking overnight.

At eight I go out to sell. The kids that go to school in the afternoon help me. We have to go to the company store and bring home the staples. And in the store there are immensely long lines and you have to wait there until eleven in order to stock up. You have to line up for meat, for vegetables, for oil. So it's just one line after another. Since everything's in a different place, that's how it has to be. So all the time I'm selling salteñas, I line up to buy my supplies at the store. I run up to the counter to get the things and the kids sell. Then the kids line up and I sell. That's how we do it.

From the hundred salteñas I prepare, I get an average of 20 pesos a day, because if I sell them all today, I get 50 pesos, but if tomorrow I only sell thirty, then I lose out. That's why I say that the average earning is 20 pesos a day. And I'm lucky because people

---

4. Bolivian small pie, filled with meat, potatoes, hot pepper, and other spices.

know me and buy from me. But some of my women friends only make from 5 to 10 pesos a day.

From what we earn between my husband and me, we can eat and dress. Food is very expensive: 28 pesos for a kilo of meat, 4 pesos for carrots, 6 pesos for onions. . . . Considering that my compañero earns 28 pesos a day, that's hardly enough, is it?

Clothing, why that's even more expensive! So I try to make whatever I can. We don't ever buy ready-made clothes. We buy wool and knit. At the beginning of each year, I also spend about 2,000 pesos on cloth and a pair of shoes for each of us. And the company discounts some of that each month from my husband's wage. On the pay slips that's referred to as the "bundle." And what happens is that before we've finished paying the "bundle" our shoes have worn out. That's how it is.

Well, then, from eight to eleven in the morning I sell the salteñas, I do the shopping in the grocery store, and I also work at the Housewives' Committee, talking with the sisters who go there for advice.

At noon, lunch has to be ready because the rest of the kids have to go to school.

In the afternoon I have to wash clothes. There are no laundries. We use troughs and have to go get the water from the pump.

I've also got to correct the kids' homework and prepare everything I'll need to make the next day's salteñas.

Sometimes there are urgent matters to be resolved by the committee in the afternoon. So then I have to stop washing in order to see about them. The work in the committee is daily. I have to be there at least two hours. It's totally volunteer work.

The rest of the things have to get done at night. The kids bring home quite a lot of homework from school. And they do it at night, on a little table, a chair, or a little box. And sometimes all of them have homework and so one of them has to work on a tray that I put on the bed.

When my husband works in the morning, he goes to sleep at ten at night and so do the kids. When he works in the afternoon, then he's out most of the night, right? And when he works the night shift, he only comes back the next day. So I have to adapt myself to those schedules.

Generally we can't count on someone else to help around the house. What the husband earns is too little and really we all have to help out, like my making salteñas. Some women help out by knitting, others sew clothes, others make rugs, others sell things in the street. Some women can't help out and then the situation is really difficult.

It's because there aren't any places to work. Not just for the women, but also for the young men who come back from the army. And unemployment makes our children irresponsible, because they get used to depending on their parents, on their family. Often they get married without having gotten a job, and then they come home with their wives to live.

So that's how we live. That's what our day is like. I generally go to bed at midnight. I sleep four or five hours. We're used to that.

Well, I think that all of this proves how the miner is doubly exploited, no? Because, with such a small wage, the woman has to do much more in the home. And really that's unpaid work that we're doing for the boss, isn't it?

And by exploiting the miner, they don't only exploit his wife too, but there are times they even exploit the children. Because there's so much to do in the house that even the little kids have to work; for example, they have to get the meat, fetch the water. And sometimes they have to stand in line a long, long time, getting squashed and pushed around. When there's a shortage of meat in the mining camp, those lines get so long that sometimes children even die in the crush to get meat. There's a terrible frenzy. I've known children who died like that, with fractured ribs. And why? Because we mothers have so much to do at home that we send our children to line up. And sometimes there's such a terrible crush that that happens: they squash the kids. In recent years there've been various cases like that. And there's also something else you should take into account and that's the damage done to the kids who don't go to school because they have to run errands. When you wait for meat for two or three days and it doesn't come, that means lining up all day long. And the kids miss school for two or three days.

In other words, they try not to give the worker any sort of comfort. He's got to work it all out for himself. And that's that. In my case, for example, my husband works, I work, I make my children work, so there are several of us working to support the family. And the bosses get richer and richer and the workers' conditions get worse and worse.

But in spite of everything we do, there's still the idea that women don't work, because they don't contribute economically to the home, that only the husband works because he gets a wage. We've often come across that difficulty.

One day I got the idea of making a chart. We put as an example the price of washing clothes per dozen pieces and we figured out how many dozens of items we washed a month. Then the cook's wage, the babysitter's, the servant's. We figured out everything that we miners' wives do every day. Adding it all up, the wage needed to pay us for what we do in the home, compared to the wages of a cook, a washerwoman, a babysitter, a servant, was much higher than what the men earned in the mine for a month. So that way we made our compañeros understand that we really work, and even more than they do in a certain sense. And that we even contribute more to the household with what we save. So, even though the state doesn't recognize what we do in the home, the country benefits from it, because we don't receive a single penny for this work.

And as long as we continue in the present system, things will always be like this. That's why I think it's so important for us revolutionaries to win that first battle in the home. And the first battle to be won is to let the woman, the man, the children participate in the struggle of the working class, so that the home can become a stronghold that the enemy can't overcome. Because if you have the enemy inside your own house, then it's just one more weapon that our common enemy can use toward a dangerous end. That's why it's really necessary that we have very clear ideas about the whole situation and that we throw out forever that bourgeois idea that the woman should stay home and not get involved in other things, in union or political matters, for example. Because, even if she's only at home, she's part of the whole system of exploitation that her compañero lives in anyway, working in the mine or in the factory or wherever—isn't that true?

WORKERS' ORGANIZATION

Basically we owe the Bolivians' tradition of struggle to the working class, which hasn't let the unions fall into government hands. The union must always be an independent organization and must follow the working-class line. This doesn't mean that it's apolitical. But under no pretext can the union place itself in the service of the government, because if we consider that our capitalist governments represent the bosses, defend the bosses, then the union must never be in their service.

The working class in the mines is organized into unions. Where I live, for example, there are five unions: the miners of Cataví, the locatarios of the "20th of October," the veneristas, and the lameros.

The unions are in turn grouped on a national level in the Federación Sindical de Trabajadores Mineros de Bolivia (Union Federation of Mine Workers of Bolivia), or FSTMB. But there are also the unions of construction workers, factory workers, teamsters, peasants, railroad workers, etc. And each union group also has its federation.

All these federations are grouped in the Central Obrera Boliviana (Bolivian Workers' Union), or the COB. All the union groups are pretty much organized through joint agreements and congresses. And if, for example, the miners have a particular problem and the factory workers have another, everything is written down on a piece of paper and in a congress they say: We're going to do this for the miners, and that for the factory workers, and every single one of us is going to join in and shoulder to shoulder we're going to work out these problems. That's how the Central Obrera

Boliviano works. For example, when the factory workers are being badly attacked, being wiped out, the Central Obrera Boliviano calls out a demonstration of all the sectors, supports those factory workers. And if the miners are in trouble, then the Central Obrera Boliviano also calls out the other unions and everyone helps out.

I think that the union, the Federación, the Central Obrera Boliviano are our representatives, are our voice, and that's why we should take care of them as our most prized possessions.

I also think that in this job of organizing ourselves we have to pay special attention to the development of leaders. In the past, because of our limited preparation, because of our lack of revolutionary watchfulness, because of our lack of solidarity, many leaders have sold out to the government. Sometimes because we chose them badly. For example, we used to make the great mistake of noticing someone who spoke very well and right away we'd say: "Wow! That guy sure talks well! He must be a good leader!" And many times it wasn't true. Not everyone who speaks well acts well, right? Other times we found a really healthy, honest guy who wanted to serve the working class. We'd elect him and then forget about him, we'd leave him alone to face the government, the company. And they made lots of problems for him. And in the end, what would happen? Some of them sold out to the government; others were killed or simply disappeared. And that way we never had a good leader. Why? In large part it was our own fault.

But through the years we learned to understand the value of solidarity. And some committed revolutionary leaders have arisen from the working class, who began to guide the people correctly. Of course, the governments have used armed force to make us give in. So you have the massacres of 1942, of 1949, then two more in 1965 and 1967. Really ugly massacres, where hundreds and hundreds lost their lives.

But instead of this being something which scares and holds the people back, it's strengthened them more and more. And correcting the errors of the past, in the last twenty years several healthy leaders have been developed and we've learned the importance of broad solidarity with them, controlling them, supporting them, and criticizing them when they don't act as they should.

Here in the mines, the compañeros really control us leaders, and if they aren't convinced by something we do, even the most humble worker draws our attention to it and criticizes us. For example, many times they've made me cry. All excited, I used to leave the kids at home and go to present a problem at a meeting or over the radio. On returning, a worker comes up to me and says: "What was that shit all of you were saying over the radio? What shit!" Like that. And that hurts, no? But then afterward you think it over and say: "Yes, I put my foot in it, I should've thought more, I should've sounded people out more." And that's how you learn.

And when a leader's in prison, it's very important that he or she feels our solidarity, not only personally, but also with his or her family. Well, any comrade who lands in jail should be able to count on this attitude on our part, right? You forget the personal suffering of the beatings undergone in jail, or that your face has been disfigured, when you come home and the children say: "Daddy, Mommy, the union, the companeros, gave us a little bread." Then if you're honorable and honest, you commit yourself forever to your people and there's no force on earth that can separate you from the people who showed you that confidence and that solidarity.

We've had that experience. We've had compañeros who've preferred to die rather than betray us. Many leaders have been deported, tortured, killed. Just to name a few, I'd like to mention Federico Escobar Zapata, Rosendo García Maisman, César Lora, Isaac Camacho. In different circumstances they were made to disappear. Maisman died in the massacre of San Juan, in 1967, defending the union. César Lora they followed to the countryside and there they killed him. Isaac Camacho was arrested and the DIC agents made him disappear. Federico Escobar was killed: first they paid a truck driver to overturn a truck; Federico was wounded and they took him to be operated in a clinic in La Paz, and at the beginning of the operation he died, and they haven't to this day cleared up the circumstances of his death. We still think they killed him.

Those leaders used the years they were in leadership to teach the working class how to organize well and not let itself be deceived. And today, even if they kill fifty of them, a hundred more appear, or if they kick out five hundred, the government can't make the working class give in.

What haven't they done to destroy the strength of the unions, the unity of the people! First they brutally repressed us, many times, even massacring us on some occasions. Then they sent people from the ORIT [*Organización Regional Interamericana del Trabajo*—Regional Interamerican Organization of Labor] to give courses in the mines. The ORIT is an international organization directed from the United States that has created some "independent unions" or affiliates, which instead of defending the worker defend the company, the bosses, you see? In Bolivia we call them "yellow unions." But the ORIT wasn't able to set up those unions in the mines. Today, the point has been reached where the government totally ignores our union organizations and wants to impose on us, the rank and file, coordinators who are elected and directed by the government itself. But the working class as such hasn't accepted that. Either openly or underground, the workers know what they want and they choose their own representatives so that they can "stand up united" before the exploiter.

Of course, there have been and there are errors committed by the leaders. Someone made me see how time and time again the workers were somewhat manipulated by the leaders. Yes, indeed, that has also happened. There are some political leaders who get a little euphoric and don't see further ahead, and think that the working class has to be at the service of their interests and their party. But I think that a leader has to have the maximum respect for the people. And if they have elected us as leaders, we must be at the service of the working class and not vice versa.

It's possible that there've been errors; that without a real reason or cause the workers have been hurt. I think that this has happened mostly because of lack of experience. When someone who hasn't lived, who hasn't known, wants to go along a new road, they always have to fall a few times and then pick themselves up again. That's why we need to learn from experience, either from our own history, from the struggles that took place before in Bolivia, or from the experience of other peoples.

And there should be testimony. That's been our mistake, not to write down everything that happens. Very little has been set down in writing. Like the testimonies that we had in the union, or on the miners' radio stations, like for example recordings; they were taken or destroyed by the army. And all of that would have been so useful to us, even just to think about what we were doing and criticize it, you know?

So, that's what I say, that to carry on the organization of the working class you've got to be very careful and choose good leaders. It's also the duty of the rank-and-file, of the masses, to control those leaders. That's very important in order to prepare ourselves for taking power.

Of course, right now we don't know who'll be our president when we're in power. But we have so much confidence in the working class that we know we'll find one. Our fight is so big, so long, and so important. There are thousands of leaders. Not only among the men, but among the women and the young people there are people of great, great courage. Here and there we see people emerge who surprise us by their great knowledge. The people are an inexhaustible source of wisdom, of strength, and we should never underrate the people.

We women, the compañeras of the men, work with them in the job that they're involved in. We women were raised from the cradle with the idea that women were made only to cook and take care of the kids, that we are incapable of assuming important tasks, and that we shouldn't be allowed to get involved in politics. But necessity made us change our lives. Fifteen years ago, in a period of tremendous problems for the working class, a group of seventy women organized to win freedom for their compañeros who were leaders and had been imprisoned for demanding higher wages. The women got everything they asked for, after a ten-day hunger strike. And from then on they decided to organize in a group which they called "Housewives' Committee of Siglo XX."

Since then, this committee has always been in step with the unions and other working-class organizations, struggling for the same causes. That's why they've also attacked us women. Several of us have been imprisoned, interrogated, jailed, and we've even lost our children because of being in the struggle with our compañeros. But the committee hasn't died. And in recent years, after a call from its leaders, four or five thousand women have come out to demonstrate.

The Housewives' Committee is organized like the union and it functions almost the same way. We also participate in the Federation of Mine Workers and we have our place in the Central Obrera Boliviano. We always make our voice heard and are careful to carry out the tasks undertaken by the working class.

Our position is not like the feminists' position. We think our liberation consists primarily in our country being freed forever from the yoke of imperialism and we want a worker like us to be in power and that the laws, education, everything, be controlled by this person. Then, yes, we'll have better conditions for reaching a complete liberation, including our liberation as women.

For us, the important thing is the participation of the compañero and the compañera together. Only that way will we be able to see better days, become better people, and see more happiness for everyone. Because if women continue only to worry about the house and remain ignorant of the other parts of our reality, we'll never have citizens who'll be able to lead our country. Because education begins from the cradle. And if we think of the central role played by women as the mothers who have to forge future citizens, then, if they aren't prepared they'll only forge mediocre citizens who are easily manipulated by the capitalist, by the boss. But if they're already politicized, if they're already trained, from the cradle they'll educate their children with other ideas and the children will be different.

That's more or less how we're working. Many of my sisters have demonstrated by their actions that they can assume an important role alongside the worker. And our committee has given proof that it can be a strong ally for the interests of the working class.

Someone said that "a bullet can't kill the ideas and hopes of the people." I believe that this is a great truth. Many have fallen and many more will fall, but we know that our liberation will come one day and that the people will be in power.

Of course, that won't be given as a gift. It's going to cost a lot of blood, a lot of struggle, like what's happened in other countries. That's also why it's so important for us to have contact with people who already live in socialism, to know about the conquests by the people who are already free from imperialism. Not in order to copy their experience, but to compare it with our reality and to see what the experiences which have taken them to power can contribute to our cause. In Bolivia we try to do that and socialist ideas have penetrated the working class to such an extent that in the last congress of the Central Obrera Boliviana, in 1970, they voted for the resolution that "Bolivia will only be free when it becomes a socialist country."

We know there's a long struggle ahead, but that's what we're all about. And we aren't alone. How many peoples are in the same struggle! And, why not say it? Every people needs the solidarity of others, like us, because our fight is big. So we have to practice the proletarian internationalism that many people have sung about, and many countries have followed. Many other countries suffer persecutions, outrages, murders, massacres, like Bolivia. And, how beautiful it is to feel that in other peoples we have brothers and sisters who support us, who are in solidarity with us, and make us understand that our struggles aren't isolated from one another. This solidarity means a lot. We always try to show it in Bolivia in some real way.

For example, in the past few years we were in solidarity especially

with Chile and Vietnam, Laos and Cambodia. We were overjoyed
by the triumph of Vietnam, which was able to deal one more blow
against imperialism. And in various ways we let the Vietnamese
people know that we were with them, even though we didn't go
and fight beside them.

When Allende was overthrown, we protested against what the
Chilean people were suffering. And, look, we have this problem
because the Chileans have taken away our access to the sea. [In
the war with Chile in 1879, Bolivia lost its access to the Pacific
Ocean. The Bolivian people have always considered this a usurpa-
tion and wish to regain their coast.] But we don't have any hatred
for the Chilean people, although the governments try to make it
seem as if we do. Because that too was a product of the system of
oppression in which we're living. And it wasn't the ordinary people
who stole the sea from us. The rulers did all that, they planned it
all. And now they want to use that banner when it suits them. For
example, when Salvador Allende was in power, in the streets of
La Paz there were parades with modern weapons and it was said:
"With these weapons we'll take our access to the sea away from
the Chileans." But when the Pinochet government came along,
as the most loyal friend of my present government, my government immediately changed its tune and went to make treaties with
Pinochet in Charaña [Bolivian village on the border with Chile
where Banzer and Pinochet reestablished diplomatic relations
which had been suspended in 1963].

Those are weapons that the enemy uses very successfully to keep
us constantly fighting among ourselves, so that way we can't unite
and form a common front, you see? They always try to control us
that way, making us angry in order to divide us.

And this doesn't only happen with the government, but also in
the organizations. In those organizations that are about to come
out a little stronger and more united, the enemy treads very subtly
. . . it takes careful note of who is the person it can trick and it
uses that person to foment resentments and disagreements. So the
organization sinks and those who reap the benefits are always the

enemy. We must be well prepared for all of that so we won't be easily fooled. That way we'll be able to keep our organizations alive.

Last of all, I think that it's essential to know that we're all important in the revolutionary struggle . . . no? We're such a large machine and each one of us is a cog. And if one cog is missing, the machine can't work. So we've got to know how to assign each person his or her role and know how to value each one. Some are good at making pretty speeches. Others at writing well. Others of us are good for providing bulk, at least to be present and be one more in the crowd. Some of us have to suffer, play the role of martyr, others have to write our history. And that's how all of us have to work together. And like a leader once told us: "No one, no one is useless, we all have our roles to play in history. And we're even going to need a person who knows how to nail a shoe well, because for just that reason a battle can be lost, or even a revolution." So nobody should think of himself or herself as useless; in one way or another, we can all help. We're all indispensable for the revolution. We're all going to contribute in our own way. The important thing is that we be well directed in the struggle of the working class and that each one carry out what is assigned him or her in the best possible manner.

Her Life

PULACAYO

I was born in Siglo XX on May 7, 1937. When I was about three years old, I went to Pulacayo and lived there till I was twenty. That's why it's not fair to tell my personal story without referring to that village, which I owe a great deal to. I consider it a part of my life. Both Pulacayo and Siglo XX have an important place in my heart. Pulacayo, because it sheltered me in my childhood; I lived my happiest years there. Because in childhood, when you've got a piece of bread to fill your stomach and a piece of rag to keep you from the cold, you feel happy. A child doesn't really notice too much about the reality he or she is living.

Pulacayo is in the department of Potosí, in the province of Quijarro, at about 4,000 meters above sea level. It's a fairly combative and militant mining district. It participated actively in the revolution of April 9, 1952,[5] disarming the government forces of

---

5. Although it was fought by the people against the hacendados and resulted in a land reform program under which serfs were given the land they had previously held on loan from the feudal landlords, this revolution was bourgeois-nationalist in character, bringing to power the Movimiento Nacionalista Revolucionario (MNR), or Revolutionary Nationalist Movement, under Paz Estenssoro. Known as the Bolivian Revolution, it also brought about the extension of universal suffrage.

Uyuni. That revolutionary effervescence of the working class was a fundamental reason for the closing of the mine. Nevertheless, because of the will of its sons and daughters, the village hasn't died. They've turned it into an industrial town where there are wool, nail, and spike factories and the foundry, which is very important, despite the fact that today it only has about four hundred workers and before it had two thousand.

My mother was from the city of Oruro. My father is Indian. I don't know if he's Quechua or Aymara, because he speaks both languages very well, very correctly. Oh, I know he was born in the countryside, in Toledo.

My parents loved each other very much. But my father got mixed up in political activities and he was also a union leader, and that's why he suffered a lot and we suffered with him.

Since before he was married he'd worked politically. Even before he was married he'd been in jail. He was educated first in the countryside and then in the mines. And he also learned a lot in the Chaco war.[6] He fought in that war and realized that Bolivia needed to have a left-wing party. And when the MNR appeared, he trusted it and joined its struggle.

First they deported my father to Coati Island, which is on Lake Titicaca, because he was a political and union leader. Then to Curahuara de Carangas. Later he returned to Siglo XX and they arrested him again. They kicked him off his job and deported him to Pulacayo. "Let him die of the cold," they said. Because Pulacayo is a pretty cold place.

When he got there, my father couldn't find work anywhere, not in the mine or anywhere, because his name was on the "blacklist." That was in 1940. And that's how my daddy, my mama, my newborn sister, and I lived.

---

6. War between Bolivia and Paraguay (1932–35). The absence of defined territorial boundaries led to a dispute over oil reserves in the region between the two countries, behind which were oil interests of the United States (Standard Oil) and England-Holland (Royal Dutch Shell).

Luckily my father was a tailor by trade and he began to work; but he had very little income and he needed material to set up a good tailor's shop. Once he went to an officer's house to mend his clothes and the officer made him join the mine police force. They gave him a uniform, he passed muster, but they mostly used him as a tailor. And sometimes they'd give him a suit that he had to deliver in three days, and then my daddy had to work day and night in order to finish it on time; but they didn't pay him anything extra for that work, just the small policeman's salary, which was very little. And so we had hard times. My mother would have to help him and she'd make some suits, she'd embroider some things and she was always working with him. I remember how we loved each other and how happy I was.

But I don't know if my daddy was still involved in political things after we went to Pulacayo; the problem is that when one of my little sisters was born, he disappeared. That was in 1946, when they killed President Villarroel. We heard about it on a Sunday, I'll always remember. My mother was still in bed because she'd just given birth. And the army guys came into my house at night and searched through everything. They even made my mother get out of bed. And everything we had, a little bit of rice, some noodles, well, they mixed it all up and threw it on the floor. They even offered to give me candies, chocolates, if I'd tell them if I'd seen weapons in the house.

I was about ten years old then, and I hadn't started school yet because we didn't have enough money. My daddy was gone for a long time and my mother went looking for him everywhere. And then, after several months, my daddy came back. It seems that some compañeros had taken him someplace.

Then everything was back to normal, my daddy went back to work, and I was able to go to school. But we had such bad luck that my mother got sick because of all those things that happened to us. She was having another baby at the time. And my mother died, leaving five little orphaned girls; I was the oldest.

So I had to take charge of my little sisters. I had to miss school and my life became pretty hard. First, my father started drinking a lot because of my mother's death. He could play the piano, the guitar, and people would invite him to any party so he could play for them. That's how he began to drink a lot. And when he came home drunk, he'd beat us a lot.

We lived all alone, with almost nobody. We didn't have friends, we didn't have toys. Once, in some garbage, I found a little bear without feet, really dirty and old. I took it home, I washed it and fixed it up. That was the only toy we had. We all played with it, I remember very well. It was a horrible toy, but it was all we had to love, all we had to play with.

At Christmas we'd leave our shoes on the window sill hoping for some little present. But there wasn't ever anything. Then we'd go out in the street and we'd see that all the little girls were playing with pretty dolls. We wanted at least to touch them, but the little girls would say: "You mustn't play with that, dirty Indian child." I can't understand it, but there was real unfriendliness on the part of the other children. That's why we lived in a world apart. Us and no one else, we'd play in the kitchen, we'd tell each other stories, we'd sing.

On the night she was dying, my mother called my father and made him promise never to get involved in political activities again, because she was going to die and he'd have to take care of us. "We've got daughters, just women," she said to him. "And if anything happens to me, who's going to take care of them? Don't get mixed up in anything anymore. We've already suffered so much." And she made my father swear that he wasn't going to get involved in anything again.

After that, my father stopped getting involved like before. But he was very nostalgic about it. When the revolution of 1952 triumphed, for example, he felt very happy. And he was sad not to be with the people who went to meet with President Paz Estenssoro. I've realized that we daughters were a hindrance to him in his activities. Of course, he didn't stop participating or helping people understand the situation. He'd get groups together in the house, he held political meetings, he participated politically, but he was no longer as deeply involved as before.

The revolution of 1952 was a great event in Bolivia's history. It was really a people's victory. But what happened? The people, the working class, the peasants, we weren't ready to take power. And so, since we didn't know anything about the law, about how you govern a country, we had to give the power to the people of the petty bourgeoisie who said they were our friends and agreed with our ideas. We had to turn the government over to a doctor, Victor Paz Estenssoro, and other guys. But they immediately made up a new bourgeoisie, they helped make new people rich. Those people began undoing the revolution. And we workers and peasants lived in worse conditions than before.

This happened because we'd always been taught the idea that only someone who has studied, who has money, and who's gone to the university can govern a country. They don't educate us and they look down on the people, so we weren't prepared to take power ourselves, despite the fact that, yes, we had made the revolution. And those middle-class people that we put into power and in whom we placed our trust betrayed everything we'd wanted to do.

For example, they said that the mines would belong to the people, that the peasants would own the land. The agrarian reform was carried out, that's true; the mines were nationalized, that's also true. But, in reality, to this day we aren't the owners of the mines, nor do the peasants own the land. Everything's been betrayed, because we left the power in the hands of greedy people.

That's brought us to the conclusion that we, the people, have to prepare ourselves in order to reach power. Why should we allow a few to benefit from all of Bolivia's resources while we go on forever working like animals, without having higher aspirations, without being able to provide a better future for our children? Why shouldn't we aspire to better things when our country is rich thanks to our sacrifice?

That's why I think that if we're going to make a revolution in the future, our government will have to come from the people, it will have to be working class, it will have to be peasant. That's the only way we'll make sure that it's us who are in power. Because only those who know what it's like to dig into a rock, only those who know what it's like to work every day and earn your bread with the sweat of your brow, are going to be able to make laws that control and watch out for the happiness of the great majority, the exploited people.

With the experience and knowledge I've picked up, I now understand that the MNR wasn't what my father had always wanted. I remember, for example, that when the mines were nationalized, he was happy. But he said that the "tin barons" shouldn't be paid. And he protested strongly and insisted to the people who met in our house: "How can we indemnify them?" He'd say that they shouldn't do that. My father thought we were asleep while he argued with the compañeros, but lots of times I stayed awake and would listen to what they said, even though I didn't understand what it was all about. So one day I asked him: "Daddy, what's that about indemnifying? And why don't you agree that it should be done?" Even then, when I was still a girl and didn't understand politics, my daddy tried to explain it to me with a story.

"Suppose," he said, "that I bought you a beautiful doll or one of those puppets that can talk and walk. With that doll you could make propaganda, earn your living, and so forth. But, let's suppose that you've loaned that doll to a man and he's taken it on tours and has made it work a whole lot. You've already asked him to return it to you because the doll is yours, you've fought with him, and nothing. Instead, that man has hit you and has won, because he's big and strong. But one day, after so much fighting, you grab him and you hit him hard and you take the doll away from him. And the little doll is yours again. But after so many years of work, it's totally broken and old. It's not as useful as when it was brand new. Now then, after taking your doll back from the man, should you pay him for the way the doll has aged? Don't you see that you shouldn't? It's the same as the 'tin barons' who've gotten rich with our mine. The mine's being returned to the people. But what's happening? They're going to pay them, they're going to give indemnification to those men for the damage they've left us. And that's what I don't want to happen."

That time I more or less understood what my father meant. With what I know today, I understand why he was so saddened when the indemnification decree, Number 53, came out.

Ultimately, the nationalization of the mines has only meant that they pass over to other owners and other people get rich. In other words, nothing has changed. In 1942 and 1949, the government massacred the people of Siglo XX to support the "tin barons," who were the mine owners. After the revolution of '52, which cost the people so much, in the same way, or even more cruelly, the government was responsible for two massacres at Siglo XX, in 1965 and 1967. Not only that, but when they nationalized the mines the machinery was already old, the government didn't have parts, so everything went from bad to worse and it's always the miners who pay.

Why were the mines nationalized? The people in the government and in the management of the company aren't so dumb. No, they're people who've studied. They are economists, sociologists, people who know about laws and everything. Is it possible that they don't know how you should do things in order for the people to get ahead? Can it be that they don't know how to solve the problems without repressing and massacring the people? Yes, they know. But the thing is that they are given money from outside. And so that's how they've been corrupted; they've been bought off, in other words.

Well, in 1954 it was hard for me to return to school after the vacation, because we had a house that was just a little room where we didn't even have a yard and we didn't have anyplace to leave the kids or anyone to leave them with. So we talked with the principal of the school and he gave me permission to take my little sisters with me. Classes were in the afternoon and in the morning. And I had to combine everything: house and school. So I'd carry the

littlest one and the other one hung on to my hand, and Marina
carried the bottles, and my sister, the other little one, carried the
notebooks. And that's how all of us would go to school. In a corner
we had a little crate where we'd leave the baby while we studied.
When she cried, we'd give her her bottle. And my other little sisters
wandered around from bench to bench. I'd get out of school, I had
to carry the baby, we'd go home and I had to cook, wash, iron, take
care of the kids. All that seemed very hard to me. I wanted so badly
to play! And there were so many other things I wanted to do, like
any other little girl.

Two years later, the teacher wouldn't let me take my sisters
because they made too much noise. My father couldn't pay for a
maid, since his wage wasn't even enough for the food and clothing
we needed. For example, at home I always went barefoot; I only
used my shoes to go to school. And there were so many things I
had to do and it was so cold in Pulacayo that my hands would split
open and a lot of blood would come out of my hands and feet. My
mouth too, my lips would crack. And my face would also bleed.
That's because we didn't have enough warm clothing.

Well, since the teacher had laid down the law, I began to go to
school alone. I'd lock up the house and the kids had to stay in the
street, because the house was dark, it didn't have a window, and
they were terrified if I locked them in. It was like a jail, with just
one door. And there wasn't any place to leave the kids, because
at that time we lived in a neighborhood where there weren't any
families. Only single men lived there.

Then my father told me to leave school, because I already knew
how to read and I could learn other things by reading on my own.
But I didn't obey him and I continued going to my classes.

Then one day the little one ate carbide ashes that were in the
garbage pail, the carbide that's used to light the lamps. They'd
thrown food on top of the ashes and my little sister, who I think
was hungry, went to eat out of the can. She got a terrible intestinal
infection and then she died. She was three years old.

I felt guilty about my little sister's death and I was very, very depressed. And even my father would say that it had happened because I hadn't wanted to stay home with the kids. I'd brought up that sister since she was born, so her death made me suffer a lot.

From then on I began to take much more care of my little sisters. Much more. When it was very cold and we didn't have anything to cover ourselves with, I'd grab my father's old rags and cover them with those, I'd wrap up their feet, their bellies. I'd carry them, try to entertain them. I devoted myself completely to the girls.

My father arranged it so that the mining company in Pulacayo gave us a house with a little yard, because it was very hard living where we were. And the manager, whose suits my father fixed, ordered them to give him a larger dwelling with a room, a kitchen, and a little corridor where we could leave the girls. So we went to live in a neighborhood in the mining camp, where the majority of the families were mine workers.

Sometimes we went hungry and there wasn't enough food, since my father could only afford a little. When you're small, it's hard to live in poverty and with all kinds of problems. But that developed something strong in us: a great sensitivity, a great desire to help all the people. Our children's games always had something to do with our kind of life and with how we wanted to live. Also, during our childhood we'd seen that even though we didn't have much, my mother and father were always helping different families in Pulacayo. So when we saw poor people begging in the street, me and my sisters would start dreaming. We'd dream that one day we'd be big, that we'd have land, that we'd plant, and that we'd give those poor people food. And any time we had a little sugar or coffee or something else left over, and we heard a sound, we'd say: "A poor person's passing by. Look, here's a little rice, a little sugar." And we'd wrap it up in a rag and throw it out into the street for some poor person to pick up.

Once we threw out some coffee when my father was coming back from work. And when he came into the house he really scolded us and said: "How can you waste the little that we have? How can you throw out what costs me so much to earn for you?" And he really beat us. But those things were things that just occurred to us, we thought that that way we could help someone, see?

And so that's what our life was like. I was thirteen then. My father always insisted that I shouldn't go on with school, but I would beg him and I kept on going. Of course, I never had enough school supplies. Some teachers understood, others didn't. And that's why they'd hit me, they'd beat me terribly because I wasn't a good student.

The problem was that my father and me had made a deal. He'd explained that he didn't have money, that he couldn't buy my supplies, that he couldn't give me anything for school. And so I had to arrange things as best I could. And that's why I had problems.

In the sixth grade I had a great teacher who knew how to understand me. He was a pretty strict teacher and on the first day that I didn't bring in all the supplies, he punished me very severely. One day he pulled me by the hair, slapped me, and, in the end, threw me out of school. I had to go home, crying. But the next day I went back, and through the window I watched what the kids were doing.

At one point the teacher called me:

"I suppose you haven't brought your supplies," he said.

I couldn't answer and started to cry.

"Come in. Go ahead, take your seat. And stay behind when school's over."

By that time one of the girls had told him that I didn't have a mother, that I cooked for my little sisters and all that.

At the end of school I stayed and then he said to me:

"Look, I want to be your friend, but you've got to tell me what's wrong. Is it true that you don't have a mother?"

"Yes, sir."

"When did she die?"

"When I was still in first grade."

"And your father, where does he work?"

"With the mine police, he's a tailor."

"Okay, what's the matter? Look, I want to help you, but you've got to be honest. What's the matter?"

I didn't want to talk, because I thought he was going to call my father in, like some teachers did when they were angry. And I didn't want him called in, because that's what the deal had been with him: I wasn't supposed to bother him or ask him for anything. But the teacher asked me more questions and then I told him everything. I also told him that I could do my homework, but that I didn't have notebooks, because we were very poor and my daddy couldn't buy them, and that years ago my father had wanted to take me out of school because he couldn't pay for it anymore. And that with a lot of sacrifice and effort I'd been able to get to sixth grade. But it wasn't because my father didn't want to, it was because he couldn't. Because, in spite of all the belief there was in Pulacayo that a woman shouldn't be taught to read, my father always wanted us to know at least how to do that.

It's true, my father was always concerned about our education. When my mother died, people would look at us and say: "Oh, the poor little things, five women, not one man . . . what good are they? They'd be better off dead." But my daddy would say proudly: "No, let my girls alone, they're going to live." And when people tried to make us feel bad because we were women and weren't much good for anything, he'd tell us that all women had the same rights as men. And he'd say that we could do the same things men do. He always raised us with those ideas. Yes, it was a very special discipline. And all that was very positive in terms of our future. So that's why we never considered ourselves useless women.

The teacher understood all that, because I told him about it. And we made a deal that I'd ask him for all the school supplies I needed. And from that day on we got on very well. And the teacher would give me and my little sisters all the supplies we needed. And that's how I was able to finish my last year in school, in 1952.

In school I learned to read, to write, and to get along. But I can't say that school really helped me to understand life. I think that education in Bolivia, despite the various reforms there've been, is still part of the capitalist system we live in. They always give an alienating education. For example, they make us see the motherland like a beautiful thing in the national anthem, in the colors of the flag, and all those things stop meaning anything when the motherland isn't well. The motherland, for me, is in every corner, it's also in the miners, in the peasants, in the people's poverty, their naked-ness, their malnutrition, in their pains and their joys. That's the motherland, right? But in school they teach us to sing the national anthem, to parade, and they say that if we refuse to parade we aren't patriotic, and, nevertheless, they never explain our poverty, our misery, our parents' situation, their great sacrifices and their low wages, why a few children have everything and many others have nothing. They never explained that to me in school.

That's why I feel that we all have a responsibility to our children so that at home they learn to see the truth. Because if not, we're preparing future failures. And when they're a little bigger, they begin to resist, and in the end, they turn out to be misfits, they don't even want to greet their parents anymore. But I think that we ourselves are to blame when we make our children live in a world of fantasy. There are times when parents don't even have a mouth-ful to eat, but they always get something for the children. And they don't show them how difficult the life we lead is and the children don't realize what reality is. And when they go to university, they don't want to say that they're miners' children, that they're peas-ants' children. And they don't know how to speak our language, I mean that they analyze everything and they explain everything in such a complicated way that we can't understand each other anymore. And that's a great mistake, because those who go to uni-versity learn so many things and we should all take advantage of that, shouldn't we? I do think that they should be able to speak and write in a scientific manner, but also one that we can understand and not always in a language which only they understand, with drawings and numbers, if you know what I mean. Because the military also understands numbers. And when they come to Siglo XX to talk over a problem with us, the first thing they do is bring a gigantic blackboard and gather us together and a guy comes out who starts to talk about money and stuff like that. The workers don't listen to them, they boo at them and tell them that they can take their numbers and go home. It's true, they boo at them.

So I think that the people who have had the chance to go to the university should talk our language, because we haven't been in the university and we don't understand much about numbers, but we are capable of understanding our national reality. That's why I say if they really want the people to be happy, those who study should maybe learn something about how to speak in our language with all the knowledge that they have, so that we too can understand everything that they learn. That would be very important and it would be a way to contribute, you might say, to the achievement of better living conditions for our country.

Thanks to all the consciousness of the Bolivian working class, the students really have changed a lot in the last few years. I see that in Bolivia the student movement is very strong, not only in the universities, but also in the colleges and schools. And a proof of that is that the government resorts to closing down the schools. Because that's the way to shut the students up, when they can't be shut up either with the tanks or planes which are used to attack the university. And each time the students rise up, the government begins to repress the movement leaders. Still, the students are always supporting us in our demands and are present with their solidarity when we go out on strike or have demonstrations or when our compañeros are put in jail.

But I also realize that many young people who supported us, and who seemed to be good revolutionaries, moved far away from us when they graduated as professionals. You no longer hear people talking about the student who'd say: "We'll bear the arms our fathers leave behind because we, their children, who have studied politics, economics, law, know how the people are deceived, we know what our fathers' lungs are like . . ." and so forth. Out of the university comes the doctor, the lawyer, he or she gets a little job and the revolutionary disappears. We have to be careful that that doesn't happen, we have to be responsible to our class, we have to be consistent, do we not?

When I finished school, they gave me a job in the company grocery store in Pulacayo. That was in 1953. The next year my second sister also finished grade school and she also was able to get a job in a pastry shop.

About that time, my father felt the need to get married again. But with his second wife, our life was more unbearable. I tried to win her affection, because I needed a mother. I'd lost mine so early . . . I needed someone who'd understand me, encourage me, caress me, take my hand. And my daddy, in spite of loving us so much, was pretty cold with us. So when this woman came to the house—she had two children of her own—I felt that it was the loveliest thing to have someone who'd prepare our food, someone who'd be there to try and stop my father from hitting me. And it all seemed good to me. And we really welcomed her. During all those years I'd gotten used to getting up early, so in the mornings I'd help her, I'd start cooking, I'd peel potatoes for her to cook, all that before going to work. And on Saturdays and Sundays I'd wash her skirts.

But, I don't know why, the stepmother didn't like us. Especially my sisters. One day I caught her hitting my little sister and we began to argue. And after that she began to take food away from us. She'd cook in a little pot and from there she'd serve my daddy, herself, and her children. And she'd give us leftovers. She'd add mote, or stewed corn, and would make us eat that. Nothing else. My daddy didn't realize what was going on because he'd go out to work and we didn't say anything to him so as not to make trouble between the two of them.

One day I caught her hitting the little one again because she didn't want to eat the leftovers with mote. So I slapped her and asked: "Why are you hitting my sister?"

She stood up too and, well, we started fighting.

And my daddy came home from work and he beat me too. But I wouldn't leave her alone.

"It's going to get worse, Daddy," I said to him. "If you go on hitting me, I'm going to go on hitting your wife. I won't stop. The more you hit me, the more your wife will suffer. You'd better let me explain, Daddy! She was hitting my little sister and me too."

In the end I had to go to the police, because I couldn't take it anymore. And there, in front of the police, I said to my daddy: "Daddy, choose between us, your wife or us. I'm leaving with my sisters. I work, I'll be able to support my little sisters. I would rather live in another house. Don't worry about us. Stay with your wife, be happy. We're leaving. We can't go on like this."

Well, my father, because of how much he loved us, had to get rid of his wife and stay with his daughters. But from that day on another torture began. No one would talk to me. My stepmother would tell my daddy that I was misbehaving in the village, that I wasn't a worthy daughter of my father. And he believed it. And he became much harsher with us, much stricter. He'd drink all the time and hit us a lot. Until I had to tell him to go back and live with his wife. And she came back to live with us. But the situation was really tragic.

One night my daddy and she hit me really hard. They'd come home drunk, both of them. So my sisters defended me, they got him away from me, and they said: "Run away, Domi!"

I ran out and stayed there in the street.

My future husband was then a civilian policeman, something like the people who walk in the streets at night picking up couples, taking people to jail or notifying the parents. I didn't know him. When he saw me in the street, he shined a light on me and asked:

"What are you doing here?"

And he wanted to arrest me.

"Aren't you Don Ezequiel's daughter?"

"Yes," I answered.

"And what's happened?"

"My father's drunk and he's hitting me. Now I'm waiting for them to go to sleep and then I'll go back inside."

"But how can you be outside like this, at night? You should go back home. Come with me."

So I went back home with him. When we entered, René said to my father:

"Don Ezequiel, here's your daughter. How can you hit her like that, how can you throw her out into the night, how can you treat her like that?"

"There he is, there he is, there's her lover!" shouted my stepmother.

And my daddy, since he was drunk, went to take out the gun he had in the house, because he was also a policeman. And he wanted to hurt me.

So a very odd thing happened: we had to escape from my father. We ran, we ran as far as we could. There was a field. My father ran after us and we ran without turning around, without stopping. From so much running, we fell into a ditch. We threw ourselves on the ground, waiting for daylight.

It was a really odd situation. And the next day René took me to his mother's house. And she tried to help me live in this new situation.

SIGLO XX

Almost by coincidence, a little while after I met my husband I came to live in Siglo XX, the village where I was born and which later taught me how to struggle and gave me courage. Thanks to the wisdom of the people here, I was able to see injustice more clearly and this lit a fire in me which only death will put out.

When I lived in Pulacayo, I wanted very badly to go back to Siglo XX, to see the village where I was born. In Pulacayo they talked a lot about Siglo XX and they even sang some songs about the place. And when someone would ask me where I was born, I'd say in Siglo XX-Llallagua. And I was always curious about really knowing the place.

After getting married, that was the first thing I thought: I want to know the village where, by a strange coincidence, my husband was also born.

That was in 1957. The first chance we had, when I was on vacation, we got some money together and came to Siglo XX. But my husband loved the place so much that he never went back to Pulacayo again and he stayed there looking for work. I went back to Pulacayo to work in the company grocery store a few months more.

When I came back to Siglo XX, I spent almost five years reading the Bible, since my father had converted to the Jehovah's Witnesses. I'd go to their meetings, I'd practice a lot of what they told me. But later on, I left them, especially when I joined the Housewives' Committee, because I discovered other things that were, well, more important for me and that they didn't want to accept.

I joined the committee from necessity, in order to be with the other women who along with our compañeros struggled for better living conditions. Then the Jehovah's Witnesses told me that I shouldn't get involved in that, that the Devil was in it, that in religion you weren't allowed to mix in things that were pure politics.

And, well, I stayed on with the committee. Later on, they called me and said that they were going to punish me, they were going to make me spend a year thinking over my sins. I'd have to go to their meetings every assembly day and no one was supposed to talk to me for a whole year. And if after a year I didn't stop doing what they'd forbidden me to do, then they'd kick me out of their religion. They said I was doing bad things because I was in the committee.

I answered:

"In the first place, God says we shouldn't judge anyone. And who are you to judge me like this? Anyway, you analyze things your way, and you only think about the little group that goes to the meetings. That's why you don't see how most of the people live. You aren't interested in that, are you?"

I told them all that. And more:

"For example, let's suppose that there's a widow who has lots of children and that, to support them, someone's told her to lie and that they'll give her some bread if she does. Later, let's say that she's had to steal because she didn't have any food for the kids. Let's say that then one of the kids has gotten sick and she needed money so badly that, in her despair, she's even agreed to prostitute herself to save her child's life. Now then, according to them, in the other life prostitutes, liars, and the like won't know God's kingdom. That widow isn't going to see God's face in the other life, she won't be able to enter paradise. I can't accept that."

Not only that, but in Siglo XX-Llallagua, the Jehovah's Witnesses are pretty rich, they don't suffer like us. I don't know how it is in other countries, but here it's like that. So I said:

"Brother Alba"—who was the richest man in Llallagua at the time—"lives happy in this life because he doesn't lack anything. And since he knows the word of God, he won't prostitute himself, he won't lie, he won't do any of those things. And so he'll enter the Kingdom of Heaven. But that widow who's suffering so much in this life, in the end God will say to her: 'Well, I told you not to do those things. Now go to hell.' Is that going to happen? What about the person who was born poor? Is that person never going to reach God's glory, while brother Alba will? Will he reach God's glory because he knows the Bible? That doesn't seem fair to me. And even though you think that spiritual help is the only important thing, I think that you have to begin with material help. If I get a job for the widow, for example, I can say to her: 'Look, work here, come to live here with your children,' and then later on I can say to her: 'Look, in the Bible it says that you shouldn't lie or steal or prostitute yourself.' Of course by that time she won't have desperate needs any longer and she'll have work, she'll be able to live by that rule, don't you think?"

Then they answered that I was really doing the work of Satan and that they didn't agree with what I was saying. I told them I was leaving. So I left.

Afterward, little by little, I began seeing how they were just one more group at the beck and call of imperialism. They said that we shouldn't get involved with politics, yet there in the temple they talked politics all the time, in the very way they dealt with everything. They'd hand out leaflets to us and in one of them it said "freedom of religion," but in a picture where there were some boots trampling some religions it said "communism, Marxism," and in another leaflet, for example, there was a picture of Marx— at the time I didn't know Marx, I knew him later—like an octopus strangling the world, that had to be killed. You know what I mean?

So I had to choose: work with the Housewives' Committee to struggle side by side with the workers, or stay with the Jehovah's Witnesses, going to their services and not getting into any of those things they called "works of Satan." It was important for me to make a decision.

There were other religions in Siglo XX, especially Catholicism. But I didn't get involved with the people of that group either, because in those days the Christians, and especially the priests and nuns, were really against us. They had a mission that Pope Pius XII had given them to fight against communism and that's why they made life difficult for us; they didn't understand us and they often took sides with our oppressors.

That happened a lot in Bolivia: religion put itself at the service of the powerful, listening to their points of view. And the people who say they follow Christ's teachings in favor of the oppressed, they really look out for their own security, in order to be well off and have lots of money and everything. And so they just make religion to serve the capitalists. Up until now there have been only a few Church representatives who understand what's really happening in Bolivia. And even when they see the injustice, for their own personal safety they prefer to keep quiet. That's why the Church almost doesn't count among the miners, despite the fact that, in the last few years, several priests, nuns, and even bishops have changed and are on our side; some of them have been beaten, deported, jailed, and interrogated alongside us. But the image of the dominating Church, hand in hand with oppressive capitalism, is still very much alive.

So ever since my fight with the Jehovah's Witnesses, I haven't joined any religious group, even though I haven't lost my faith in God. And maybe that's one thing that I really don't share with what I've read in the books on Marxism, where they always deny the existence of God, at least that's what I've seen, you know? But it seems to me that denying God's existence would be to deny our own existence.

Well, after we arrived in Siglo XX, I lived alone with my husband for only two years. Afterward, my sisters came to live with me, one by one, and I had to take care of them once again. None of them could get along with my father's second wife and they didn't have anyplace to go.

After two years I had my first child. Suddenly my family was large and my husband didn't like that. My mother-in-law died and my husband was very unhappy. There were days when he'd work and days when he wouldn't. With all those problems, he'd also get drunk sometimes and when he'd come home, he'd say he hadn't married my sisters, that it wasn't his obligation to support them. Things like that.

My sisters looked for work for a long time. But it was really hard to find, especially being women. Besides that, we lived in such scarcity that we had to share one pair of shoes among all of us sisters. We'd put them on when we went out. Our economic situation got worse and worse.

When we got to Siglo XX, we looked up two leaders, Federico Escobar and Pimentel. It was said in Pulacayo that they were good leaders. And I wanted to meet them.

I met Escobar when they took our house away. My husband and I moved in with someone else. My mother-in-law died and he went to Pulacayo to bury her. I was expecting my first child. The man we moved in with had retired and they were kicking me out because they said my husband didn't have a right to that room. They told me I had to leave right away. I told them they should wait till my compañero got back, because I was still pregnant and how could I move in that condition? Anyhow, we had to look for another place to live. But the company only gave me that morning and then the watchmen came and dragged all my things out. The watchmen are workers who can't work any more or are disabled because they've had an accident in the mine and lost an eye, an arm, a leg, or because they have mine sickness. Then they work in the section of the mining company called social welfare and that way they have an easier job that doesn't require so much physical effort.

So the watchmen came and evicted me like an owner evicts someone for not paying the rent.

I was outside crying and the neighbors saw me. At about three in the afternoon, a neighbor of mine got back from work and his relatives told him what had happened. He told me I should look for the leaders.

I agreed, but I was frightened and suspicious because I didn't know them. Anyway, we went to Federico Escobar's house. His wife greeted me very cordially. The compañero told her what it was all about and she said: "Don't worry, my husband will help you and everything will work out fine." And she tried to comfort me.

My few belongings were still out in the street in front of my house. We covered them with a tent and a neighbor agreed to watch everything.

At seven that night, I think, Escobar arrived home from work. And, well, he was different from what I'd imagined. I thought I was going to meet a dominating man, a man used to giving orders. I'd never seen such a simple, good man. It was the first time I saw him and he stretched out his hand to me as if he'd known me for a long time. He was so nice to me.

But before talking about our problems, Federico made sure we had some supper. Then my neighbor said to him: "Look, they've kicked this woman out of her house. For a year now she's lived with some other people in a room. Her husband's out of town and now they've kicked her out into the street."

Federico was very angry and immediately he asked the union for a car and he went to Cancañiri, where the company's social welfare office was. He called the watchmen and really bawled them out because they'd done such an awful thing to me. Then he made them open the room and put everything back inside again, scolding them and asking them why they'd done that to me, asking them if my husband wasn't a worker like them. And he made them put everything in its place. Then he said to them:

"Look, a woman lived here, a lady lived here, and ladies don't have their things thrown all over the place that way. Do me the favor of putting everything the way it was, because she can't be expected to clear up this mess you've made."

I was embarrassed and I said:

"Thank you, sir, it's all right. I'll fix it up."

"No, señora, you just rest."

He made them put the bed back together and said:

"And didn't you even stop to think that this lady can't go looking for another place to live?"

And he said to me:

"Now look, you just rest, because you aren't well, you're expecting."

I really was about to give birth, because that happened on November 3 and on November 7 my son Rodolfo was born. That's another reason I was so nervous, also, because I was alone. Escobar was aware of the whole situation and that's why he made the watchmen put my things back in order. Then he handed me a note and said:

"Look, Señora, this is so you can live here. No one has the right to evict you. Your husband works for the company and no one can kick you out."

That was the first time I ever saw Escobar. Before leaving, Federico told my neighbors that they shouldn't leave me alone and that someone should stay with me in case my time came. I learned a lot from the leaders. I owe part of my personal growth to them.

THE PEOPLE'S WISDOM

In those years the MNR governed Bolivia, first with Paz Estenssoro, then Hernán Siles Zuazo, and then again Paz Estenssoro. That government called itself "revolutionary nationalist" and we had put them into office, but it began not to pay any attention to what

the people said and wanted. For example, the nationalization of
the mines was badly done, the company was terribly impoverished by the indemnification, and the people were deceived. Also
we wanted, for example, Bolivia to have its own metal foundry,
because we had to transport the ore from the mines, pay customs
and transportation, take it to England by ship to be melted down,
and then put it on a ship again for the United States, in order to
deliver it to the boss's door. Yes, it's us who in the long run pay for
all that, because the money that gets used up in that whole trip
could be saved to make the country progess more and more, and
to pay the workers better. That's why the miners said that one way
to end the problem would be to have our own foundry and sell
the metal ingots right here. And not give them away to the United
States at any old price, but rather say: "Let's see . . . who'll pay us
best?"

But our MNR governments didn't want to listen to us; instead,
through the U.S. Embassy, they made plans and imposed their policies. They decreed a "monetary stabilization"[7], and they made the
"Triangular Plan,"[8] all to their advantage. And when the workers
opposed this, immediately there was a crackdown. In those days
we suffered quite a lot in Siglo XX because of their policies.

Really, the people of the MNR who'd been put in power after
the people's revolution in 1952, were, well, pretty greedy, don't you
think? And imperialism took advantage of this to corrupt those
who called themselves "revolutionaries." And with the nation's
money a new corrupt bourgeoisie was created. It was corrupt in

7. Promulgated by the government of Hernán Siles Zuazo in 1956, based on
a plan prepared by Jackson Eder, North American adviser.
8. Plan to rehabilitate nationalized mining, in which the governments of the
United States and West Germany, as well as the International Development
Bank, participated. Among other things, it meant a decrease in the number
of mine workers, the freezing of wages, total control of the union process
and particularly of the activities of the mine leaders, and the suppression of
worker control with the right of veto. These were the conditions imposed on
the Bolivian government by the financiers.

every way: in its agents and labor representatives, peasant leaders, and authorities. As if that wasn't enough, the MNR reached the point of setting up Nazi-style concentration camps in Bolivia. For example, everyone knows the sad story of San Román and Menacho, who were chiefs of political security for the MNR. In his own house, San Román had a kind of jail where he brutally tortured the people. San Román was the terror of all the political prisoners.

Well, the workers, and especially those of Siglo XX, criticized the situation we lived in. When all of these steps were taken against the people, there was fighting in the mines, and protests and demonstrations. They cracked down hard on us: they didn't send groceries, they didn't send wages, they even cut off our medical supplies. And they put the leaders in jail.

I remember that in 1963 the leaders spoke out against one of the government's measures. The Mining Corporation of Bolivia, COMIBOL, said that it didn't have money to send medicines to the hospital. There was a terrible flu epidemic then, with diarrhea and everything. There was no medicine for the children. And it turned out that at that same time COMIBOL contracted with a group of international performers,[9] with Japanese, North Americans, Africans, etc., to give shows in the mines. The people who went to see them told us they were anticommunist-type shows and that COMIBOL had paid for their trip.

Well, the leaders, and especially Escobar, had already sent telegrams to COMIBOL, saying that the company's workers weren't going to respect the performers and that they'd take them as hostages if COMIBOL didn't send the medicines we needed. Some workers went to pull the train off the tracks so that the foreigners couldn't leave. I saw them when they were in the Cancañiri station

---

9. From "Moral Rearmament" a crusade made up of intellectuals, athletes, and performers of all nationalities. On some occasions, like the one Domitila refers to here, it was used by the United States in its worldwide anticommunist campaign.

waiting to leave. We'd gone up there out of curiosity to see. All day long those foreigners waited. And they'd ask: "What's happened?" And we'd tell them that the rain had washed out part of the tracks and they were being repaired, or something like that. But the problem was that the rails had been taken away by the workers.

As it turned out, COMIBOL had to send the medicines right away by plane, to get the foreigners out fast so that nothing would happen to them. So about ten that night they left. Immediately they announced on the radio that the medicines had arrived, that the persons who needed them could pick them up with their vouchers, and that the hospitals were open that night. And that in case of emergency, we should take the children there.

I also had a little daughter who was sick with diarrhea and needed a strong medicine, so I went to pick it up. And I saw a long line of people and the hospital really was open. It was one o'clock in the morning.

So COMIBOL and the performers, with their anticommunist propaganda, had come to fool us, to lie to us, to hurt the people, but in the end, the tables got turned and they did us a favor.

The workers always analyze the situation. But the owners don't listen to them; they don't listen to them, and that's why they have to take other steps. For example, when they criticized the Triangular Plan, the monetary stabilization, when they made clear the need for our own foundries, no one paid attention to them. And yet all those ideas came from the people. Look how recently those ideas are made to look like President Ovando's brainstorm. But the truth is, it wasn't like that at all. Various leaders have died demanding things that we needed because they had a very clear vision of the situation and openly stated: this is what has to be done, not that.

Ever since I've been in Siglo XX, I've always tried to keep in touch with everything. I listened to the news on the radio. I went to the demonstrations and tried to know how things stood, partly because it was all new to me. I don't mean that in Pulacayo I didn't do the same. Could it be because in Pulacayo I lived in a world apart and that's why I didn't realize what was going on? But in Siglo XX I really began to get interested, to learn about the struggle and about the people's sufferings. And that awoke in me a great respect for my father and for the cause he had devoted himself to.

Siglo XX made me understand the wisdom of the people. How many great men struggled for us, people from our own village! And how many women too, like, for example, Bartolina Sisa in the Indian Rebellion [1781–1783], Juana Azurduy de Padilla in the War for Independence [1825], the heroines of La Coronilla, in that same war. We also have great women intellectuals who've reached a pretty high level, like Maria Josefa Mujia and Adela Zamudio, who were great poets.

And closer to home, we have our own experience, no?

For example, I've known a lot of women who maybe haven't learned to speak a little more, like I have, but who are anonymous heroines, who've bravely defended the people and have died for them.

And how many things have been worked out by the people through their own experience! Every day we see things that we can learn from the people. And that's why I think that if we'd only stop and look at each step—even the steps that the most humble citizen takes—we'd see great intelligence, great wisdom. I think it's very important to point this out and to look carefully at the people's work to find out what makes them what they are, so we can appreciate their values.

Everything I know and am I owe to the people. And also the courage they've inspired in me.

THE HOUSEWIVES' COMMITTEE

The mine workers' wives organized a committee in Siglo XX during that very difficult period of Paz Estenssoro. Seeing all the struggles the people were involved in, they couldn't stay on the sidelines.

At the beginning, we had the mentality they'd taught us, that women are made for the home, to take care of the children and to cook, and that they aren't capable of assimilating other things, of a social, union, or political nature, for example. But necessity made us organize. We suffered a lot doing it, but today the miners have one more ally, a pretty strong one, an ally who's sacrificed a lot: the Housewives' Committee, the organization that arose first in Siglo XX and now exists in other nationalized mines.

This committee was formed in 1961. At that time, we were living through a pretty rough economic situation: the company owed our compañeros three months' wages, there was no food to eat, there were no medicines and no medical attention.

So the miners organized a march which consisted of everyone, miners, women, and children, going on foot to the city of La Paz. This was a very long march, because La Paz is really far away [335 kilometers]. But the government types found out about our plans and they stopped us. They arrested the leaders and took them to jail in La Paz.

So one by one their compañeras went to find out about their husbands. But in La Paz the women were treated badly and they even tried to put them in jail and abuse them. Each one of the women would return completely demoralized. In the union hall they met with us and began telling angrily about what had happened to them. And that's when an idea came up: "If instead of going like that, each one on her own, we all got together and went to claim our rights in La Paz, what would happen? Maybe we could all take care of each other and get better results."

And they decided to go to La Paz. They had no idea even about where they should go to make their demands, nor how to do it. It seems that someone told them that in those days there was going to be a ministers' meeting and that a workers' representative was going to be there. And that they should take advantage of that opportunity and support the compañeros' demands by shouting: "Freedom, freedom for our husbands!" And that's what happened. But then the so-called *barzolas* began to shout and threw rotten tomatoes sprinkled with pepper at the compañero. They went over to the compañeras and hit them and even tried to take their children away from them, in order to intimidate them. There was a real run-in, until the police arrived and broke it up.

The *barzolas* are part of a tragic chapter in the history of women in Bolivia. They were women who the MNR people organized and who took the name of María Barzola, but who didn't play the role she had played when she asked for fair treatment for the workers. Because, according to what I've been told, María Barzola was a woman from the village of Llallagua. In 1942 there was a big demonstration demanding a wage increase from the old mine owners and she led the march with a flag. When they were getting near Cataví, where the main office was, the army arrived and massacred a whole bunch of people. And in that massacre, she died. That place is now called the Plain of María Barzola.

But the MNR's barzolas began to serve the interests of their party, which was part of the government and, in fact, they helped repress the people. They served as an instrument of repression. Because of that, there's a bad feeling against the barzolas in Bolivia. For example, in La Paz, when a sector of the working class demanded something, the barzolas went out to confront them with knives and whips; they attacked the demonstrators who were protesting against government policies. In the parliament they also stood up and if someone spoke against the MNR, the barzolas were there with rotten tomatoes and other things to throw at them to make them shut up. So instead of advancing the cause of Bolivian women, this movement only served as a repressive weapon. That's why, when someone sells out to the government or there's a female police agent, people say: "Don't get involved with her, she's a barzola." It's a shame that this historic figure of our people has been so misused.

After the confrontation with the barzolas, the compañeras who were in La Paz went back to the place they'd been thrown out of and declared a hunger strike. That night San Román came, the terrible San Román whom no one wanted to meet. And something happened there. One of the compañeras stood in front of him and said: "San Román, you know very well that we don't have arms to defend ourselves from your hangmen. But if anything happens, we'll all blow up together, at this very minute. We and you will blow up, because all we've got here is dynamite." And she took something out of her pocket and asked for a match. But while the compañeras were looking for a match, San Román and his group went running out.

Fortunately, the factory workers immediately supported the women and that night moved them to a room in the Federation of Factory Workers, where they continued the hunger strike. And they sent out a document in which they asked for freedom for their compañeros, payment of the workers' wages, stock for the grocery stores, and medicines for the hospitals.

The hunger strike meant that none of the compañeras could eat anything. They could only have liquids. They lasted ten days; some of them were with their children.

They were joined by university students, factory workers, and even women from other mines began to arrive, in solidarity with the compañeras.

The government had to accept their demands so that the strike wouldn't get any bigger, and the housewives won. They returned home with their freed compañeros, the company paid the workers, and the grocery store was well stocked. It turned out to be a pretty good thing in our favor.

But since we had been educated like most women, thinking that we shouldn't get involved, immediately we forgot the great sacrifice of those compañeras.

The women who'd taken the initiative to carry out the hunger strike thought it was necessary to organize in order to continue struggling side by side with the compañeros. They all got together to do a little propaganda work in the streets: "We're going to have a meeting, we're going to organize a committee." And that's what they did. They organized, they appointed their leadership, and they called the organization Housewives' Committee of Siglo XX. There were about seventy women.

But you should have heard the guffaws from the men at that

time. They'd say: "The women have organized a committee! Let them! It won't last even forty-eight hours. They're going to organize among themselves and it's all going to end right there."

The truth is it didn't happen that way. On the contrary, the organization grew and now it's very important, not only for the women themselves, but for the whole working class.

Of course, at the beginning it wasn't easy. For example, in the first demonstration in Siglo XX after they came back from La Paz, the compañeras went up on the balcony of the union hall to speak. The men weren't used to hearing a woman speak on the same platform as them. So they shouted: "Go back home! Back to the kitchen! Back to the washing! Back to your housework!" And they jeered and booed them.

But the women were strong and really wanted to work, so they didn't give up. Of course, they wept with rage and a sense of impotence, but they went right ahead. They got hold of a typewriter and began to write. They sent out communiqués of support for the workers and had them read on the miners' radio stations, stating their point of view about the situation we were living through then. For example, they said that as workers' wives they didn't agree with the government's economic program and urged everyone to think seriously about it. They sent letters to the president and his ministers, telling them their point of view. They sent letters to COMIBOL, to the Mine Workers' Federation, to the COB. They went to the grocery store to make sure they gave us good service, to the schools to see that our children were well cared for, that the school breakfast was adequate, to the hospital to see that the sick were taken care of properly. They really worked a lot.

The hardest worker was Norberta de Aguilar, wife of an old company worker. They told me that at the beginning of the committee, a doctor's wife called Vilma de Garrett was organizing. But it was Norberta who really made the committee go. I think that she's a great woman, because she knew how to make the organization work according to its principles, which is very difficult. At least that's how I knew her, although they say that today she's changed.

Along with Norberta others worked very hard: Jeroma de Romero, Alicia de Escobar, Flora de Quiroga, María Careaga, Angélica Osorio, Cinda de Santiesteban, Simona de Lagrava. They are many, many, I can't name them all. And each one contributed to the committee's work as much as she could. For example, one of our compañeras died during the second hunger strike, which was in 1963. She was compañera Manuela de Sejas, whose intestines dried up too much; they had to operate and she died, leaving eight children orphaned. Many compañeras had miscarriages in the hunger strikes. In the case of others, their children are very anemic because of what their mothers suffered. Several compañeras are sick because of what they've gone through. So it was a very special kind of work that they did, standing guard at night with the compañeros, going on strike, taking care of union property, like the union headquarters, the radio station, the library, and things like that. Sometimes the women would grab the microphone at the union radio station and would talk to us, helping us to know what to do.

Well, all of that drew attention to us and when General Barrientos came into power in 1964 he immediately saw the danger in women's organizations. During 1965 there were many problems. They arrested our leader, Lechín Oquendo, and deported him to Paraguay. Immediately they arrested a bunch of people from the radio, the press, and various other leaders. They also attacked the Housewives' Committee: "Let's see," they said, "who is the leadership? Who makes it up? Who are their husbands?" And they deported those husbands to Argentina, saying to them: "You, sir, are being thrown out not because of political or labor problems. You're an honorable and hardworking man and we're satisfied with your work. But we aren't satisfied that you allow your wife to lend herself to foreign interests." And so on and so forth. "Out you go!" And his wife would be thrown out of her house. Now "Let her support her family!" That was the first measure they took against the committee.

At that time the committee didn't have as much popular support as we do now. For example, when they arrested me, the workers went out on strike for days, demanding my freedom. And that made it much easier for me. But the earliest compañeras received very little solidarity, because the men didn't see the importance of women organizing, they didn't want to understand, it didn't seem right to them, it seemed out of place.

In the beginning, the committee also had problems with other women's organizations. For example, there were always clashes with the Christian women. This was a group of women from the Christian Family Movement who despised us, detested us, and called us heretics, and did anything to discredit the committee. Now we work together and things have changed. Because, after being imprisoned, I reached the conclusion that it's not worth fighting among ourselves. With everything I'd learned and everything I knew about the Bible and all those things, well, I went to talk with the Christian women and asked them whether, when a government massacred people, it was right to protest or not. And whether they agreed with the economic measures the government had taken. In the end I asked them whether the government said to the Christian women, "Well, they're Christians, we have to pay them a different wage . . . " or whether the economic measures affected all of us the same. And if for love for your neighbor it was fair or not to unite and demand workers' rights. Then they said yes, that I was right in what I said. And in a joint meeting we held, we reorganized the committee to cooperate with them and since then we've worked together.

But there's still a long way to go for women to reach the level of participation we think is needed. There are even women who don't understand why they should participate. To me it seems like a crime and I get very angry when some compañeras begin to say: "Why gripe so much and get involved in demonstrations and strikes? After all, we're fine now, we were much worse off before!"

What do you mean, we're fine? Our oppressors surely are fine. And they're fine thanks to us, thanks to our compañeros' work. We don't even have a roof to die under, because the housing in the mining camp is just on loan and ninety days after a worker dies we're out in the street. What do you mean, we're fine? When there are massacres, we end up alone with our six or seven children, with all that responsibility!

Our work wasn't always easy, even with the leaders. Not all of the union leaders understood or helped. Of course, sometimes we put our foot in it, because of lack of experience. Sometimes, when the men began to confront a problem, we women had already planned and made some progress, and some men didn't like that at all. On the other hand, with other leaders, especially in the most difficult periods, we really worked together. Escobar in particular helped us quite a lot. When he came to a meeting he'd help us and say: the situation is this way, this is how we have to organize things, we have to fight for this and in this manner. Then we understood the whole situation better and that was great for us. With other leaders we also had the opportunity to work well and discuss problems together. And that's very important, isn't it?

I think that there are still about 40 percent of the men who are against their compañeras' organizing. For example, some of them are afraid they'll get fired from the company, or that there'll be reprisals like those my husband had to suffer because of my involvement. Others are afraid people will say bad things about their wives. Because, in spite of our behavior, in spite of the fact that the men in the leadership respect us, there are still people who speak badly of us, especially people who don't understand, those who are *machistas,* you know, people who say that women should stay at home and only live for their family and not get mixed up in politics. Those old-fashioned people always go around inventing stories. For example, they said we were the union leaders' mistresses, that we'd gone to the union in order to get involved in a love affair. So, many compañeros don't allow their wives to participate in the demonstrations or in the committee or anything, because they're afraid and they especially don't want their wives going over to union headquarters.

But for us union headquarters is the working-class's meeting place, it's like a temple, it's sacred. It's taken a lot of blood to build that building. We meet in the union building in order to handle working-class problems and the compañeros have to treat us as their comrades, their allies, and not on any other basis.

There are some compañeras who participate when something very special happens. For example, when we organized a demonstration to demand more job openings in 1973 some five thousand women participated. And when they went back to their homes, lots of workers beat their wives and said they were housewives and had nothing to do with politics and that their obligation was to be at home. Until, finally, we said we were going to criticize them on the radio, which we did. We said: "Those compañeros who beat their wives must be government agents. That's the only thing that can explain the fact that they're opposed to their compañeras' demanding what in all justice is ours. And how can they be annoyed by a protest which in the end benefits everyone?"

In any case, we've really advanced a lot. And you can see how much: in 1973, I was sent to a Workers' Congress in Hua-nuni, where five hundred companeros were meeting. Three delegates from the Housewives' Committee went, but the other two couldn't stay on, so I was alone with five hundred men. We were housed several to a room, because we didn't have the money to pay for separate rooms. We were given school cots and, well, "the compañera can sleep over there." So I went to the corner they assigned me. My compañeros, all of them without exception, respected my being a married woman with children. There were twelve or thirteen of us in one room. We talked about the problems of the working class, we told each other stories about things that had happened to us in previous congresses. And it didn't occur to anyone to get out of hand with me. My compañero knew that I was going to be in that situation, but he didn't doubt me or mistrust me. And that's how I was able to participate in the congress, representing the Committee and taking our message there.

Happily, these new ideas concerning women have jelled very well, and we've won our place in the struggle. For example, it's a great relief for all of us when a compañero comes over to us women and says: "In the union they've forgotten to ask for such and such, so why don't you women see how this problem—a problem that affects the whole working class—can be solved." Yes, that's very encouraging.

In broad terms, that's how we've won our participation. The capitalists repress the people, they're organized. Their wives are also organized in those groups like "Lady Rotarians" and "Lady Lions" that exist in Bolivia and that surely exist in other countries too. So we, the wives of the workers, need to be organized too, don't we?

JOINING THE COMMITTEE

I wasn't in the Housewives' Committee right from the beginning. I liked it, I liked to listen to what the compañeras said and to go to their demonstrations. When the compañeras got their husbands out of jail in 1961 and came back with them from La Paz, I went to see them arrive, because they were announcing on the radio that they were getting in at such and such a time. I saw how happy the women were who were arriving with the freed prisoners.

In 1963 I began to participate. That same year they arrested and jailed the leaders again. They'd put them in jail any time they wanted to! They'd take them in and hold them there for months, sometimes years.

Escobar and Pimentel had gone to a workers' congress in Colquiri, together with Jorge Saral, the Huanuni leader. When they were on their way back from the congress, they were ambushed and taken prisoner.

The miners of Siglo XX found out what had happened and, at the same time, they found out that there were four foreigners in Cataví. A certain Tom Martin, labor attaché for the American Embassy, was there with three other gringos in a meeting with the management of COMIBOL! They were seventeen in all, I think.

Well, the miners decided to take these guys prisoner so that they'd give us back our leaders. They did it during a banquet that management held for them, at which all those representatives were present. They stormed in and took away every single one of them.

Everyone was pretty jumpy, because a compañero had arrived wounded by a bullet which had grazed his head. He told us how they'd been taken in an ambush and had been made to lie facedown with their hands tied. And he said that he tried to escape over a wall and rolled down and only one bullet had reached him and so that's how he'd managed to escape and tell what had happened. He said that when he'd escaped he'd heard a burst of machine-gun fire really loud and that's why he figured that the leaders had probably all been killed already.

The workers were furious because they thought their leaders had been killed. That's why the miners wanted to hang the four foreigners, to get back at them. All of the townspeople went to the square to see what was happening. The foreigners were there and the miners wanted to do them in.

So then when Norberta, president of the Housewives' Committee, turned around and faced the workers in all her anger, we thought it was the right thing to do. She said that these foreigners shouldn't be killed yet. Instead, they should be taken as hostages and exchanged for the leaders, whom she hoped were still alive. And only if they weren't should we decide whether or not to kill them.

"Let's think things through before doing anything," she said. "Because there could be a terrible massacre here in the village."

The workers weren't sure what to do and they asked: "And who's going to be responsible for seeing that the gringos remain as our hostages?" Because they knew that Tom Martin had fought in wars and had been trained with the Green Berets and "crime aces," and that at any moment he could escape. No one wanted to make a decision.

It was then that the women answered, with great courage, that they'd do it. There were about twenty women. Right away they organized the thing, they put the hostages in the union library and, on the radio, compañera Norberta immediately called for all the women to carry out their responsibilities.

"Compañeras!" she said. "The leaders have been taken. As wives of the mine workers, we have to support them." And she went on to explain that, in order to gain their freedom, we had other prisoners who the women were keeping as hostages, and that all of us should collaborate. And that she was calling on all the women to do guard duty. We agreed to do what she was asking and we started to help out. So at night some of the women stayed there on guard.

My husband had gotten lost that night. I waited for him to come back from work . . . and he didn't, and since I wasn't used to that, I went back to my house and stayed there crying and waiting and wondering what could have happened to him.

Well, the next day at dawn I made a small breakfast and went to my husband's job to ask for him. They told me that all the workers had left, that no one was working, that a strike had been declared. "Go to union headquarters to ask about your husband; he's probably over there on guard duty," they told me.

So I went over to the union. They made me go in. I saw how well prepared the women were. They searched me all over.

I asked if my husband was there, and he came out to see me. He'd been there all night standing guard. He was happy and said:

"You see, they've taken our leaders prisoner in La Paz, but we've brought the gringos here and the compañeras are holding them and we're standing guard."

And all excited he told me what they'd done. Then he said:

"Look at that lady over there . . . she's really old."

I looked at her: she was really old, with very white hair. She was sitting near the window, doing her guard duty.

"And you, you cop-out, I bet you were happy, sleeping all night long," he said to me.

That hurt me a lot. But compañera Norberta, who'd overheard him, said:

"You better not believe it, I don't think she was cool and calm. I bet she couldn't sleep all night, thinking about our situation."

I liked the fact that she stuck up for me. And I thought: she's imagined that I didn't sleep all night because I was worried about what was happening, but I was really waiting for my husband to come home so he could tell me what he thought.

"Well," Norberta told him, "if the compañera hasn't done anything up to now, it's surely because she hasn't been given a chance. But I bet that from now on she's going to help us out."

My husband said:

"What? . . . This little fool? . . . Why she can barely take care of her kids!"

"No," said Norberta. "It's that she hasn't been given a chance."

So she said to me:

"Look, compañera, we're here standing guard, we have to make sure that none of these prisoners escapes. It's a pretty difficult job for us, and we need people to work with us. And so we'd like it if you could come and help us by standing guard too."

So I told Norberta I could.

"Which shift do you want to be on?" she asked me.

"How many shifts are there?"

"Three."

"Good. Put me on all three," I said.

I went home to get my children and went back to the union to stay.

Norberta was a very dynamic woman. She was on leave from the committee for a few days, because her husband was sick in the hospital. But she divided her time between her husband and the people on guard duty, helping them in everything. During that time they operated on her husband and he died. That really got to me. Just imagine this woman's courage, with her husband that sick and at the same time she takes on the responsibility of the hostages! Her commitment to the people was admirable. I didn't see her cry even once.

Jeroma de Romero, the committee's interim secretary, was with Norberta. She was also a great woman. She took over the responsibility in those difficult moments, especially when Norberta would have to go to the hospital for a while and take care of her husband. There I also met Pimentel's wife and I got to know Escobar's wife better, and also her mother and his children.

Life there at union headquarters was very special. We shared everything, just everything. If someone brought one of us some food, we'd share it. Our children were there, in the large hall. There were also other people in the corridors, everyone doing guard duty, watching out so that no one could escape, some watching the hostages, others in contact with the leadership.

Everything was well organized. Norberta was always up to date on any news, but she still didn't have any exact information. We were just there doing guard duty. The women in the leadership came and went, had interviews, all those things. But aside from that, since we had to keep a certain discipline, there are things we didn't find out about from inside the union hall. Any communiqué they got was read over the union radio and that's how we found out about it.

Once, when it was my turn to stand guard at the door, a compañero knocked. I thought it was eleven at night. Since he was a miner, I opened for him. He was tipsy and he said: "You're on the gringos' side; you're treating them like kings here, you're not bothering them at all, while our leaders, how do you think they're being treated in the political prisoners' cells? San Roman must be killing the leaders by now and you're siding with the gringos. Let me in!"

Then, as we had arranged, I said: "No, compañero, go home, no one can come in here. Tomorrow, when you're sober, then we'll talk about it and you'll understand the situation better. It's true that we treat the hostages well, but the leaders aren't too bad off."

I tried to explain, doing the best I could. But the compañero couldn't understand; he said that I'd sold out to the gringos and that he wanted to kill all of us. And he showed me that he was carrying dynamite. I hadn't had any experience so I got scared, I ran inside shouting:

"Dynamite! Dynamite! We're all going to be blown up! We'll all be blown up!"

I'd never seen dynamite explode, but I knew it was very powerful; after all, it can destroy really hard rock.

Norberta came out and I shouted at her: "They're throwing dynamite!"

Norberta went down the steps and there was the lighted stick of dynamite. Completely calm, she took the stick of dynamite outside. She had no time for anything else except to get out to the street and throw the stick. It exploded immediately; it was a small explosion, not full force. And so we were safe from any danger. Of course, we got a bit shook up, but no one was hurt. That showed me that she was a very firm woman with a very courageous attitude. And she also served as an example for me.

Another important thing happened in those days. Paz Estenssoro's lackeys set the peasants against us and there was a kind of army that wanted to attack us inside union headquarters.

One day two men came to tell us: "Look out, the peasants from Ucurena have attacked a small village and they've burned the fields, they've stolen cattle, they've raped the women. You women here should support those compañeras. You're organized, you have the radio station, so you should protest and be heard."

Well, we thought that was true. And we spoke out on the radio station called "The Miner's Voice."

And it turned out that the same people who had come to tell us were also instigating the people from Ucureña: "The miners are insulting you. You've got to get back at them."

It was all a maneuver to set the miners against the peasants and the peasants against us. A little later we caught on. And we were able to see how intelligent and keen the enemy is in sowing discord and making us fight among ourselves.

In the Ucureña region, the peasants were organized into commandos which supported the MNR government, because that's the village where the agrarian reform decree was signed. When they heard the news that we'd insulted them, they decided to come to Siglo XX to "get revenge" and help save the gringos.

One day we were told that the Ucureños were coming closer in order to attack us. They said that helicopters were going to come, that parachutists would come to rescue the gringos. In other words, that we'd be attacked by land and by air.

On the radio they said they wanted to send greetings to Tom

Martin and his companions. They spoke in English. And they told them that they should take advantage of the fact that at dawn the commandos would come in and help them. The son of one of the women, who knew a bit of English, translated the conversation for us. So that way we knew that the peasants, helped by the army, were going to break into union headquarters.

So we had a meeting, and Jeroma spoke to us. She said that the responsibility we had undertaken was a big one, but that she felt happy and that we had to carry out to the end the task we'd been given. But we couldn't leave our children behind to suffer in the hands of those people. So our obligation was to die with our children.

Then we decided that all of us, with our children and our husbands, should move into the union building and place dynamite in such a way that, if necessary, we'd be blown up with the building, but so that no one would come out of there alive, not us or them. That was our final decision.

There were about five or six cases of dynamite which we divided among ourselves. We put dynamite on the tables, by the doors, by the windows, and also on our bodies, on our children's bodies, ready to be lit in case of an attack.

The secretary-general of the committee stood in the doorway of the union building and said: "They better not get their hopes up, because we're not going to let them escape." And she also said that if one of the hostages tried to escape when the peasants arrived, we women, with the dynamite, could blow everything up. They could come by land or by air. We weren't armed, but we'd light the wicks and blow up everyone and everything.

So the decision we took was pretty brave and I'm sure that if the moment had come, we'd have carried it out. There was such a feeling of confidence! We had set ourselves such a special goal that we had to live up to it. Besides, what did we care about freeing the hostages and escaping, only to suffer later the worst things imaginable at the hands of the peasants?

My husband was there too and we said to each other: "If you die,

I die, the children die, no one will be left to go on suffering at the hands of those people."

But we waited all night and nothing happened.

Juan Lechín, who at that time was secretary-general of the Mine Workers' Federation, also came to the union building. First he came to speak with the prisoners. Then he spoke to a group of us women, to convince us. He told us that the gringos had to go to Cataví to communicate with La Paz by radio. That they couldn't talk over the phone from the union building, but would have to go to Cataví, but that they'd come right back. He wanted us to trust him and said:

"Look at my white hair, white from so much suffering and work. Trust me. The hostages have to go, but they'll come back. You know that I too am a longtime struggler, tireless like the leaders who are in prison. You all know how much I've already lived through, both victories and defeats. Compañeras, try to understand the situation."

At the beginning, I was very impressed by his words and I thought that we should pay attention to him and trust him. I was surprised by Jeroma de Romero's attitude, which was very courageous. She understood the situation and answered:

"Compañero Lechín, you really know how to sugar-coat the pill before making us swallow it. If you want to have something to do with the gringos, you can do what you like, you can even put them on golden thrones, but you have to do it inside the union building and no place else. You may have white hair, but the people are also tired and getting older because of all the failures, imprisonments, and struggles they have to face. You know that we have a commitment and as long as we don't have our leaders right here with us, we aren't going to let the gringos go. It's a deal we made with the workers. You know very well that the gringos are here so that we can exchange them for the leaders and that under no circumstances will we let them go until these conditions have been met."

Lechín got furious and said: "How is it possible for me to come to an agreement with ten thousand workers and here, with ten women, I can't get anywhere?"

And he left, very angry. What I'd seen and heard seemed very important to me, especially what that compañera had answered so bravely.

Another thing which impressed me was that those gringos wanted to buy us off and offered us chocolates, cigarettes, candies, and if they were eating, they'd invite us to have some of their food. And we women, because we were inexperienced, would accept. Even me; sometimes I'd accept some things, cigarettes for example. But one day Jeroma drew our attention to it:

"What are you doing? We didn't come here to share things with them. They're our enemies. And that should be really clear, especially in this situation. We shouldn't take anything from the enemy," she said. And she made us give back what we'd taken.

At about that same time, a group of Church women came to see us. They wanted to speak with us. Of course, in those days the Church was also controlled from abroad. So they took the gringos' side. They said that we women were heretics, communists. They cried, they screamed, they said that because of us, all of them were going to suffer at the hands of the peasants. We answered them, really furious. Then they got really shocked and said: "My good-ness! What kind of women are there around here?"

The Bishop of La Paz also came to talk to us. He got very angry with us and told us that we should free the foreigners, asking us what they'd ever done to us and saying that we were very arro-gant. At that time the Church treated us badly. Even in 1961, when since the government was starving us already the compañeras were on hunger strike, asking for their husbands' freedom. The bishop excommunicated us. He said that we were heretics because we'd gone against God's law, and that God didn't pardon the fact that, even though there was food, we voluntarily went on hunger strikes. But I can see that he didn't understand why we did it, that it was a final resort in the terrible situation in which we lived—you know?

Well, after talking with the women, the Bishop promised us that he'd do everything possible in La Paz so that they'd free our leaders. The news that the peasants from Ucureña were going to enter our village had left the population terrified. People were taking their things to Llallagua where they rented housing. Others went to Uncía from Llallagua, so they'd be further away and safer. There was a really peculiar kind of panic. And I think that they wanted to confuse us women, no? But fortunately the leaders' firmness helped a lot. They kept us going. Of course, there were moments when we were afraid too, but in the end we were all very firm in our decision.

Compañero Lechín went to La Paz to explain the situation, to convince the leaders to write us. So the leaders wrote us a letter. And we got their letter with their signatures which we knew well. In it the compañeros told us that they were still alive and that we shouldn't let ourselves in for a massacre in the village.

Then there was a workers' assembly and the union resolved to free the gringos and the other people who were with them. We women had committed ourselves to returning those men when the union asked us to. So we signed a document where we said that we were returning "every single one" of the hostages, because the union wanted it that way. That we'd known how to fulfill our obligation and that we no longer assumed any responsibility. And that it was into the hands of the workers that the hostages were freed.

And the hostages came out. That group of women that had insulted us came to the door of the union building to insult us again and applaud the gringos. They screamed at us and wanted to hit us.

We felt really low, as if it had been our defeat, because all of our efforts hadn't been enough to meet the objective we'd set, which was the swapping of the hostages for our leaders.

They told us that the peasants of Ucureña had, in fact, arrived pretty close to Siglo XX, after several days' march. And that it was very difficult to convince them to return to their villages without doing anything to us.

The leaders remained in jail for a long time more. Of course, we were allowed to organize a commission which went immediately to La Paz to speak with them and see that they were alive and well. So we went, and afterward, every now and then, we had free access to the jail. We were able to get them moved to the San Pedro jail, which was healthier. Each week a committee from Siglo XX went to La Paz to visit them and take them food, literature, and other things; because, even though they were prisoners, they were still treated as our leaders. The other leaders were just temporary. Not only that, but when a worker went on vacation, the first thing he did was go to the jail to visit the leaders. Federico always, always clued them in. He had his little radio and, with the literature we took him, he knew all about what was going on. He'd always talk to us about the problems, about what was going to happen, what we should do, how we should stick together. That's what he especially recommended us to do.

And, well, the leaders were there more or less a year. With the coup in 1964, [10] the workers took the opportunity and went into the jail and got them out, along with others.

What I saw and lived during those events, in all those days we spent in the union building with the hostages, will help me all my life. And from that experience on I began to participate regularly in the Housewives' Committee.

THE SORA-SORA PAMPAS

In 1964 there were lots of problems, especially in La Paz, and they came down hard on the working class.

There was a demonstration in Oruro, where several students were killed. The secretary of the committee left me as interim secretary and went to Oruro for the funeral services with some of the compañeros. There they were arrested, beaten up, and put in jail.

The government wanted to take over the mines' radio stations so that no solidarity campaign could be carried out. They told us

---

10. MNR was overthrown and General Barrientos seized power.

that the army was about to enter the mines. The radio at Huanuni was hooked up with Siglo XX and they asked for help. The workers of Siglo XX, as always, mobilized to help them.

The news of an encounter between the workers and the army reached us, and we heard there were several wounded and that a truckload of people had disappeared. In the union building we stood guard over union property. The wives of the compañeros who had gone to help were around the union building, trying to find out something about what had happened, who were the dead, who were the wounded.

We heard a communiqué over the radio that said that the truck with the wounded had been located on the road. And that the army wouldn't let anyone get by, not even the ambulance.

And the people asked us to help. "We've got to go there, we've got to go there," they said to us. But we didn't have any transportation. So we housewives carried out a campaign asking for solidarity from the inhabitants of Llallagua, who responded quite well. And we named representatives to go collect food, medicine, and funds. After that, we were able to rent a vehicle in which seventeen of us women fit. Halfheartedly the driver agreed to take us. And he didn't want to go as far as the place where everything had happened; he just left us near Huanuni. We thought even that was all right and we went with him. I named another interim secretary-general who remained in Siglo XX.

When we reached Huanuni, we found out that the people from Siglo XX were no longer there, that they were much farther ahead, fighting in the Sora-Sora Pampas, because at night they'd advanced and had surprised the army. It was a very special thing, because the workers had no weapons, they only had dynamite.

I ran into the secretary-general of the Housewives' Committee of Huanuni. She was about seven months pregnant and I was four months pregnant. And she said to me:

"Compañera, there are wounded people that the army won't let us pick up. But we women are going to figure out how to do it. Get into the ambulance."

On the way, as we got near the place where the wounded were, they began firing at us. They made us stop and said:

"You can't go any farther."

The woman told the stretcher-bearers to go get the wounded, but they didn't want to. So then she ordered them:

"Take your work coats off."

And she told me to put one on.

"Or are you frightened?" she asked me.

Quite honestly, I was afraid, because it was the first time I'd faced something so big and dangerous. I made myself a little strong and answered her:

"All right, Señora, let's go."

I put on the work coat. We both got down from the ambulance.

"Make sure they see that we're women," she said. "Let your long hair show."

Then she got a stick and a white cloth. Using it as a flag we began to walk and walk. She and I, across the pampa. A shot passed really close to us. I was almost deafened.

"You mustn't show you're afraid, you've just got to keep on going," she said.

And we saw how they were watching us through their binoculars. But we kept on going forward, and then they didn't do anything to us.

We began to observe the ground carefully where we saw signs of blood and we began lifting up the wounded. But it was a giant's task that we had to do between the two of us. Because, just imagine: she was pregnant, I was pregnant, we had to lift up the bodies and take them somewhere. From there we signaled the ambulance and the stretcher-bearers came to get them and take them away. We'd return again to find another and then another. The army just wouldn't let the ambulance come any closer.

We got totally exhausted, because we worked almost the whole day. In the end, the stretcher-bearers helped us, because we couldn't have lasted all alone. So then we'd team up, one man and one woman, and the army didn't bother us anymore.

When we got back, we realized that the other women had prepared food and they were serving it to the people from Huanuni
and not to the people from Siglo XX, who were up on the hill. So
I said that the food shouldn't be dished out there. We returned to
Sora-Sora in a truck, as far as we could go. Then we had to climb
the hills on foot to where the compañeros were keeping a lookout
so that the army wouldn't move in.

Absolutely exhausted, we came down from the hill and went
back to Huanuni. The compañeros had asked us to get help and
dynamite, because what they had was running out. But in Huanuni
they didn't listen to us and no one went to relieve them. Since they
couldn't defend themselves anymore, the workers finally returned
to Huanuni, absolutely let down.

And it turns out that a truck had continued to follow the army
and, suddenly, when the army pulled back, the compañeros in the
truck realized they were alone. So they turned around. But they
found many workers on the road, begging them to please take
them along. So the driver returned to the pampa three times and
brought three truckloads of workers to Huanuni. The compañeros
were very thirsty, they were hungry, and there wasn't any tea, there
wasn't any water. It was after midnight. We were in the Huanuni
union building.

Their leader said to us women:

"Compañeras, maybe the army will come in tonight and take
it out on everyone who was out there. So I'd like you to go to the
hospital. We've been able to get a few beds there. You'd better go
there and lie down. It's not fair for you to have worked so hard and
have something happen to you now."

Both of us thought that it was the most correct thing to do and
the most prudent, so we went to the hospital to sleep.

The next day, very early, we asked the hospital director to help us
and we got breakfast ready for all the compañeros from Siglo XX
who were in Huanuni. They lent us tons of stuff. And, of course,
the staff was suspicious about lending us the things. So we left
three women from our group as security; they were to stay there

until we returned with all the utensils. And then, with the money that the people of Llallagua had given us, we went to the bakery and filled our shawls with bread. We bought all we could. So the fourteen of us women went to give breakfast to the compañeros at the crack of dawn. You should have seen how happy they were to be able to eat a little something.

We went to the hospital to see the wounded, to find out which of them could be moved to Siglo XX and which of them couldn't. We saw some of them who we thought were already dead, but who we'd saved, even though they were badly wounded. And one of them was even a leader until just recently.

The army didn't come that night. There were already lots of problems in La Paz. And some weeks later, there was like a coup d'état and President Paz Estenssoro had to flee the country.

THE WORKERS WILL PAY THE COST

On November 4,1964, General Barrientos took power.

Right from the beginning, thanks to the clarity of their leaders, the working class began to say that Barrientos was a military man and that we shouldn't trust him. That way, they began to help the people understand things. In other words, the people showed their disagreement with the government and knew right away that it wasn't a people's government, that it wasn't going to save Bolivia. And they warned us that moves would begin to be made against the people. What I mean is that the people were already seeing the difference between a government that's led by the people and one that's imposed from above. And if it's imposed from above, then that government shouldn't be trusted.

Barrientos came with the army to Siglo XX. They sounded the union building siren and the soldiers almost dragged us out of our homes to take us to the plaza. Barrientos made a speech there: "Why do you slander me before knowing what my government will be like? I'm going to do many good things. But one thing is clear, COMIBOL is bankrupt and all Bolivians will have to make sacrifices. I'm giving up half my own salary and everyone in the army is doing the same. And why do we do this? To help the miners, because COMIBOL's bankrupt. And it's not my fault if we're in this situation. It's because Paz Estenssoro pilfered. And look, that's why more than thirty-five thousand workers are going to be in the streets. And what will happen then? That's going to mean chaos for Bolivia! How is it possible? I'm sure that the workers are going to make sacrifices. For just a year I'm going to take half your wages and after a year, when COMIBOL is well capitalized, then we'll give it back to you. And if there are profits, they'll be distributed among you."

Well, everything he said gave the impression that COMIBOL was really collapsing. He said that COMIBOL had to pay its debts, otherwise it would be embargoed. And a whole bunch of things like that. And some people said: "If things are like that . . . how can we do anything but save our company? We've judged too fast . . . this government just came in. . . ."

And so the decree calling for a wage reduction was issued. And when they told us the news, everyone was unhappy about it. The Housewives' Committee also issued a manifesto. How could they take away such a big part of our wages, which were already pretty low?

And there were various measures taken against the economy. That was in May 1965.

So the protest demonstrations began, Then the people from the government began to take it out on the leaders.

First they arrested Lechin, and exiled him to Paraguay. And, well, the Mine Workers' Federation declared a general strike.

Then an ultimatum came: "All the leaders must leave." And it also said that if they didn't leave, the army would come to kick them all out. A lot of blood would be shed. And so on and so forth.

We convinced Federico Escobar to leave. He didn't want to go. We went to talk to him about how they wanted to kill him, that he had to get out. But he didn't give in and said to us: "I'll go into the mine, and if they want, let them drag me out of there. I won't leave." But the people knew that if Escobar entered the mine, they'd grab him and kill him. And, well, we didn't want to lose a man like him. We made him understand. And his comrades also made him see that it was better to have a free compañero than one in jail and much better a live one than a dead one. And then we asked the parish church for help and they helped sneak Federico out.

They got the union leaders, the journalists from the radio station "The Miner's Voice," the husbands of the women who led the Housewives' Committee. They got about a hundred people or more. And they took all of them away in planes, deporting them to Argentina. What a scene!

They also began to disarm the people. For example, they offered all the workers who handed in their weapons a medal or something like that. Not that all the workers had arms. No. How could they? A section of the MNR, its aimed militia, had weapons. So there were very few who were armed.

If the leaders hadn't left that time, a lot of people would have been killed, a whole lot of blood would have been shed! We didn't have weapons. What would we have defended ourselves with? The miners thought of all that.

SEPTEMBER MASSACRE

After the leaders had been deported to Argentina, the workers, and especially the Trotskyists, organized a sort of underground union. Isaac Camacho was at the head of it, as secretary-general. From inside the mine he directed the union movement. The people from the government were looking for him, because they'd discovered that he led the clandestine union.

One day, on September 18, 1965, Camacho came out to meet with the people at the door of the union building. And that's where they arrested him. And in order to get him, they had to arrest a lot of others, and they also killed some students, some women, several people. There was a confrontation because the people tried to defend him. That was on a Saturday. Camacho disappeared.

On Sunday they buried the dead and on Monday the workers went down into the mines. The workers from the clandestine union said to the miners: "Look at what happened . . . we can't let things go on this way."

The workers reacted, because it wasn't fair that the army could just kill so many people like that. And they decided to organize a protest demonstration. And they also armed themselves: they took dynamite out of the company's storeroom.

But the army had found out about everything and had already installed the soldiers with their submachine guns and heavy weapons at the mine entrance, which was so thickly surrounded the miners couldn't get out.

The army cut off all lines of communication. The microphones, the telephones, everything was cut. We women wanted to let the miners know what was going on, to tell them not to go out, that the soldiers were waiting out there in order to wipe them out at the mine entrance, to tell them that there were weapons all over the place. We were dying to communicate with the mine interior, but we couldn't.

We were afraid and we thought: in a little while the miners are going to come out and the soldiers are going to open fire on them with their guns.

Fortunately, the workers realized what was going on. I don't know how they found out about everything. So they came out from the other side, through the Cerro Azul entrance, on the opposite side of Siglo XX. And from that side they took the army guys by surprise.

There was a confrontation where the workers really defended themselves with a lot of courage, because the only thing they had was dynamite, while the soldiers had really modern weapons.

But when we thought that we had the situation under control and things were quieting down, the worst part began: the army came in planes to machine-gun us. For the first time, we could see how a plane flies, dips down or noses in, and how some little rays of light came from the inside of the plane and there were the bullets falling: pa! pa! pa!

They fired on the Plaza del Minero, on Cataví, on the rock pile. The bullets came toward us from everywhere, like rays of light. And not only that, they also attacked the ambulances, something that can't be accepted in any war, in any battle; it's an international crime, isn't it? There were many dead and there were so many wounded that they didn't fit into the Cataví hospital.

That year I was just beginning as secretary-general of the Housewives' Committee and I was just another citizen who didn't understand enough about the situation; I wasn't very up to date. But I *did* see that massacre. And I had seen how, for example, they put agents of the Ministry of the Interior into the ambulances, disguised as stretcher-bearers, who went to pick up the wounded, but they were there with their cameras snapping pictures of the people running around taking care of the casualties. And it turns out that when that massacre took place, they began to use the photos to pick people up. They'd show them to the agents in Siglo XX and would ask: "Where does so-and-so live?" And they'd begin to look for him. They also took all the young people whose pictures they'd taken out into the school playground. And all of them were taken to prison. It was a terrible haul-in, terrible! It was atrocious. Zacarías Plaza did all that. He was in charge of the occupation of the mining camps.

Zacarías Plaza was a military man who had gotten lots and lots of money and lots of medals for having massacred so many workers in Siglo XX. But in 1970, I think, after having suffered various attempts on his life, Zacarías Plaza turned up dead. At dawn, on the feast of San Juan, thanks to a group which called itself "Eagle Eye," he appeared . . . dead! They made a mess out of the guy. I found that out from the newspapers. And they said that everything that had happened to Zacarías Plaza was vengeance for what he'd done in Siglo XX. And that was the fate which awaited all those who'd massacred the people.

Those two massacres, the one in September 1965 and the San Juan massacre of 1967, we owe to Zacarías Plaza. He took charge of everything. And he mocked us: "Why do you want to get into the dance if you can't dance? Okay, dance now if you want!" And he gave the order to massacre us.

Well, the army, triumphant, entered the mines, because we didn't have weapons or anything to defend ourselves with. And they began a house-to-house search and took in all the men.

The army spent their time communicating among themselves over the radio: "Now we're in the north, in the south, now we're doing a general mop-up of these reds, these cowards, these bastards. . . ." And so on and so forth. Yes, all of us were "reds" as far as they were concerned.

Some very sad things began to happen. In Catavi, for example, the following happened: In one house, the husband had gone traveling because he was on vacation. With all the ruckus, all the shots and fighting, the wife had hidden her children under the bed, as was the custom here. There's a belief that when there's shooting, the children should always be put under the beds and wrapped up in mattresses so that the bullets won't get to them. The bullet just gets tangled up in the wool and doesn't reach the children and so doesn't wound them. So in that house that's how they did it: they put the kids under the bed, and when the soldiers knocked on the door the mother didn't want to open. So they began to bang on it and then they went in. The kids were crying and the soldiers said: "There's someone under the bed. Come out before I count to three." But the kids were afraid and didn't come out. And the soldier counted: "One, two, three!" And the mother shouted: "But it's only my children! Please!" As the woman was kneeling to beg for mercy because the order to shoot had already been given, the guy thought she wanted to grab his gun and . . . bang! bang! . . . he took his pistol and killed the woman. And the others also fired. We went to see and the kids were under the bed. When the husband got back, he no longer had children, no longer had a wife, and the oldest daughter had lost both legs. All the others died immediately.

In another home, the same thing happened. It was closed and the soldiers knocked on the door. The woman was going to open and . . . bang! bang! . . . they shot her. And she died right there.

A worker was escaping over the rock pile and one of the soldiers came through the door of my house and stood there and began firing. He almost got him. Then the worker hid, see. He threw himself down and we could see him rolling and rolling downhill.

And another worker, for example, who never got involved in anything, who didn't even go to meetings, was in the doorway of his house, but he didn't want to go out: "Sir, I haven't done anything," he said. And the soldiers said: "Ha, coward! Come out!" And they hit him real hard.

They've committed all kinds of abuses.

So all of Siglo XX was declared a military zone. A curfew was established, and we only had the right to be outside until eight o'clock at night. For example, we had to go to the baths—a public place because we don't have them in our houses—accompanied by the soldiers. And when I went with my children, the same thing: with soldiers. It was worse than a concentration camp!

Every night you had a soldier posted at your door. It was like that in all the camp's houses. That's why I say it was a military zone. The camp filled up with so many soldiers that at each door, at whatever signal, they'd shout: "What's up?" Then you had to say, for example: "Please, sir, I want to go to the baths. Could you do me that favor?" Then, only then, would they let you open your door. You had to go to the baths together with the soldier, go back home with him, and close your door. The same thing with the light: after a certain hour, everything had to be dark. And if it wasn't, they shot in the air or a soldier would shout: "That light ought to be out by now. Why's it on?" That's why I say it was worse for us than in a concentration camp in those days at Siglo XX.

Some days after the massacre, the Manchego Regiment[11] from Santa Cruz arrived. Since they're people from western Bolivia

---

11. This part of the account takes place before Che's guerrilla warfare began, when the Manchego Regiment was made up only of regular conscripts. Subsequently it became a regiment of "rangers"—troops specializing in counterinsurgency, trained and equipped by the Pentagon. The ranger regiment mentioned here is the one from Challapata, a town near Siglo XX.

and they don't know the highlands, they'd been told: "Let's go to Cochabamba."

The poor things, who'd never been out of Santa Cruz, when they landed in Uncía they were trembling. And they said:

"Boy . . . Cochabamba . . . it's pretty cold, isn't it?"

That's what a couple of guys told us, who afterward became our friends.

When they got here they were told:

"Well, you're in Siglo XX. You're in the red village of Bolivia. Only communists live here. Here you can't trust anyone. You mustn't talk to anyone, not even the kids. Because those kids know how to use dynamite. And if they do, you're the ones who'll be blown to bits. It'll be so bad we won't even be able to pick you up with teaspoons."

That's how they frightened them. That same morning they brought them to begin the "cleanup operation." They went into every house in the camp. They looked into everything, they broke everything. They even pried up the floor boards and checked out every single thing.

"You got weapons? You got dynamite? Communist propaganda? Political propaganda?"

What didn't they do and what didn't they ask! And that's how they carried out their "cleanup." We couldn't do anything, not even take out a package, without them opening it first. Because, according to them, we were all armed.

That morning I was coming from the grocery store and a soldier stopped me:

"Let's see, Senora, let's see . . . halt! What've you got there?"

And he searched through everything. After seeing that all I had was food for dinner: "Okay, you can go."

It was like that with all of them.

Well, it turns out that at dinner time, the top brass went to eat. And the soldier boys were left alone in front of our doors, as far as they'd gotten with their "cleanup operation" at that point. And since they hadn't even had breakfast, the poor boys were hungry.

Aren't people funny: sometimes the soldiers kill them, they fill them full of bullets, blood is flowing all around them. The shooting ends . . . and the women come out with their bread and give some to the soldier boys.

That really made me angry and furious. And I'd say to them:

"But how can you? How can you practically say 'thanks' for having come to kill us like dogs?"

And they'd answer:

"But no, Señora! These are our sons! They're like our own sons! It's the ones at the top who give the orders, Señora. It's not these boys' fault. And the day after tomorrow, maybe the same thing's going to happen to my son, when he's drafted: he'll be sent to kill people. How can we not give them a piece of bread?"

Everyone reacted like that. And after a while, I understood them. How wise my people are! Really! Why this madness to kill everyone? What terrible men! What bad men! How can they do this to my people?

You know, once a woman recognized one of the soldiers, who was her nephew. And she went to hug him and offered him food. But the boy didn't want to take it. And he told his aunt that they'd told them at Siglo XX the inhabitants would try to poison them. He was really scared. And that's how they all were. They'd been told that so they'd be afraid to get close to us. But little by little they began to accept the things we offered them. Soon everyone was giving them things to eat.

When they returned to their barracks, the Manchegos began to ask the rangers: "How can you have been so stupid as to kill such beautiful people, such good people? All of them are sharing with us, all of them treat us well. Are you savages? Couldn't you see what was really happening?"

The officers of the occupation army found out about the conversations. And then, as punishment, they took the Manchegos to the top of the hill. The young soldiers were dressed in their clothes from the east, where it's so hot, and they weren't used to the very cold climate of the highlands, and several of them died there in the cold. And they took away the ones who survived. What became of them? I don't know.

In my house, three of the Manchegos had become our friends. And during the time they were there, sometimes they'd knock on the door:

"Señora, could you invite us to lunch, please? Today we're on leave and we don't have anywhere to go."

And between this and that we'd begin to chat about the situation. We even shared things with their families. The soldiers would give us chestnuts their parents had sent them and we'd send their families things that we had, like canned goods, or noodles.

Everyone knew how to distinguish between the Manchegos and the rangers. Everyone hated the rangers with their green berets who were trained to fight against the guerrillas with a really special preparation, really fascist-like; they were responsible for the massacre. On the other hand, the Manchegos weren't trained like that, they were simple conscripts. I wonder what happened to them when they were taken away?

Sometime later, a commission from outside came, made up of university people, the press, and the Church, in order to find out "what happened in September." Because, as usual, the government made out that it was the victim and made us look like we were guilty for everything that had happened.

The commission arrived. But there was so much repression that no one wanted to talk. No one even felt like it. No one. I remember very well that they called us over the radio to go and denounce what had happened. But not one worker felt like speaking. Everyone was silent, absolutely everyone.

I was with my husband and he said that he wasn't going to talk either:

"Look, they fired my compañeros from the company; they'll fire me too, and we have such a big family (at that time my sisters were still with me), you've got to think about all that. Don't go to speak."

I would listen, and I listened to the people from the commission . . . and it drove me crazy that people couldn't talk, couldn't say anything, even though they were drowning in pain and anguish. But they couldn't talk because everyone was afraid, you know? It made me sad, it made me distressed. Speak, speak! I'd say.

And I turned around and saw a woman who was there with her little children, crying because they'd killed her husband. So I said to her:

"But, Senora, don't cry. Stand up and denounce your husband's murder."

The woman looked hard at me and said:

"But, Señora . . . well, you're our president, so you go and speak. You're a housewife . . . so go and speak."

That was enough to make me begin to think about my role as a leader: it's true that I'm a leader, I'm also part of this. And I'm asking that others speak and I'm not doing anything.

The other people who'd heard what the woman said also said:

"She should speak, she should speak!"

So I stood up and began to speak. And I denounced everything that had happened. I explained our whole problem, how we wanted them to give us back our wages and how we'd asked for them. How the repression was killing us. And I spoke of all the things I'd seen, including how I'd seen them attack the ambulances. And I told them that the whole world must find out about our situation.

And when I finished speaking, I sat down. And, well, my husband was no longer beside me. But many workers were surrounding me. Some, who'd seen other things, whispered to me and said: "Such and such happened too . . ." And I'd repeat what the compañero said to me. And in the end, every single one of the people near me embraced me and kissed me and said:

"It's a good thing you didn't leave, that you didn't abandon us." And one of them said to me: "Now I understand why it's necessary for women to participate in everything."

The solidarity the compañeros were showing me made me very happy. Because I'd spoken for them, and it was for the press, the radio, for many commissions that had come from La Paz, from Cochabamba, from Oruro, and from abroad.

And that time, in spite of everything I said, nothing happened to me or to my husband. And it turns out that all the villages supported us and sent help to the widows.

Even the army brought food and distributed it, like some kind of bad joke. It's the kind of thing that really, really hurts. But that's how it happened. The army distributed food, after massacring us. And the worst thing is that the people live so miserably, that many of them, especially from the non-mining population, lined up and fought for the food. It was humiliating and painful to see such a thing. I'll always remember it. They'd killed so many people and now they were coming to shut us up with a piece of bread, a can of sardines. It wasn't fair, was it? How beautiful it would have been to refuse all that and, even if we had to die of hunger, not accept anything! But, unfortunately, it didn't happen that way. It was very painful to see those lines of people, shoving one another, fighting to get a little rice, a little can of milk.

In 1970, there was a congress of mine workers in Siglo XX. General Ovando was already in power; Barrientos had died in a helicopter accident in 1969. At that congress we stated, among other things, that the widows should receive an indemnification, and that all the orphans should get scholarships to study. But nothing has been done. We also mentioned that General Barrientos had left a lot of money, thousands and thousands of dollars, which should be expropriated; I told the miners the money could be distributed among the people who'd been affected by his massacres and all his repression. But that hasn't been done either.

THE ROCK-PILE WOMEN, OR *PALLIRIS*

At that time there were a lot of unemployed women, especially the widows of workers who'd died in the mine or in a massacre. Unemployment was so terrible that every day women came to the union or to the management office looking for work. Two of my sisters were among them. They had to go every day. And every day they came back without an answer.

So it occurred to me to organize them into a Committee of Unemployed, or something like that. We began to take a census. And we were able to prove, for example, that there were families that weren't very large and where both husband and wife worked. And there were widows with six or seven children who didn't have any income whatsoever. That didn't seem right to us. And so we began to look into the situation of the people who didn't have work and we organized this committee so that their situation could be kind of investigated. We wrote down everything we found out. We took it all to the management and we told the manager that it didn't seem right to us that while some women were dying because they didn't even have bread, other women had work at the same time their husbands also worked for the company.

We argued so much that the manager had to pay attention to us. He fired nine people who didn't need work so badly, and nine of the women who needed work and who were organized in the Committee of Unemployed were given jobs. The women who'd done all the work and who wrote up the document to present to the management were mostly young. But look at what happens because there aren't enough jobs: right after they found out about this, some of the widows met and asked the sections where their husbands had worked to support them and the sections sent letters to the manager, saying that the women who most needed the jobs were the widows. And so we had to make an arrangement and nine widows went to work for the company. The young women were pretty let down, but we couldn't go against the workers' decision.

When people saw that nine widows went to work, our original list of forty people grew rapidly to more than two hundred. There were lots and lots of women who came to us daily, who never got tired of showing up at my house, saying, "Señora, I'm also a widow." They'd cry and tell me what they and their children had to live through. "With all the work that my husband did in the company, with everything that's been sacrificed, this is how we live. . ." and so on and so forth. It was a terrible mess! They'd come and tell me all kinds of problems . . . it really made you feel terribly sad. I'd write down every single thing and we went on like that, looking for solutions. We continued going to see the manager to ask how the situation was. The manager said he was going to try to fix the thing up some way or other, that maybe we would form some cooperatives.

One day, really at their wits' end, the girls started crying and said they were willing to work at anything. So much walking and they hadn't gotten anywhere! They couldn't take it anymore. And so they went to the manager's office and said to him:

"Señor, if you don't do something about our situation we're going to go on a hunger strike, it doesn't matter if we die, because in any case, we can't go on like this any longer."

So he said:

"You're willing to work at anything?"

"Yes, at anything," they answered.

"Okay, we have a plan. Why don't you come back tomorrow? Then we'll talk it over with you."

When we returned the next day, they told us that we could go work up at the rock pile. That was the plan they had for us.

The rock pile is a place that's like a hill made of stones taken from the mines, stones which have been next to the ore. At the beginning, when they began exploiting the mine, the stone came out black as coal, it was very high-grade ore. Then they'd take just the ore, and some stones which were half mineral, half stone, and just throw the rest away. And that began to form a sort of mountain. That's why there was good ore on the rock pile. And that had to be sorted out.

The work they proposed to us was the following: the girls would have to move those stones, pick out the ones with ore in them, put them in some little bags, go to the grinder, grind them, and give them to the company. And the girls would be paid by the company according to the bags they handed in. It would be done experimentally for three months. And after three months they'd have to sign a work contract.

The manager asked me: "How many people want to work?"

"Two hundred," I told him.

"Well, we can hire all two hundred. Tell them to come here and we'll talk it over."

I called all the women together. I explained everything to them. And then many of them, especially the widows, said:

"Ay! Not on the rock pile. No, no, and no again. We don't want to. We aren't *palliris*." [Aymara word meaning "one who collects by choosing."]

That's what the palliris are, the people who collect rocks with ore.

The girls we'd begun with looking for work stayed on. None of them walked out on the group. They began to work. Every day they'd get home really bushed, with their hands very sore. Because they had to do everything by hand: collect the ore, sort it, put it in bags. Absolutely everything by hand. Their hands would be bleeding.

They were each paid 400 pesos and they worked like that for a month. Wow! They thought that was heaven! You should have seen how happy they all were. As soon as they were paid, they'd come running over to my house and say: "We've got 400 pesos! They've paid us, Señora!" And they felt happy, despite so much sacrifice, because that was an important change.

Well, the other people found out that the women working on the rock pile had earned 400 pesos the first month and they wanted to work too. About five hundred women went to Catavi to ask the management to give them work.

Management told them they couldn't take on everyone at once, but that they could increase the group by a hundred people a month. So we made a list and, a hundred a month, four hundred more women started working as palliris. But they lowered the wages of the first group of women as they increased the number of workers: the second month they were paid 300 pesos, then 200, and, in the end, 180 pesos a month.

When the three trial months were up and the moment had come to legalize things with a contract, we went to Señor Ordóñez, who at that time was secretary-general of the union, to talk to the manager. We'd made a plan for a collective contract with the company, with full benefits. We said that, after having completed the three trial months of work on the rock pile, the main thing was that these women workers be contracted as company workers, with social security benefits, grocery discounts, medical services, everything. We said that if they didn't meet our demands, we'd take steps against them, and we were a pretty strong group.

That's what we wanted to say, but it turned out that a government agent, who'd been sent from Oruro, won over the women's confidence, so much so that he got himself appointed as their work adviser. Without our finding out, they'd sent a letter saying that mister so-and-so was adviser and representative for all the demands that the women working on the rock pile wanted to make. In a word, they turned their backs on the union and the Housewives' Committee.

So we got to the managers' office. He had us come in and asked us: "What brings you here? Whatever do you want?"

It wasn't the same manager as before. They'd changed him. We told him that the time for an agreement had come, like the company had promised the women working on the rock pile three months ago.

We were inexperienced and had accepted the oral agreement of the previous manager, so we didn't have any papers to prove what had been settled on.

"Ah! . . . Let's see," said the manager. He called in the secretary: "Bring me the memo the women working on the rock pile sent. Let's see what it says."

Then he read the memo to us, in which the women said that they'd "unanimously" named a certain fellow-worker—that guy from Oruro—as their representative and adviser.

Then the manager told us:

"Look, señoras, in this letter the rock-pile workers have openly turned to other leadership."

We didn't know anything about the change and we asked ourselves: what could have happened? How strange! Why?

"So, señoras, I have nothing to talk over with you, absolutely nothing to say about the problems of the women working on the rock pile. You can only come here on other matters. We've already been over this with the women's adviser and everything's well taken care of."

That shut us up, like a bomb. We felt very upset and asked ourselves: what could have happened?

And the manager said:

"Why are you so surprised? If that's what the women decided, it means that you must have done something wrong. You can't fool around with people that way!"

When my sister came home I asked her:

"Why did you do all that without telling us? What happened?"

"I don't know anything about it. They didn't tell us anything," answered my sister. So she went to tell the other workers.

The worst part is that in the agreement which was signed by the group and the "adviser," there was absolutely nothing that helped the workers out. Nothing. They continued slaving away as always.

Federico Escobar had been freed by then and he had returned to Siglo XX. But he wasn't in charge of anything because worker control was outlawed. Worker control had been created by law in 1953 by the MNR, when the mines were nationalized, so that the company's activities could be controlled: how much tin was taken out, how much profits were taken in, how they were distributed, how marketing contracts were made, or the grocery store contracts, and so on. It meant that the mines were in the hands of the people, because worker control functioned through a freely elected representative.

The bosses of the mining company, however, had a lot of problems with Federico Escobar, an honest man who never sold out. So they decided to outlaw worker control. That was in 1965. Afterward, we got it back again. For several years we struggled to establish worker control again, because it arose as a law. In other words, what one hand had given, the other took away, see?

Well, I went to speak to Federico and said:

"Look, these women workers should have gotten a contract by now, or signed a document or something. What can we do? They're really suffering terribly and the company's lying to them. They earn very little and work much too hard. At the beginning they paid them well, but now they earn too little. Besides, they don't have grocery store rights, they don't have benefits, they don't have anything. Their children need to get educated and they can't send them to the company school. They also need medical care. Recently, for example, there was an accident, one of the women fell down because they'd dug a hole, and she smashed her hip and couldn't get medical attention."

I told him all that, and little by little we pressured in the right places. Through Escobar they got some things, for example, they got the right to the grocery store, and their children could go to the company school. That way, we got a few small concessions.

But time was slipping by . . . and that wasn't the solution we'd proposed at the beginning. If we'd stayed united, I think we'd have gotten much more.

The palliris worked like that for six years. There were more internal splits and a pretty large group began to be led by two activists who used the compañeras politically. They took them away in trucks when there were demonstrations, so that it looked like they were supporting Barrientos.

A small group stayed independent. In 1970, when General Torres took power and it was said that it would be a democratic government, we thought: "We've got to take advantage of the moment." So I told my sister who also worked on the rock pile: "Do something so that after six years, things don't just stay the same." According to the law, after three months, part-time workers have the right to become regular workers. I wanted that to be presented as a proposal.

My sister began talking with the women. They also went to the church to ask the priests for help. The church published some pamphlets that sort of told the group's story and showed how the women worked in really humiliating and difficult conditions. And the women working on the rock pile got organized and asked to be recognized as regular company workers, with all the fringe benefits.

But another commission of the same women workers held a meeting with COMIBOL, and COMIBOL made them agree to be paid off and fired. The majority of the women agreed. Only a minority struggled to keep their jobs and improve working conditions. But what the majority says, the minority does, and that's how it had to be.

Juan Lechín was at the workers' assembly. I stood up and said:

"It's not fair for the women working on the rock pile to be laid off like that. And if there's a majority who wants to leave, let them leave, but the women who want to continue working should be able to stay on. What we want is for their living and working conditions to improve, not for them to be laid off. Because where are the compañeras going to work? They don't have any other place to work. Besides, they don't have any savings. And the meager severance pay they're going to give them . . . what good will it do? Many of them have debts, many are sick. Are they going to sleep in the street, sick and in debt? They won't have money or work. How will they live? As workers, you can't allow this to happen. We have to support them."

Then many of the women who worked on the rock pile asked me what I had to do with all of that. They said that they were "workers, not housewives." Well, the point is that the Housewives' Committee had organized them. And we were within our rights to do that. Because we have our declaration of principles where it says, for example, "that we should fight for good conditions for the widows." So as an obligation to the widows, the idea of organizing them to get work had been born. At that time I was the organization secretary in the committee and that's why this job was given to me and I did everything I could to do it well. That's how it was, see?

The small group that wanted to go on working asked for my help. So we went to La Paz to discuss the problem with COMIBOL, and we managed to get something for them. COMIBOL agreed to open a sewing cooperative. The government was going to donate the sewing machines. But since none of the women knew how to sew, we agreed that they'd be paid three months' wages so that they could learn with teachers. And we also agreed that afterward the company would employ the women, giving them work for the company itself. At least we tried to get something for the workers. And the co-op exists to this day. But it's a very small group.

Another thing we got for the women rock-pile workers had to do with severance pay: those who agreed to leave were going to get a total of 800 pesos. But according to the law, and with the help of the union and compañero Lechín, we got them to agree to give them the other benefits that people leaving the company are entitled to. And that way the women got about 2,000 pesos, more or less. We were able to help them with that, too.

I thought like a real leader, so in spite of all the opposition, I had no reason to feel bad nor to say, "They've done bad things to me, so I'm not going to get involved anymore." I knew that people behaved like that out of ignorance, you know? Because they didn't understand labor laws.

The whole problem of the women rock-pile workers made me think a lot about that: that both men and women should begin to understand labor laws, so we can organize our demands. The majority of us don't know what rights we have, what laws protect us, what decrees are in our favor. And that's why we're even afraid to ask for things that are state obligations, or that the boss must give to the workers. For example, I know several cases of mine workers and widows of workers who lost their benefits because they didn't know how and when to ask for things; they're careless, they don't know about the law. And that's why they're even tricked by the welfare service.

In the Housewives' Committee we still have a long way to go in terms of knowing about all that. But you can't ask the compañeras for more than they can give. Everything here is so different, and we have to work hard just to survive and we have so many problems to solve that we still haven't been able to organize ourselves to study all these really important things more carefully.

I haven't had the opportunity to read all the labor legislation either. But when there's a problem to be solved, sometimes I go to the union and borrow the legislation. I tell the secretary that I want to look up material on a certain problem and he tells me: "It's in such-and-such an article on such-and-such a page." The leaders know all that very well.

I think that that was the main problem of the workers on the rock pile, don't you?—that they didn't have a clear idea about the laws that could protect them and at the same time they let themselves be influenced too much by those two leaders who betrayed them. And that's why, when we wanted to help them, we were really rejected. And finally, in order to put an end to that "national shame," as it was called, they've preferred to close that source of work for women; just close it down and put an end to that "shame" for Bolivia. But the truth is that they've condemned four hundred women to death by starvation, instead of looking over the situation and seeing what other way there was to solve the problem.

Many of those compañeras today say: "We made a mistake, we could still be working today." Many of them spend every day looking for work wherever they can. Many of them want to organize. But it's too late now.

The situation of the palliris, the conditions they were forced to work in, really constituted a "national shame." But it's also a shame for Bolivia not to have work for women, isn't it? Especially for the widows of the workers who've died or been deported or fired by the company, who live in misery because they can't find work. Well—isn't it?

CHE IN BOLIVIA

Che's guerrilla activities in Bolivia took place in 1967.

The guerrillas arrived at a really special moment for the people. Since 1965, the government had owed us 50 percent of our wages that it had cut. Barrientos had promised to give it back when COMIBOL got stabilized economically. But years went by and, instead, a new bourgeoisie was formed from the military men who began to buy big houses, Mercedes-Benzes, and who lived very well, while we were starving to death. They also created the DIC, a new secret police organization.

That's why we lived with constant demands, trying to solve our problems. But the government always gave us the same answer: firings, arrests, prison.

Suddenly we began hearing that there were guerrillas and that the government was going to take strong measures against them and anyone who supported them.

In the beginning, we didn't pay any attention to that. And we would say: "The guerrillas exist only in their imagination." We thought it was a pretext to massacre a lot of people, both with blood massacres and white massacres. We call the massive layoffs of workers "white massacres," when they're thrown out into the street. And ever since Barrientos came into the government, there had been a lot of white massacres: every worker who complained was kicked out of the company, was laid off. More than five hundred workers in Siglo XX had no right to anything: the right to work had been taken away from them. So we thought that, with all the talk about the guerrillas, the government just wanted to have a pretext to step up the repression even more.

But later on we saw a communiqué from the guerrilla group and it was signed by Moisés Guevara, Simón Cuba, Julio Velasco, Raúl Quispaya, and I don't remember who else, but all of them pretty well known in the mine. In the manifesto they said that just as the government had an army to defend it in order to stay in power, by the same token the working class needed an armed group to defend the workers. And that various sons of the people had gone to the mountains to put an end to that dictatorship, to all that fascism that had covered the people with blood. And that they'd gone to the mountains to begin the struggle from there. They were conscious that this system of exploitation had to be changed and that power had to be given to the working class. And that once the working class was in power, only through socialism would we get a more just, a more human world, without hunger, without misery, without malnutrition, without injustice, without lay-offs by the company.

There were two pages with a very deep analysis of the situation in which we lived and the things we needed, signed by those leaders. And since we had certain connections with them, we could identify their signatures. And so we no longer doubted the truth about the existence of the guerrillas. All of this was publicized a lot, and we even read the communiqué over the radio, which was, maybe, an error on our part.

And in those days, they decided the Mine Workers' Federation should immediately call a plenary meeting of the secretaries-general in Siglo XX, to demand from the government the wages it owed us. Some miners also said that, if they didn't get their wages, they were going to openly support the guerrillas, because, with so many white massacres, it seemed to them that it was better to die in the mountains than to die from starvation without work in the mines. And there were even some demonstrations of spontaneous support for the guerrillas.

The plenary meeting of the secretaries-general was to open on June 25, 1967. But the day before, at dawn on the 24th, which is the traditional feast of San Juan, when there are bonfires and we all have the custom of drinking with the neighbors, of singing and dancing, the army entered and killed a lot of people. And all of us who, according to them, had supported the guerrillas, were arrested, beaten, mistreated, and several were killed. For example, I lost my unborn child in prison because they kicked me in the stomach, saying that I was the liaison with the guerrillas. So, many of our comrades and even some of our children went with Che, because many of us had lost our most beloved ones for the sake of Che's guerrillas in Bolivia.

It seems that Che had the idea that he had been deceived. At least that's what he says in his Diary, no?—that they'd painted another picture of Bolivia, other possibilities. But I think that Che made some mistakes. For example, the mistake of trusting a political party too much, and of not establishing contact with the real people's organizations, the working-class organizations, so that they could give him their sincere opinion. And then, the people who'd committed themselves to his struggle pulled out afterward. All this is there in Che's Diary, no? It's not something I made up. Anyhow, I don't know too much about it. But anyone who wants to find out about it can read his Diary, where he mentions this and many other things.

Until the moment that Che died, none of us in the mine knew he was in Bolivia. There were comments. But only when the photo of his corpse came out in the papers did we know that Che had been with the guerrillas. In other words, we only knew that there were some miners involved. And because of the support we gave them, many of our comrades suffered and died.

That's why I was so hurt when, one day, after I spoke at the International Women's Year Tribunal in Mexico, a man came up to me and said:

"Are you a Bolivian?"

"Yes," I answered.

"Ah!" he said. "You're the cowards who let the great *comandante* Che Guevara die without punishing his murderers."

That hurt me. Because when you don't know much about a thing, before giving an opinion, you should be sure, you should investigate before saying anything, right? And I know that all the things that happened in Siglo XX in the San Juan massacre and afterward were because of the existence of Che's guerrillas. And it doesn't seem fair to me to say to me that the Bolivian people are cowards and that we betrayed him.

THE SAN JUAN MASSACRE

So the other big massacre [after the one of September 1965], which we call the San Juan Massacre, occurred at dawn on June 24, 1967. It was terrible, because it took us all by surprise.

All through the mining camp you could hear the rockets, the firecrackers we explode on that feast day as a way of showing our happiness. And the army came in and began shooting. That confused the people a lot, since at first they thought all that noise was only the firecrackers.

The army had planned everything. People dressed as civilians arrived. They came in freight cars to the Cancañiri Station. They got off, they shot at everyone in sight. It was terrible, terrible!

At dawn the union siren went off. That siren only goes off once a day, at five in the morning, to wake us up. It only sounds on other occasions when there's some other emergency. It's really, really loud. They say it used to be a ship's siren.

So the siren was sounding and we turned on the radio. And we heard that the army was attacking and that we had to go defend our radio transmitter.

We opened the doors. But no sooner had we opened them than they began shooting again. They were already in position. They fired at everyone and everything.

And why? Well, because the government had found out that the next day there was going to be a meeting, a plenary meeting, of all the secretaries-general to talk about our problems again. And the government didn't want it to take place.

At the train station, we had to convince the women to go pick up and save the wounded and make sure that the compañeros, furious by now, wouldn't go out to face a hail of bullets.

How many things we saw that night! For example, I saw a worker, with his leg in a cast, go out with his old pistol to face the army. But we were able to take his weapon away from him and hide it. Since they saw that he was in a cast, they didn't do anything to him.

I saw a pregnant woman in an ambulance who had been shot in the stomach. Her baby died.

Another woman shouted at me: "What happened to my son? Help me! Help me!" I picked up the boy and took him out of the house. And when I was about to put him into the ambulance, I put him on my lap and . . . I saw that his skull was empty.

Well, there were scenes I'll never forget, that are still vivid and that were really ghastly. Entire families died. Rivers of blood flowed!

There were people who died in bed, because the soldiers were shooting wild, really wild, at everything.

In one house, for example, a bullet came in and killed a man, and by a horrible coincidence, it ricocheted off the wall and also killed his wife. The child is an orphan and still lives in Siglo XX.

The army surrounded the radio station and the soldiers wanted to kill everyone working there. The leader, Rosendo García Maisman, came out of his house to defend the transmitter. His compañera wanted to stop him, but he said that his duty came first. When he got to the radio station, they'd already wounded the commentator in the leg. A soldier was going to shoot him down. Rosendo killed the soldier and saved the wounded man. But there was an exchange of bullets, more soldiers arrived, they grabbed Rosendo and killed him, shooting him twice through the nose. And that's how he died, defending something that belonged to the people.

No one knows how many people died.

And the next day, when they buried the dead in the cemetery, hundreds and hundreds of them, I stood up on top of a wall and from there I spoke out:

"We can't stand for this. How can they kill the working class this way, kill the people who make so many sacrifices, who are working, who are making the country rich? What they've done to us isn't just. Why? The government itself took our wages away, and all we ask for is what we're entitled to in all justice . . . And then they kill us this way, it's unfair. Cowards! Bastards!" I shouted.

And since there were guerrillas at that time, I said:

"Why don't they go up into the mountains? There are armed men there, waiting for them. Why don't they go and fight from there? Why do they come here to kill defenseless people? And how dare they come in here, when it's thanks to the workers that they enjoy a comfortable life, with houses, cars, and vacations?"

That way, I did an analysis of everything. And I also said: "And do you think that because you've got weapons you can walk all over us this way? We wear pants too, we've got brave men. And it's only because we don't have guns that we can't defend ourselves against your massacre."

Well, that was June 25.

WHERE'S THE MINER WOMAN?

That was enough so that, two days later, they came to arrest me. They broke the window of my house in the night and came in like prowlers. They searched the whole house and said I'd killed a lieutenant in the doorway of the union building on San Juan night. That was a lie, I hadn't even been in that doorway.

Some man showed up in a *jucu* cap [wool cap covering the head and face, leaving only the eyes showing], which they wear when it's cold. And he said that I was the women's leader.

"She's the one who's asking for the general's head," said another.

"Bitch! Bitch who's paid by two masters! Communist!" shouted another man.

Then I got mad and began to take the things out that I had in a drawer.

"Paid by two masters! Where would I get paid by two masters from? Why, I don't even have enough to buy myself any decent clothes!" I answered.

They pushed me. My baby daughter Alicia woke up. They threw her in the air and I was able to catch her.

Everything that I had of value, papers, the Housewives' Committee documents, they tied up in a sheet. And they dragged me out. And they also took my compañero, just as he was, without any shoes on.

They tied him to an army truck, with his hands behind his back. They barely allowed me to get a coat for my little girl.

And we got into the truck. We found some of the Siglo XX leaders there. Up until then I hadn't been afraid.

When we got to the Llallagua exit, there was a military truck full of prisoners tied to each other, with bloody faces. They turned the headlights so that I could get in and I saw blood flowing. I thought they'd killed them right there. And I said to myself: "They're going to kill me." I thought about my orphaned children. Then I felt really scared. I didn't want to show it, but I was really afraid.

With a shove they put me into the truck. I fell down and then someone shouted. Then I realized that they were alive. They were about to tie my hands like they'd done with the men, but my little girl began to wail.

Colonel Acero came and asked whose child it was and who was that woman.

"She's the leader of the women," said the man wearing the cap.

The colonel made the truck stop, he made me put on my poncho, and he took me off the truck to the pickup where the chief agents were riding.

We stayed in Llallagua a long time, until the truck was loaded with about forty or fifty prisoners, and then they took us to the Miraflores barracks. They put us in an empty room. They told us that from that moment on we were political prisoners, that we were forbidden to do anything, and that if we tried to escape they would shoot us "for trying to escape." Then they left.

The prisoners were all tied up. I put my little girl on a table in the room and began to untie the men. It was difficult, they were tied so tight, but finally I was able to do it.

The next day we left there and they took us to the Uncía landing strip to fly us by plane to La Paz. But the weather was bad and the plane didn't arrive. We waited a long time on the landing strip.

Meanwhile, the compañeras had mobilized a demonstration and were coming from Siglo XX to Uncía. The agents telephoned the barracks saying that they were approaching, that they were there.

When they announced that the women had passed the police checkpoint at Miraflores, they made us go back immediately. At the barracks there was another vehicle ready to take us out by another route. They put me in the front with my little girl, as a kind of shield. And an agent was beside me with his gun pointed at me. They drove out behind the barracks to take us to Oruro, so that from there they could take us to La Paz. I could see the people running with banners and they ran toward the barracks. But they couldn't see us.

On the way to Oruro the vehicle broke down. Then they made me get down and sit on the ground. The soldiers stood around with their submachine guns covered with blankets so it didn't look as if they were armed. And they told us: "Be very careful. We're aiming at the child and her mother. And if anyone tries anything, calls for help, or tries to escape, we'll shoot, starting with the child and then her mother."

We stayed that way for several hours, until they'd fixed the truck. Lots of trucks went by, lots. And they didn't realize anything was going on, because the men in the truck were covered with a tarpaulin.

When we reached Oruro, I found Nabor, a schoolmate of mine who was there as a government agent and was coming to pick us up. My little girl was very hungry and was crying. One of the agents gave me 5 pesos so I could buy her something to eat. I went up to Nabor and asked him to help me. But he said:

"What do you think? What makes you think I'll help you?"

And he wouldn't help me. I couldn't believe it, but he wouldn't help me.

We reached La Paz. My little girl was dying from the cold. She was two years old. And everyone said: "What? The little girl too? It's not her fault." Some of them, the more sensitive ones, began crying. So then I tried to calm them, saying that my daughter would never forget what happened. And that it was good for her to be toughened and realize about injustice from her earliest childhood.

In La Paz they put us next to the government palace, where the DIC is. They put the men downstairs. And that was the last time I saw my husband. They left me outside.

My little girl began crying from hunger. She screamed. . . . How she screamed!

An agent approached me and asked:

"Why's that baby crying?"

"She's hungry," I said.

"Well, give her your breast."

"What do you mean? She doesn't get the breast anymore. She's two years old."

A little while later he came back with a little jar of coffee and a sandwich.

"Take this," he said. "And don't say I gave it to you. It could cost me my job."

We slept. It was very cold.

In the morning, I got up and asked them to let me go to the bathroom. I wanted to see my compañeros. I went down to the floor where they'd put them and didn't see anyone. When I was passing through a patio, I saw a tall man. I looked around everywhere and, without meaning to, I bumped into him. He insulted me. He almost spat in my face. I thought he was an agent.

Later, when I was coming out of the bathroom, a dark-skinned man recognized me. Then I asked about my compañeros. And he told me:

"At four in the morning they took them to Puerto Rico." Puerto Rico is a very unhealthy, deserted island in the state of Pando.

They pushed me on and I left. And then I got a big surprise: everyone there was a prisoner. They gave me things to eat. I gathered them up in my poncho. And there were oranges, apples, everything. And they said to me: "Courage, compañera. You're not alone, our cause is great."

It was like a narrow little street full of people. I got to the door and bumped into the man who'd insulted me. And he said:

"Forgive me. I didn't know you were a prisoner. Forgive me." He looked through his pockets and gave me all he had: cigarettes.

I left. They searched me all over and took everything away from me. I protested, but they didn't give it back, even though the food was for my child.

I went back to the cell. At the rear there was a young woman. I didn't trust her, thinking she was an agent.

At three in the afternoon they called me for my statement. During the interrogation, they shouted at me to make me cry:

"Helping guerrillas, eh? You'll see. . . !"

They insulted me horribly. I couldn't stand any more . . . I was afraid. My little girl was crying, and I tried to calm her down.

I said to the soldier, trying to appear calm:

"What are you talking about? I don't know anything. No, sir, I don't know anything."

He got furious and began yelling:

"This one's pulling our leg! Take her away before I kill her!"

I didn't eat a thing all that day. The young woman who was in the cell gave my daughter a sandwich.

They took me the next day and asked me the same things all over again.

They took pictures of me. They covered my eyes and took me to a building with an elevator. They put me in a room and the first thing I saw when they uncovered my eyes was the United States flag and on the other side the Bolivian flag, and a framed picture with two hands that said "Alliance for Progress." The room was all painted blue. You couldn't make out the door or anything. The desk was full of rubber stamps.

I sat down. They showed me a photograph of my father and began saying that I was poor and that most likely it was out of necessity that I'd gotten involved. And the lieutenant said:

"These foreigners are looking out for you, because the Bolivian government wants to take drastic steps against you. And they're going to help you if you help us, so that way you'll save your children and your husband and also yourself."

But since in Siglo XX there was already talk of the CIA and since in the movies I'd seen how the intelligence service acts, I had some idea of what was going on.

So then they began:

"We want to help you. Your children will go abroad to study. . . ."

I asked them what they wanted.

They told me they wanted to know who were the guerrilla liaison people, where there were "arms," etc., etc.

I told them:

"Who are you to ask me that? If I have union or political problems, well, that's for my government to deal with. And it seems to me that I should be asking you: who are you? And what are you doing here? I'm a Bolivian citizen and not North American."

They began speaking English. They rang the bell, and they brought in a dossier. Then they said:

"It makes us happy that you're proud to be Bolivian. That's wonderful. And the foreigners you got involved with are bad. What are those people doing who've taught you to hate the gringos so much? We gringos do everything for you. Look at the school in Siglo XX, in Uncia, schools for the miners' children. And now, look at this . . . Everything is from the Alliance for Progress. All of that is our work. And tell me: what's Cuba done for Bolivia? Or China? Have they built one single school? No! What they want is to make slaves out of you."

"I'm not going to answer a single question," I told them.

The lieutenant laughed and laughed and said that I was just making things worse for myself.

They took me out of there. The agents by now were only leading me by the arm, not pushing me. They blindfolded me again, they took me to the cell, and they took the blindfold off.

Two hours later the agents came in with blankets and food, being very attentive. And they said to me:

"Mr. Quintanilla sends you greetings for your pride in being Bolivian." Mr. Quintanilla was one of the heads of the DIC and a CIA agent.

I didn't trust the food. And my little girl ate it all.

The foreign woman at the rear of the room came over to me and spoke. I was rude and very unpleasant. I asked her not to bother me. She laughed and understood my mistrust. She said she was from Brazil and that in Brazil she'd faced a death penalty and that her comrades had helped her escape to Uruguay. And that she entered Bolivia clandestinely and they arrested her because of the guerrilla problem. They were about to take her to the border, but she had a lawyer.

I didn't answer anything.

"Your little girl's so pretty."

The agent was in front of us and so very softly she said:

"You're not alone. The miners are on strike. Be calm."

And she went on pretending, until she left.

The agents would come to frighten me. Then I'd say that I'd heard that's how they always treat women, that they even rape them.

"And now I'm seeing the proof," I said. "You can do whatever you want to me. But I'll tell everyone all about it when I get back to Siglo XX. And if you're from the Christian Party, you'll have to answer to God."

The Popular Christian Movement was Barrientos's official party. That's why I talked to them like that. But later I was afraid of making the situation worse.

I was incommunicado. I didn't have any news from the outside, not a word. Only what the lady lawyer told me whenever she came.

An agent came and explained to me that he didn't support the government, but "I've got three little children and I have to do it for them," he said.

He brought me a little pair of pants that had been his little girl's. I accepted them for my daughter. Later he told me:

"Last night I was on duty at the ministry. There's an underground place there where they put criminals. And I heard babies crying there. I asked my colleagues what was going on. One of them, the most cruel one, told me: 'That's where they've got the kids of that communist woman from Siglo XX.' I went to see them."

And the agent described each one of my children perfectly. With details.

Then I asked him:

"And now what?"

"That's how this government is. They aren't feeding them.

And that's why I want to help you. That's why this has got to be a dark secret just between the two of us. Have you heard about the Minors' Council?"

"Yes," I said.

"Well, I'll send them a letter so that they can take charge of your children until you get out."

"Yes," I said. "Please do me that favor."

And I believed him.

"You've got to save your children," he said. And he left.

I was desperate and I told the young woman about my conversation with the agent, and I cried a lot.

But she told me angrily:

"Listen, I'm going to tell you something: in Brazil we've heard a lot about you and the committee, and I thought you were a brave woman. And now, when I get out and say that I was with a woman from Siglo XX, they're going to be surprised. And I'm going to have to tell them that at the first lie they told her, she started crying like Mary Magdalen."

I felt very upset about what they were doing to my children. It was the first time in my life that I had to go through that, and I was horrified to think that they were in prison and sick in a damp cellar, without food and without anything to cover themselves with in the cold. The agent had told me they were crying, shouting: "Daddy! Mommy!" When I thought about that, my heart ached. I was all broken up and went on crying.

Finally the Brazilian woman said:

"Well, Senora, I think you've gotten yourself into a tight spot. Your people must have seen something good in you in order to appoint you to the position you have. You shouldn't think only as a mother, you've got to think as a leader, which is the most important thing at this moment. You aren't only responsible to your children, you're responsible to a cause and it's the cause of your comrades, of your people. You've got to think about that."

Then I told her:

"Well, yes. . . . But if they kill my children? And if they die?"

"If they die, senora, you must live to avenge their death."

That's how she answered me, she said nothing else. She went back to her side of the cell and didn't say anything else to me.

I spent the whole afternoon crying, tremendously upset. Until about three in the afternoon. Then the doors opened wide, they were never opened like that for anyone. The door opened and the first thing I noticed was a strong perfume, like someone with lots of makeup on. Three ladies came in with their handbags, really elegant. They came with the agent who'd talked to me about the Minors' Council.

The agent told me:

"This is the president of the Minors' Council, and the other lady's her secretary."

"Pleased to meet you," they said to me. And they began to tell me about the Minors' Council: that the Minors' Council fights for minors, doesn't let them suffer injustices, doesn't let them be exploited . . . things like that. And they spoke wonders about children. That the council always looks out for them, and this and that.

Then they told me they'd seen my children.

"Horrors! What savagery! How terrible!" they exclaimed. "How is it possible that mere children are treated that way? How terrible! Now Señora, the object of our visit is to find out if you really want the Minors' Council to take charge of your children. In order to do that, we need a letter from you authorizing it. You've got to give us the letter. And that letter has to be signed, so that we can take charge of them and take them to the hospital immediately, because they're pretty sick by now, and if we delay the children could die."

The idea seemed marvelous to me.

"Yes," I said. "I'll do it."

"Very well. Let's see, let's see, dear . . . We've got to write out the letter for the lady, so that she can put us in charge of the situation."

The other lady looked for her notebook.

"There's the letter. Is it all right like that, Señora?"

And she read it to me.

It said that I, Domitila Barrios de Chungara, originally from

Siglo XX, of such and such age, married and in full command of my faculties—something like that—voluntarily gave the Minors' Council authorization to take charge of my small children who were in prison, until I could be freed or arrange my situation.

"Sign here, Senora," the president said.

"All right," I said. "But look here, Señora, it seems to me that to sign a document like this one, you've got to make up this kind of authorization letter with the competent authorities, with a lawyer and with a special paper and with a stamp."

"Yes, yes," she said. "Yes. Let's see, where's that paper? Take it out."

The other looked and looked for it.

"Oh, how terrible! In all the rush I forgot it. But there's no problem, I think she can sign on any piece of paper."

And the other lady said:

"Let's see, Agent, please get us a little piece of paper."

And the agent ran out fast and brought a big sheet of paper, with a letterhead, the DIC's letterhead.

Then I said:

"No! I won't sign it that way. That's got the DIC letterhead . . . Let's tear off that part on the top."

But the agent said:

"How can you tear that? You might tear it crooked and then it would be ruined."

Then I said to him:

"But I won't sign anything with the DIC letterhead on it. I can't sign anything like that on a blank sheet of this paper."

"But we haven't got any more . . . And it was so difficult for us to get in here. . . . Don't make things difficult. Think of it, it involves your children."

And so on and so forth. And they began pressuring me.

Then I said:

"No."

"Well, since you won't do it on the letterhead, then sign here, on the back."

I felt so scared! I looked at the Brazilian woman in the cell with me, so that at least she could signal me or guide me, because it was a terrible moment of indecision. The others were pressuring me. I needed someone to say to me: "Don't do it" or "Do it." I looked at the other woman and she had a newspaper over her face and wouldn't look at me. It was a desperate moment!

And the lady was saying:

"Hurry up, Senora, we don't have much time."

The agent, from outside, was saying:

"It's time! Hurry up!"

To myself I was saying: "No. My God! . . . What have I done? What have I done?"

In those days I had very religious ideas.

And very quickly I analyzed the situation: "Have I killed anyone? No. Others have killed and I've denounced them, because that goes against God's law. And so, if they kill my children now, they've got to pay for it with their conscience. Because if I sign a blank sheet of paper . . . how many innocent people will I be putting on the line! I'd better not sign."

"Look, Senora," I said. "My children are my property, not the state's. And so if the state has now decided to murder my children in that underground room where you say they are, well then, let them murder them. I think that will weigh on their consciences, because I won't be guilty of their crime."

"Ay!" shouted one of them. "I told you, I told you. That's what these heretics are like, that's what these communists are like." She said to me: "Look, all animals, lions, even wild beasts defend their young with their lives. Listen, you savage!" And they grabbed me, pulled at me, and pinched me. "What kind of mother are you that you won't defend your own children? Ay! How horrible, how terrible, what a disgusting woman!"

And she left.

The other one said: "In any case, Señora, I understand you're especially nervous right now. But if you want to change your mind, all you have to do is call me."

And she gave me her card. And she left too. Then the agent said to me:

"Ay, Señora, how can you do this to me? Now I've really risked my job! How terrible! It's my fault for getting involved in things I shouldn't. You really deserve to be made mincemeat of here. But just remember this: your husband will hear about this, we're going to tell him you've sentenced your children to death. So don't hold your breath waiting to see your children again. You've killed them! I'm going to tell your husband about this right now."

And he left.

I said to myself: What have I done? What have I done? Have I killed my children? No, my God, no! No!

And the Brazilian woman was standing there. And she embraced me, she embraced me and she hugged me tight. I cried a lot. And she said to me:

"Domitila, I couldn't have done what you did. Not even I. You've passed your trial by fire. I was thinking: how can such a great people be wrong about their leaders? And I see that the people were right to choose you, Domitila."

And she was crying too. The two of us cried a lot. And she told me she was happy to be with me at that moment and that I should live to avenge the death of my children.

But my children hadn't even been imprisoned. . . .

And from that day on, I declared myself on a hunger strike. I didn't eat anymore, in order to avenge the death of my children. They'd bring plates of food to me and I'd return them untouched.

"If you've killed my children, why should I go on living? Kill me too. Bring me poison," I'd say. "Bring me poison. My children are dead, and now I'm going to die. . . ."

Until one day, I'll always remember, it was a Thursday, I was near the door the agents used to leave by. And in the doorway I heard the sound of a baby's laughter. Then I stretched up to peek through the glass in the door. I saw a lady sitting there. And I spoke to her:

"Señora, are you all alone? What a lovely little baby! I also have my baby here. Why are you here?"

"Ah," she said to me. "They stole my bicycle, my radio, every-thing. And now I've come here to get them but they've already closed the office. So I'm just waiting here. They told me to wait here till two o'clock in the afternoon. And you, what did you steal, why are you locked up?"

"I didn't steal anything, Señora. But . . . and your husband, where does he work?"

"My husband's a factory worker."

"Ah!" I said. "Look, compañera, I'm from Siglo XX, they've locked me up here. I'm the wife of a mine worker. Well, there's got to be solidarity among the workers, no? Couldn't you take your husband a little note?"

I already had a little note written on a cigarette paper. Because my little daughter who was with me sometimes cried a lot and then the agents would take her out in the sun. And my little daughter went from office to office. And from one of the offices she'd brought me a little cigarette paper. It was a new brand, just out, L & M, I think. And it had two wrappings, see, one white and the other silver. My little daughter had brought it along with an old ballpoint pen. So with a little piece of straw from a broom I fixed the ballpoint pen. And I wrote a letter, saying I was in prison and that maybe, in a moment of desperation, I'd lost my children. And that the only crime I'd committed was to denounce a crime against the working class, the San Juan massacre, and that I had come out against it. Because of that, my husband was in prison in Puerto Rico and I was in the DIC cells, in La Paz, where I was on hunger strike because I no longer had any reason to live. And I said: "I denounce to the Bolivian people that this is one more crime that has been committed against me and against my four children." And I signed it at the bottom.

I told the woman all that, so that at least she'd know. I asked her to publish the letter. But she said to me:

"No, no, girl. You're going to get me in trouble. No, no."

"Look, for your little girl's sake, do it. I've also got my little daughter here. Look, take this piece of paper to your husband. If your husband gets it published, good. If he doesn't, well then, he doesn't. But I want your husband to take this letter to the university so that there they'll know I'm in jail. It's just that no one knows about it."

I wept as I begged her. "And if they catch me? And if they denounce me?" she asked.

"But I don't even know who you are, I can't see your face and you can't see mine either. Who's going to know that you took it out for me? Do me this favor, compañera. It's almost time for the office to open."

"Okay, give it to me," she said.

"Hide it well. It's very tiny," I said.

So reluctantly she took it. But I think that compañera did give the paper to her husband and that he turned it over to the university. The thing is that everyone found out I was in jail.

On Friday, early in the morning, the head of the DIC came in and, kicking me, he said:

"Who took that letter out? Who wrote that letter?"

He began really walloping me.

I answered him:

"Go ahead and find out, investigate. That's your job, no? Your job is to find out, to investigate. I'm not your agent. . . ."

Then he grabbed me by the hair and put me in another cell, in a little room. And I was isolated there. And the door opened with an iron stick, but from the inside, see? And with that stick the door was bolted. I wouldn't open for anything. My little girl was crying because she was hungry, but I wouldn't open the door for them. "No hunger, no thirst, little daughter. . . . We're going to die here."

Outside the agents begged me:

"Señora, don't be so cruel. At least give your baby something to eat. Don't let her cry."

"No," I said to them. "Did you have pity on my other children? I won't have pity on my daughter either. Because that way I'd be helping you. You should really thank me, because I'm helping you to finish your job."

That's how they came and knocked on the door. They said they were going to break it down. But they couldn't, because it was pretty solid, it was made of metal and was the only door to the room. And I had bolted it firmly from the inside. So I was locked up in there till Saturday.

The agents came on Saturday afternoon and said:

"Look, Senora, there's an order here to let you go."

"Ah! . . . I can see it's another trick. I don't need my freedom anymore."

"Really, Señora, here's your freedom and your husband's. Here it is."

Then they pushed a paper under the door. And I read: ". . . by order of the Ministry of the Interior, Domitila de Chungara is freed . . ." etc., etc.

I couldn't believe it. At the same time, I wanted to believe it. Also, my little daughter was dying and I said to myself: your daughter's going to die. They hadn't cleared up if my other children's death was a lie or not . . . I thought of so many things!

Finally I thought: what can I gain and what can I lose? At least there's the chance of saving my daughter. But at the same time, with great pain in my heart, I thought: it could be a trap.

I opened the door. The agents said to me:

"Go on! Get dressed! Where are your things?"

"What things would I have? I don't have anything."

"Okay then . . . into the pickup."

When they opened the door . . . I saw lots and lots of people! And a young man near the door was shouting:

"Where's the miner woman? Where is she, murderers? The DIC guys can't get anywhere with the men, that's why they're taking children and women!"

And they began insulting them.

"Here she is, here she is. She's being set free."

Then the young man saw me and said:

"Señora, all the people are on your side. Here, take these."

And he gave me a whole bunch of papers. I began to read one of

them. It said that the Barrientos government was massacring the
people and was massacring women. "And below we reproduce the
letter which the compañera wrote from inside the prison." And
there was my letter in lots of copies. I don't know how many people
gave me papers or who they were. But lots and lots of them gave
them to me. Some were leaflets from the Communist Party, others
from the university. And there were lots of others. All of them had
reproduced my letter.

While I was reading, the DIC guys put me in the truck. And
they took all the papers away from me.

They took me out of jail and gave me provisional freedom. But I
wasn't sure if they were really freeing me or not. Because I left the
DIC and I didn't know where they were taking me. They put me in
the vehicle and it began to move. The people in the demonstration
shouted.

First the agents asked me if I had a relative or some acquain-
tance at whose house they could leave me. I answered them that I
lived in the Siglo XX mining region, that that was where I had to
be. Then they said:

"You can go."

"How am I going to travel?" I asked. I didn't have any money.

Then they went to get some money and took me to buy my ticket
and sent me off to Siglo XX, accompanied by an agent. But before
the vehicle left they told me that in their investigations they'd
proved that the Lincoln-Murillo-Castro group[12] was responsible
for the San Juan massacre. That that group of young people had
killed a bunch of lieutenants and young soldiers and that it was all
proved. They also told me that the workers believed all that and
had asked for the heads of the main leaders.

And that I was one of them. That the workers were waiting for
us at Siglo XX in order to hang us. I was petrified! They told me
lots of things.

---

12. Youth organization for political education with a Marxist orientation
whose members worked in some mining centers.

We reached Oruro after midnight. The passengers got off. There was no transportation to Siglo XX, so we had to sleep right there.

They asked me if I knew anyone in Oruro. I told them I didn't. And I stayed on the bus. The agent went in the back and spread out his blanket and went to sleep. I stayed in my seat.

After about an hour like that, a woman who'd also stayed on the bus, got off. Then, when I saw that the agent didn't move, I got off too. Since all I had to carry was the baby, I slipped off to my father's house.

I got to the house and knocked on the door. I was crying and crying. They put me in a chair. My daddy wasn't there. He'd gone to Siglo XX because he'd read in the papers that I'd been put in jail. My stepmother said: "Your name was in the papers, it said they'd arrested you. What's going to happen? It's a good thing you came."

I rested there that day. In the afternoon, after eating, my stepmother said: "You'd better leave." Because she didn't know anything about the kids; she thought they'd been lost. And the two of us cried. I told her that the miners wanted to hang us because they thought we were responsible for the San Juan killings.

Very worried, I left Oruro. Of course, I began to doubt all the things they'd told me. But I was frightened when I left for Llallagua-Siglo XX.

I got there at about five in the afternoon. It was snowing a little. Fearfully, I got off the bus. I took a few steps. And I noticed that the village looked very calm, there were people talking, like always.

A woman who had worked on the rock pile recognized me:

"Ay, Domitila! You're back!" and she embraced me.

Was I relieved! And I'd been expecting them to hang me, to beat me.

The people around me realized I'd arrived and, in a little while, first one, then another had to come up to me: "How are you? It's good to have you back with us! How did they treat you? Did they beat you? How was it?"

Uf! . . . I felt so relieved! They were all so happy and they said:

"We're on strike, we haven't worked until now. We haven't worked for many days."

In other words, since my arrest they hadn't worked, in support of all of us who were in prison. Just imagine!

I felt so relieved and I congratulated myself for not having signed that paper. I was so happy!

I was so confused that it didn't even occur to me to ask about my children or anything, but instead I thought of all the things that had happened to me, about not having signed the paper, and soon.

Going up to Siglo XX, I asked:

"And my children?"

"Well, I saw them the other day," one of my compañeras told me.

And we went toward my house. A whole bunch of people went with me. More than a hundred people were with me. And everyone who saw me would join the crowd.

When we got to the corner of my street, some kids went running to tell my family. And I saw the door of my house open and, one by one, my children came out.

You can imagine how I felt! What a relief! To think that I hadn't lost them, that they were there! I began crying with joy, jumping up and down and hugging them. Can you imagine that moment? It was great! It was like I'd come back to life. That moment was so beautiful that there wasn't anything but my kids and shouting and kissing them and holding them close and feeling them against me—alive! It was really something. There aren't any words to describe it!

Then my daddy came out. And we embraced. The neighbors came and we began to talk. I didn't have a minute's rest all night. One by one, the prisoners' wives came and asked for their husbands. I spent the whole night talking. No one left. And they told me about themselves and I told them about myself. And then we'd tell each other over again. Like that, all night long. The sun rose and the house was still full of people.

The workers told me that they'd called a union meeting and that I should go. So I informed the workers about everything that had happened. I didn't leave out a single detail. I also told them that I was afraid and that the agent who was with me as far as Oruro had told me:

"Look here, Señora, you'd better not say that it was us who arrested you. If you want to save your husband, you've got to say that you came to the DIC voluntarily because you wanted to free your husband and, since you didn't have any place to stay, we put you up in the DIC offices. If you want to see your husband alive, you'd better say that. Because, if you don't, you'll be responsible for your children all alone."

I told the workers that they'd threatened me that way, but that it didn't matter, because I had to tell the people and there was no reason to lie, right?

And it turns out that the workers protested. They decided to go back to work, but they also issued a manifesto. They asked for the freedom of the other prisoners, because I was the only one they'd let out.

And so, the next day, there was a memo on the door, saying that I had to leave the district within twenty-four hours. The memo they gave me was final. It was signed by the company manager and two other military men.

They did the same thing with the other compañeras whose husbands were in jail: they gave them a memo giving them twenty-four hours to leave the district.

There was also an internal decree from the company, ordering the children who were in school to be given their grades and kicked out, just like that, in the middle of the school year, so there wouldn't be one single pretext for us to stay there: not even because of our children, not for anything. So . . . everything was over.

Very worried and crying, the women came to me: "What shall we do? What shall we do?" And a good number of them met in my house and we discussed the matter.

And it turned out that several compañeras went to the management. I didn't go. And at the offices, the colonels really gave them a working over, so they told me. They told them that they should leave, and so on and so forth. One young woman, who had been at the meeting in my house, said to the women:

"Well, tell them what Domitila said."

An agent heard her.

"Let's see," he said. "This young lady has something to say. Someone's told her something. Someone's influenced her. What did your boss lady say?"

And they pressured the girl. She was very scared.

They called me there immediately, saying they wanted to discuss my husband's case. So I went over to the management offices. There were the officers. And we had a run-in and said some pretty rough things.

"Ah," said the manager. "Look here, what a surprise! You haven't learned your lesson yet? Do you want another lesson?"

He asked me what else I wanted. So I said:

"Look, mister. The women were in my house and I gave my personal opinion. You arrested my husband and told me to leave my house. I won't be able to leave, because, in the first place, I'm a married woman and my husband left me there and I can't leave. If I leave home and my husband comes and doesn't find me there, he'll sue me for abandoning our home. So, if my husband wants to go to Oruro and I go to Cochabamba, or if my husband wants to go to Santa Cruz and I go to La Paz, what will happen? So I can't make that decision alone. Another thing: there's the problem of his job and his severance pay. Do you think I know how much they have to give him? And how do I know if my husband will agree? They could even give me less and my husband would think I spent some of it. So, from that point of view also, I can't decide anything. If you want me to leave the house and go away, free my husband. I'll leave with him. That's what I talked about with the women."

Then they began to insult me. I also answered them with pretty hard words. And then, at one point, I said:

"Well, since you don't want to free my husband, take me and my other children to jail. Take me to where my husband is now. Anyhow, my husband's sick, take me and my children to him. There we'll live or die together. If not, will you take charge of my children, of feeding them, of their education . . . ?"

Then with dirty words they answered me and asked if they had fathered my children. So I asked them, with even dirtier words, if they thought they were men enough to do that. The women who were there got frightened. And they shouted at me:

"Ay, Señora! How can you use such words? You're condemning our husbands, your own husband!"

"Well if you want to, you can lower yourselves, lick the colonel's boots . . . I won't, not me! Why should he insult me? No, and no again!" I shouted.

And I left.

I was sure they were going to shoot me in the back or make me return. "Now they'll arrest me, now, right now," I said to myself. But I continued a good distance, I turned around . . . and nothing. Nothing happened to me. It was really surprising.

That same day they went to get my husband. About seven days after I returned to Siglo XX, they brought him back. And then the boss said to him:

"Look. It's your wife's fault we're firing you from the company, because you're a sissy. You know who's wearing the pants in your family. Now you'll learn to control your wife. First of all, your wife's been in jail and instead of shutting up she's worse than ever now: she's still making trouble, she's still getting everyone all riled up. That's why we're firing you. Not because of you, but because of your wife. In the second place, what do you want with a political wife? Go ahead, give her up, and then I'll give you your job back. A woman like that isn't any good for anything. Imagine, tomorrow, if you work really hard, you'll build a little house—who doesn't dream about a little house?—or you can even buy one. But, since your wife's political, the day after tomorrow the government will take it away. So your house isn't yours anymore. Why should you always be messed up by a woman like that? Now that you're fired, you haven't got anyone who'll support you. Well, let's see if that woman learns her lesson. That woman's too much! She doesn't even seem like a woman."

And right away they gave my husband his severance pay.

Then I said to him:

"I'm not leaving."

And we really had it out.

But one night the agents came and forced their way into the house. They came in like devils: slam! bang! And they began throwing all our things onto an army truck.

And they made us get in the truck. My children didn't want to leave, they got down, they took things off the truck. And the agents would put them back on again. It was a terrible scene. The soldiers had been very firm, standing at each door, and they wouldn't let the people behind them get through, so they couldn't do anything for us. And the neighbors cried and shouted: "Why are you taking the senora? She never did anything. She's always been a good neighbor."

The agents went on loading our things. My daughter, the oldest, grabbed onto the door. She didn't want to leave and she said:

"I don't want to go, I don't want to go."

The agents pulled at her and she resisted and bit their hands. And they made my son get on the truck, in the dark, and my son would get down again, unloading the things.

Finally I said loudly to my children:

"The owners are throwing us out. We're poor, and poor people get thrown out like that. The house isn't ours. Haven't you realized that it's the company's house and the company lends it as long as your father can work? Now they don't need anyone's services and that's how the bosses throw us out, daughter. Unfortunately, because the army helps them in these things. That's why when you're in the army you'll never do that against your people. We're people who've got their dignity. They're throwing us out, we don't need to beg or stay here any longer."

I sat down in the truck.

"Okay, María, come on up," I called.

So then my children one by one got into the truck, crying and crying. And the truck left.

I made myself strong and I said to my children:

"Why are you crying?"

And I swallowed my tears, watching my children cry. In our own country, thrown out of our own village . . . where would we go? We'd been born there, we'd been raised there, we'd lived there.

They say that the land is for those who work it. That land in the mine that our fathers have worked was the only thing we had to live from. And yet they'd thrown us off it. We were foreigners in our own country.

They took us to Oruro. There, in a plaza, they threw us off with all our things. And they left. We didn't have anyplace to go, not a single house where we could take the things. We were thrown out into the street, without anything we could even fix a meal with.

There wasn't much choice. I went to look for my father. He was very poor too. He lived in a little house with two rooms. And so he gave us one of them so we could leave our few belongings.

Fabiola, my second little girl, was in grammar school and had stayed in Siglo XX. The teacher said that the parents could be "devils," but that the children couldn't be denied an education, which was the most important thing. She said that she had sworn to teach all children, without discrimination. And that she wasn't going to accept the management's order.

"Señora," she said to me, "if you don't have anyone to leave your daughter with, leave her with me. She'll stay in my house, she'll finish the school year. Let me know where you'll be so that, at the end of the year, I can take her to you."

And my little girl stayed with the teacher. But my other children couldn't go on studying. And they cried day and night, remembering Siglo XX, the house, the food, and other things.

Then I decided to go back to Siglo XX. That was at the end of July. At seven at night I left with the kids and went to my sister's house. She worked on the rock pile and had a little house. I was there, almost locked in, with all my kids. I left almost all the money with my compañero, who remained in Oruro, because I knew that if they caught me, they'd take everything I had. I only took 500 pesos, to spend on food. We lived like that for almost two months. I had a big belly, expecting another child.

My husband said:

"I'm going to work, I'll look for work."

But, unfortunately, they'd put him on the blacklist and no one could give him work anywhere. It was an order from the Ministry of the Interior. So he began drinking and spending all the severance money. I didn't know about any of this.

On September 15, my father came and told me:

"Daughter, your husband spends all his time on binges. Why did you give him all the money? He's spending it like water. I've told him, but he says: 'That's my job now.' Tell your compañero that he shouldn't spend money that way, you both have to think about the kids' future. Maybe you could set up a little business and find a way to get out of the mine. Since you have the opportunity to leave, it would be good to try and get used to city life, for the sake of the kids."

"All right," I said.

I was already short of money, I didn't have any more food, I didn't even have anything to eat. So I went alone to Oruro, on September 15.

In Oruro I found my compañero really drunk. When he saw me he got bitter and said:

"Why didn't you bring your children?" etc., etc. Of course, he thought it was my fault he couldn't get a job, you know? So we quarreled. Finally I waited till he sobered up and then I spoke with him again:

"Look, since we have the chance to leave Siglo XX, it'd be better to stay here in the city till I have the baby. We can work here."

Well, then my husband told me that he'd found work on two occasions, but that the people from the Ministry of the Interior didn't let him work and got him fired and that he was on the blacklist and where was he going to work? He was very depressed and things didn't look too good.

So I said:

"I think it will be easier when I'm here. I can work at something too. But don't drink anymore. I'll come back with the kids."

I took the 1,000 pesos, bought flannel and other things for my baby who was going to be born and would need some things. I bought other things for the kids; I had to have shoes for all of them. The little money left over I gave to my father to keep. And I went back to Siglo XX.

IN JAIL AGAIN

When we reached Playa Verde it was late. They arrested me there, in the plaza. A captain came over and said:

"Look, Senora, I don't want problems with you. You'd better leave. There's a warrant out for your arrest. You knew Norberta de Aguilar, didn't you? She's been arrested because they say she's a guerrilla liaison and she denounced you . . . I don't know why . . . there's a warrant out for you. But since you're pregnant, go away, get lost. Because, look, if I have to arrest you, well, I don't want that on my conscience. Because it's a serious thing. You'd better leave."

"But, sir, I just want to see my children. I promise you I won't leave the house."

"No, Señora, go away. Your husband had better go see the children, if it's that urgent. There's no warrant out for him; but for you there is. You'd better leave."

And he made me take my things off the bus and put me on another one going to Oruro.

In Oruro I found my compañero drinking, drinking like a fish. When I asked:

"Why are you drinking?"

Uf! Well, he hit me. And he said that it was my fault he couldn't get a job, that it was my fault he was drinking like that, and that he didn't care about what I was telling him.

Well, he sobered up and the next day we talked.

"Look, they won't let me into Siglo XX. Now the kids are all alone, with no one, with nothing."

"I'm not going," he said. "Why should I go?"

I was really upset, desperate.

So my father said to me:

"But daughter, why get upset? And why cry, why are you being so silly? What good did it do teaching you to read, what good is it that you're involved in union questions, in political questions, and all that, what good is it if you don't learn certain things? How are you going to travel there looking like yourself, acting like yourself? You've got to disguise yourself, girl, if you want to go someplace secretly."

And so he gave me some ideas.

I was neither dumb nor lazy, and although I was afraid and time was short, I had my hair cut, made myself up, styled my hair, and bought some other clothes. I thought that that way I'd be able to get through. But it was useless.

When we reached the main gate of Playa Verde, a guy shouted: "One minute, please!"

And, pow! He went into the toll booth. Then he came back to the bus with two agents and said:

"Arrest that woman, please."

As a matter of fact, for the first time I was really terrified. My knees were trembling, they knocked against each other. I wanted to disappear. And, really, it seemed that my body guessed what was going to happen to me. I was trembling . . . and it was like my heart was being wrung by an iron hand.

"This woman gets off here," they said.

"No, no!" I said. "Why do you want me to get off? I feel sick . . ."

"No way. None. If this woman doesn't get off, the bus doesn't leave."

And they wouldn't let it go.

The people said:

"Why don't you hurry up and settle your problems? We've got to go. Hurry up! Get off!" And things like that.

So the driver came over and said to me:

"Señora, would you like us to go tell your family?"

I didn't even have time to answer him, because the agent who was behind me wouldn't let me speak. He pushed me and made me get off. And they took out all my things.

They searched me all over, inch by inch. There were three agents and the three of them searched me. My hair too, they left it all messed up. They wanted to know what those scars I have on my legs were from, what I'd done and why I'd done it. They asked about everything, absolutely everything.

That happened on September 20.

They put me in isolation and I stayed there. In the afternoon a sergeant came and asked me:

"What's your name?"

"You ought to know," I answered. "Or do you mean that you've arrested me without knowing who I am?" That's all I could think of to say at the moment.

Then he shouted:

"God dammit! Are you making fun of me? I'm asking the questions here!"

He asked my name, where I was from, where I was going, how many children I had, where my husband was, why I was going to Siglo XX. So then I told him everything.

They left me alone, locked up. The only thing I could hear were the footsteps of someone who walked like this: 1-2-3, 1-2-3 . . . I tried to distract myself counting the steps. I tried to forget what I was going through. So that's how it was. At moments I'd sit down, at moments I'd stand up. I was cold, my stomach hurt, I was thirsty, I was frightened. It was a moment like no other. . .

A guy came into the cell. Later on I found out he was a colonel's son. I don't know if it was night or day, because it was always real dark in the cell.

He told me he'd come to question me and work me over. And like he felt important, he began asking me about the guerrillas, if I knew them, if I worked with them.

But his main purpose was to make fun of me. I realized that from the start. And since he saw I was expecting, he asked me if I didn't know what women were good for. And why did we get mixed up in things, since women were made only to give men pleasure. And he insulted me, no? And he even said that surely my husband had never satisfied me, and that's why I wanted something bigger, something more. And that they were really going to work me over. That if I didn't want all of that to happen, I should start talking. That they had evidence that I was a guerrilla liaison and that I'd received lots of money and that the guerrillas had stolen it from the people.

I remained silent and didn't want to have anything to do with him. Then he began to get harsher, shouting at me, making me feel really awful. And now and then he pulled at me, walloped me, and he wanted to take me by force. But I wouldn't let him. He spat in my face. Then he kicked me. I couldn't stand it, so I hit him back. He punched me again. I scratched his face. Then he began to hit and grab me. I defended myself as much as I could. And as he continued hitting me he said:

"What about Norberta? Norberta de Aguilar has declared that you received 120 million on instructions from Inti Peredo,[13] and that you're a guerrilla liaison and have made connections with people for them."

I answered:

"That's a lie! It's true I knew Norberta. But I'm not a liaison. It's a lie, it's a lie—"

"It's true! It's true! You can't deny it. Do you want the proof? Let's see. . . ." And he called the guard. "Bring those letters we have as proof against this bitch."

And they brought a letter written in beautiful handwriting, with beautiful lettering. But precisely because Norberta was my friend, I knew what her writing was like and it wasn't the writing I saw in the letter. Anyway, the letter said that she, Norberta de Aguilar, under pressure by the government against her children, declared that on instructions from Inti she had given me 120 million pesos

---

13. Chief of the National Liberation Army, and Che's comrade, killed in La Paz in 1969.

to recruit people in the mines and send them to the guerrillas. And that I had promised to send fifty men to the guerrillas by the end of the year. And that she was declaring all of this to save her children's lives. "Let's hope my country knows how to understand and forgive me," it said. And at the end it was signed: "Norberta, widow of Aguilar."

"There it is, there it is," said the sergeant. "Your own friend has betrayed you!"

"But because she's my friend, I know her handwriting and her signature and I can tell that this is neither her writing nor her signature," I said to him. He got furious.

"So you still deny it? But here's the proof! What more do you want?"

Then he made me listen to a recording where a woman, a university student, said that she'd given me the sum of 150 million, on instructions from somebody named Negrón.

They were trying to chalk up 270 million to my account!

"Where did you put the money? God dammit! Where did you put it?" the guy shouted. And he hit me, telling me to talk. He hit me very hard, and me in my eighth month. . . .

The young soldier who was next to me with his submachine gun looked shocked at how bad that guy was hitting me. And the guy said to him that one shouldn't have pity on these heretics, these communists who have no morals, who are worse than beasts. And he went on hitting me without letup.

I defended myself as much as I could. And the more I defended myself, the more the guy got infuriated, because he was also a little drunk, see, and he hit me all the harder.

At one point, he put his knee here, on my stomach. He pressed on my throat and was about to strangle me. I shouted and shouted. It was like he wanted to make my stomach burst open. I realized he was pressing more and more, I was having trouble breathing. So then, with both my hands, with all my strength, I pulled his hands down. And I don't remember how, but I grabbed him by his wrist and I bit him over and over again. I was so furious and so nervous that I didn't realize I'd been biting his hand, see. Really, I didn't realize it. I was so desperate!

Then suddenly I tasted a warm and salty liquid in my mouth . . . I let go of his hand and I saw it: there was flesh hanging from his hand, ripped off, like that. I felt a terrible nausea on tasting his blood in my mouth. . . . Then, with all my anger . . . tcha! I spat his blood all over his face.

Well, that was the end of me. The end!

"Huah!" shouted the guy. A terrible screeching began. He began kicking me, he shouted, he called the soldiers and made four of them grab me. He had on one of those big, square rings. I don't know what he did with his hand, but he tightened and tightened it, making me really scream loud. And as I screamed he punched me all over my face. And I don't remember anything else. . . . The only thing I do remember is that I felt as if something in my head had burst open. I saw something like fire falling all around me. Nothing else.

When I woke up like from a dream, I'd been swallowing a piece of my tooth. I felt it stick here in my throat. Then I noticed that the guy had broken six of my teeth. Blood was gushing out of me and I couldn't open my eyes or breathe through my nose. My eyes were swollen closed.

I passed out again, I fainted.

Suddenly I came to when they poured water on me. Was I wet!

There were other soldiers there. And they told me that this time that was it, that I had hurt the son of a colonel, and that I was really going to pay for that.

"Take that shit inside!" one of them shouted. And kicking and screaming at me, they dragged me to another cell. Then they threw me into it. It was even darker than the first one. Much darker. You could hardly make out anything.

After a long time, I made out a shadow—a shadow that was coming toward me from the other side.

Ay! It really scared me! I felt a horrible panic. I felt like screaming. I felt a great despair just thinking about the other bastard who'd tried to grab me and take me by force. And I thought that

I was all alone face to face with someone worse. I was really in a state of shock. I moved back and back. . . . Finally I came up against the wall. And the other figure came closer and closer. . . . With difficulty, dragging itself along the floor, it came toward me.

"Who can it be? Who can it be?" I wondered. I thought it was someone else who'd come to work me over.

But it wasn't . . . it must have been a compañero who'd also been tortured. I guessed that because it was so difficult for him to move.

When I couldn't move back any farther, he put his hand on my arm and said:

"Have courage, compañero . . . our struggle is great . . . so great! . . . You mustn't weaken. You must have faith in our future."

And very softly he began to sing a revolutionary song that was well known in Siglo XX.

I almost passed out from fright and I couldn't speak. So the only thing I did was squeeze his hand. We stayed that way a long time, squeezing each other's hand. And I never dared tell him who I was, not even that I was a woman, nothing.

He continued:

"You must be brave, have faith . . . both of us have to give strength to the others. We aren't alone, compañero . . . What we're doing isn't for ourselves. It's a great cause and it won't die."

And he talked to me like that, saying things that are engraved in my memory. It made me feel so much better, in that moment of such despair. To this day, I don't know who that person was.

I don't know how many hours went by, but then four guys with flashlights came in. They shone them on my feet and then they grabbed me and led me out. And the man in the cell with me could only say:

"Courage . . . courage . . ."

Then they took me to the cell where I'd been before. I saw a man there, dressed in civilian clothes, who was very angry. As I came in, he gave me a good wallop and said:

"Is this the bitch that bit my son? Is this the bitch that scarred my son's face?"

And he knocked me down.

Then he began stamping on my hands, like that, with his feet on my two hands, and said:

"Those hands will never again leave their mark on my son's face! Neither his mother nor I have ever touched him. And this hungry bitch . . . what did you want to do? Eat my son up? You bitch!"

And he hit me furiously. Then he said:

"All right. Luckily you're expecting a baby. We'll take our revenge on your baby."

And he took out a knife and began to sharpen it in front of me. And he said that he had time enough to wait until my child was born and that with that knife he was going to make mincemeat out of my baby.

I got really scared. I felt terrified. "How can they do that to my child?" I thought.

And I said to the colonel:

"Look, mister, you're a father . . . try to understand! Your son was trampling on my defenseless child. He was kicking it and squashing it in my stomach. That's why I defended myself the only way I could. As a mother I dared to defend my child. Understand me, sir! They've accused me of a whole bunch of things I didn't do. I'm not a guerrilla liaison. I'm nothing of the kind. I've been in the Housewives' Committee. But if you let me go, sir, I won't even work with them anymore. But, please sir, let me go, let me go! I haven't done anything wrong. A mother always has the obligation to defend the child she carries inside her. And your son kicked me really hard in the stomach. That's why I defended myself. And I'm sure that any mother would do the same. Your own mother would have done what I did if she'd been in my place. Sir, please!"

He kept on sharpening the knife and he laughed at me:

"Look how the witch asks for mercy!"

And he told me he was in no hurry. And that the longer my agony lasted, the better it was for him, the better he'd take his revenge.

And he left the cell, laughing at me.

And, as if fate had a hand in it, I began to go into labor. I began feeling pains, pains, and more pains. And at times the baby to be born got the better of me. I was so nervous . . . I heard the young soldier's footsteps, and I tried to hold back. I didn't want it to be born! And I said to myself: "If it's born, let it be born dead. I don't want the colonel to kill it! Don't let my baby be born alive!" Really, I lived through a terrible odyssey. The head was about to come out and I pushed it back in. It was a terrible moment.

Finally, I couldn't stand anymore. And I went to kneel in a corner. I leaned against a wall and covered my face, because I couldn't even make the slightest effort. My face hurt so much it seemed like it would burst. And in one of those moments, I gave in. I don't remember if my baby was born alive or if it was born dead . . . I don't know anything. The only thing I remember is that I knelt there and covered my face because I couldn't stand anymore. It got the better of me, it really did. I noticed the head was coming out . . . and right at that moment I fainted.

After who knows how long, I seemed to be waking up from a dream and seemed to be in my bed. And I tried to cover myself. I wanted to move my feet, move them, but I couldn't feel them. It seemed like I didn't have feet . . . it seemed like I only had one arm, because I couldn't feel the other one. And I tried to cover myself, and there weren't any blankets.

"Where am I, where am I?"

I tried to think clearly and I heard the soldier's footsteps, click, click, click. Then I realized: "Oh yes, I'm in jail. What's happened? What's happened?"

I remembered a few things and I thought: Where's the baby?

I tried to sit up. But my whole body was numb, I was freezing right there on the floor. I was soaking wet. It was blood and the liquid you lose during childbirth that had wet me all over. Even my hair was wet with water and blood.

Then I made an effort and found the baby's cord. And along the cord, stretching it out, I found the little baby . . . completely cold, freezing, there on the floor.

I don't know now. Did the baby die inside me? Did it die after being born, because no one helped it? I don't know.

It's very painful to lose a child that way. How I've suffered because of that baby I lost! How I've wept, looking for him! My poor little baby who was the victim of those insane people who were against me.

Finally I was able to find the baby and I tried giving it warmth from my body. I took it and wrapped it up in my dress. I had it on my stomach, covering it, covering it to give it warmth, even though it was very little I could give. Its little head was like a bag of bones that sounded "poc, poc, poc." I touched its whole body and found out it was a little boy.

And I passed out again.

A soldier came to call me. But I was dreaming that my son was laughing and crying at the same time. The soldier woke me up:

"Señora, Señora . . ."

"Soldier boy, please," I said to him. "My baby's crying. Give me my baby . . ."

The soldier got scared and ran out:

"Colonel, colonel! This woman's given birth! She's given birth!"

"She's given birth?" shouted the colonel. And he came in. "Get up, whore!" And he kicked me.

I didn't feel much, because I was half frozen. From the waist down I didn't feel anything. And since I hadn't passed the placenta, I was hemorrhaging a lot. My vision was fogged.

The colonel shone a light on me, and then I was able to see my little son. The colonel grabbed him by the hands, picked him up and threw him at me with disgust. The baby fell on my belly. And the colonel got dirty, because the baby was still wet.

"Disgusting bitch! Pig!" he shouted. Then he said: "Bring some water!"

Then they brought cold water in two buckets and "pah! pah!," they threw it over me. At that moment I was able to react, I could just move and I realized that I still had feet. Because it seemed to me they'd amputated me from the waist down.

Then a sergeant came in who'd been with the cops and said:

"Excuse me, colonel. This woman is going to die soon."

He took my pulse and said: "I've had some experience. This woman is going to die and we won't be able to question her. It would be better to help her . . . she seems to have retained the placenta."

He looked at me and asked:

"Have you expelled the placenta?"

"I don't know," I said. "I don't know."

The sergeant examined me and said that I hadn't. He said he'd take charge of me for a while and that later the colonel could question me. But that I couldn't go on like that, because I'd die.

The colonel left, annoyed. And the sergeant ordered:

"Bring me warm water! Hot water!"

And he sent another soldier for two old blankets.

Then he said:

"Now I'm going to help you. You try to help also. Let's see."

And he tried to pull the placenta out, and he pulled it out, but only half of it.

Then he made me sit up and began scolding me:

"What are you up to, girl? Being a woman, being pregnant, why didn't you just keep quiet? Why did you do that to the colonel's son? What are you up to? Why are women so rebellious?"

The soldiers brought two buckets of water and the sergeant told me to wash. Then I was able to sit up a little. I undressed, I washed my hair some. The sergeant wrapped me up in a shawl he had, he put an old blanket on me like a dress and with the other blanket he covered my head.

I couldn't hold myself up on my feet anymore, I couldn't stand anymore. So I lay down right there and said:

"Well, my son has died here and I'm going to die here too. Look, why do you want to help me? I want to die! Because if I don't die . . . if I don't die . . . you've all made me suffer so much that you'll be sorry. You'll be sorry. You keep on saying I'm a communist, that I'm this and that. And, if I get out alive, now I'll become one, now that I feel a greater and deeper hatred for all of you. Why don't you do me the favor of killing me?"

"All right," said the sergeant. "You've got to be calm, you've got to have faith . . . you'd better pray, you've forgotten God. . . ."

And he left.

I remained alone in the cell. I heard the soldier's footsteps, I listened . . . and I don't remember what happened then. I didn't see anything else.

I fell into a deep sleep where I saw a real high mountain peak. I was falling from a very high cliff . . . I saw myself fall in pieces of flesh, brains . . . All of me was left on those black crags, everything was left there, until I reached the bottom. And having fallen, I got up. I was wearing a very long white nightgown, and I was lifting up a corner of the hem, and I went around collecting my flesh, piece by piece, with great difficulty . . . Clawing at the crags I went up and up. . . . And as I found a drop of blood, I'd clean it up with a corner of my nightgown. And I said in my dream: "I have to reach the top. When I reach the light I'll be safe." And so I climbed up and up, picking up piece after piece of myself, cleaning up the blood . . . I reached the light. There I saw some twisted faces, half white, half blue, that were coming at me, over me, and were looking at me. . . . And I fell again. I don't know how long I was like that. I don't know.

And then I came to, and I was in a clinic. Those deformed faces I saw became clearer little by little: they were the doctor and the nurses, with their caps and masks, who were looking at me and taking care of me. The light I saw on the hilltop was the strong operating-room light.

In my dream I also heard laughter. I heard it each time I fell to the bottom of the gulch. I heard them laughing at me: "ha! ha! ha!" I realized later that the laughter came from the police guards who were nearby, guarding me and playing dice and other things. There were agents keeping an eye on me, see. And as they played, they laughed. Little by little I got better. . . . And everything became clearer.

I had a bad headache, and my body ached all over. The agents were always close by my bed. So when the doctor came to examine me, the first thing I'd see were those faces looking at me from head to toe . . . and I saw them laughing . . . I saw them with their submachine guns, standing beside me and, well, I felt terrified, scared, ashamed. I couldn't get used to being watched. I didn't want to be watched. I covered myself again and again, I clung tightly to the bed. . . . Sometimes it seemed to me that they wanted to throw me back into that gulch . . . and I'd lose consciousness again.

I don't know how long I was there like that. I don't know how many days went by. I'd get attacks of hysteria and then I'd scream without stopping. I guess it was for my son, because I always had the idea that they let him drop and that I was still looking for him and couldn't find him. And I saw a kind of gorilla or something that grabbed my son and began to eat his legs and rip him apart. And there I was, screaming without being able to reach him. I had all of that in my head, as if it was happening in real life, see? And then sometimes, I'd look at the doctor in his white uniform and it seemed to me he was a gorilla who was eating my son's little legs and I'd start to scream: "Give me my baby back! My son! How are you going to eat him like that?" Those fits I went through were terrible. And they always had to put me to sleep to make me better. They held me down to give me a shot so I'd sleep. And then they could take care of me. I don't know what happened. The problem is that, when I was conscious, I didn't let anyone touch me.

Finally the doctor felt really sorry for me. And he told the police agents that they had to leave. Because when the doctor came and I saw the agents with their mocking faces, I'd say:

"Get away from here! I don't want you to look at me! I don't want you to laugh at me! I don't want it!" And I shouted and shouted. You know, when I saw them laughing, it seemed to me that their mouths grew and got this big. And it drove me crazy to hear their laughter.

That's why the doctor got annoyed and said to the agents:

"Look, you've brought me your broken plates so that I can fix them. If you don't trust me, you shouldn't have brought her here. I want you to please get out when I come in to examine her."

Later he told me that as a doctor he'd sworn to save lives and that if I was in his clinic it was only to save my life, to cure me, not to torture me. That I should trust him. And that if I had lost a baby, I should remember that I had other children and that they were waiting for me. That as a mother I should be brave and strong when facing those things.

So little by little, he convinced me: "It would be better to consider me your friend, I want to be your friend," he'd say to me. And finally he told me he wanted to help me, but that the agents wouldn't let him.

When the doctor finished treating me, the agents would come in again. They were always there, looking at me, they didn't leave me alone. But now it was different, because they weren't in the room when the doctor examined me.

And it turned out that someone in the hospital recognized me and got in touch with my family.

Meanwhile, what had happened to my family?

My father thought I was in Siglo XX from the day I'd left his house, on September 20. My sisters and children thought I was in Oruro. So it hadn't occurred to anyone to look for me. But on the 30th of the month, my daddy had gone to Siglo XX. And when he got there, my children asked him:

"Papi, didn't our mommy come too?"

"What do you mean, didn't she come? She came on the 20th! She should have been here ten days ago!"

That's when they started looking for me. It was pretty awful. They found out which bus I'd been in on the 20th and it was confirmed that on that day I'd been arrested and that they didn't know where I was, and that it happened in Playa Verde.

They went to Playa Verde and were told I wasn't there, that everyone who'd been arrested had gone to La Paz, to Oruro, to Cochabamba.

My husband had gone to La Paz to ask about me and they'd told him:

"Well, who's your wife? She's that communist? Ha! She must have left with all the money. Yes, she must have gone off with her lover, that wife of yours. And you're stuck with the kids, with no money. That's how the communist bitches are . . . immoral . . . and who knows what else."

And my husband went back home full of doubts. But when he spoke to my daddy it was all cleared up:

"She left the money with me. I have it here. Something's happened to my daughter."

And they were working on it when a young man came and told them that someone had some real information. In a plaza in Oruro they notified my daddy that I was in a clinic, that I was half dead, and that they had to do the impossible to get me out. They were already asking for me from La Paz and a DIC commission had already come to take me to La Paz again for questioning.

So when they heard that, my father and my husband began to get busy. They went to the university, they denounced the fact that I was half dead, and they made as much racket as possible.

They went to the DIC office in Oruro to ask about my whereabouts, and they say that my father began to shout:

"How can this be? It's unjust! I've been to war . . . I've served the country for so many years . . . I'm a veteran . . . I haven't even been able to give my daughters an education. . . . It's not fair of you to do this to my daughter. My daughter's that way because I brought her up like that. So go ahead, shoot me! Because the ideas she has are ideas that I gave her."

And they say my father walked out of the DIC office shouting like that, shouting like a madman. And in the doorway he bumped into a man who knew us in Pulacayo, when my father was a tailor for the mine police. In Pulacayo that man was the commissioner, and by then he was already a colonel and was with the police team that had come to get me. Well, my father bumped into him and looked at him. And the other man also recognized my father.

"What are you doing here, Barrios?" he asked. And they embraced.

Then my father said:

"I don't know who they've mixed my daughter up with. . . . They're slandering her, they say she's a guerrilla liaison and who knows what else. They must have her confused with a different person."

And that man was so fond of my father that he tried to help him.

The man told my father that the only way I could be helped was to take me to Los Yungas, so that I wouldn't talk.

Los Yungas is a tropical, warm region where they grow coffee, oranges, bananas, and all kinds of fruits. It's pretty far away from the highlands, which are cold, and where there are mostly minerals.

The DIC people came to the hospital and threatened that if I went back to the city and talked about what had happened, then this colonel who was freeing me would take his pistol and with three shots he'd really screw up my father. The colonel told me first that he wasn't very convinced that I was innocent. Then he said:

"Because of the respect I have for your father, because I've seen that poor man suffer so much to raise all of you orphans, because of the friendship I feel for him, I'm going to have them give you provisional freedom. But look, I'm risking my neck, I'm gambling my prestige, I'm gambling my position by freeing you. So if you leave the place we're sending you to, if you come to the city and talk, the only thing I'll have left to do is look for your father, take my revolver, and empty it into his body. Three shots through the head, and then leave him there, dying. It's up to you."

So they took me and forced me into a truck. My daddy and my husband had hired it to take me away. There was a bed in the truck and they put me into it.

The doctor gave me a little box with medicines and said:

"Good luck . . . take these pills, they're so you don't get carsick. Good luck."

And he said that in the little box there were all the directions for using the medicines.

To this day I don't know what hospital I was in. The only thing I know is that it was in Oruro. My father said: "Why do you want to know? Just be happy with the fact that there was one good person, among so many bad ones, who wanted to help you."

IN LOS YUNGAS, "SO THAT I WOULDN'T TALK"

I didn't know we were going into exile. The truck left and I fell asleep.

I woke up at dawn, It was very hot. And I seemed to hear birds singing, like this: "chiu, chiu." I looked up and saw a lot of trees.

"Where are we?" I shouted.

Then my husband spoke:

"Calm down, dear. You're all right."

And he began speaking to me gently.

I looked at him and only then did I recognize him. I asked:

"Where are we? What are we doing?"

"We're going to a place where you can get better, so you can get your health back. Calm down."

"Where are you taking me?" And I began to shout.

Then my husband made the truck stop. My daddy was in the front and he got down. He came over and hugged me, he wept and said:

"The important thing is to save your life. That's the important thing."

And since he's religious and he sees everything from the point of view of God's work, he said:

"God is so great that He's allowed you to remain alive. And He himself will allow you to be saved. We're going to a paradise where there aren't any of those martyrdoms that you've suffered. You're going to see Los Yungas, that's where you're going to live. When you're strong again, we'll go back to Siglo XX together."

That's how he tried to make me feel better.

And we got to Los Yungas. With the little bit of money we had left, we bought a tiny house and a small plot of land to plant on. Then my husband went to Siglo XX to bring the kids.

Then I found out that every single day I had to go to the local
DIC office to sign the attendance book which guaranteed that I
didn't leave there; in other words, I was, you might say, deported,
with all my family. I didn't have the right to leave the place.
There were no medical facilities there. There was no one who
could inject me with the antibiotics the doctor had prescribed.
And with the heat that I'd never known in the highlands, with
those bugs I'd never seen . . . with all that and with the wounds
I had, I began to rot. The wounds began to get terribly infected.
My body released foul-smelling secretions . . . I realized that I was
about to die. I had terrible chills. And I felt bad, so bad, that in my
desperation I took the medicines I should have been injected with
and drank them in my tea. I took cold baths all the time. I put on
damp rags. I was barely able to save myself. How long I've suffered
with that!

In addition, the baby never left my dreams. And when my husband went back to the mine to get the rest of my kids, at night I'd
run out of the house screaming. I saw the baby. It was horrible . . . I
felt oppressed by something . . . I saw the faces of my torturers . . . I
heard their laughter . . . I saw them eating the baby. . . . It was enough
to drive me crazy . . . crazy! At times I felt like throwing myself off
the highest peak and ending it there. The bugs bit me. Everything
drove me crazy. If it hadn't been for the powerful idea of seeing my
children again, I think I'd have killed myself that time, because I was
wiped out, really wiped out. I didn't want to suffer anymore. My
wounds hurt me, I couldn't rest. And when I slept, I'd dream horrible things. Ay! It was really terrible.

Then my husband arrived, the kids arrived, and I felt a little
better. He brought me some medicines, some bandages. And I
was able to cure myself and all that helped me get better. But just
barely. It took a lot out of me.

Everything was different in Los Yungas. In the highlands we ate
meat, bread, sugar. In Los Yungas, we only ate yucca, plantain, and
things we weren't used to.

My husband felt very bad because of all our problems. And he told me that it was all my fault. That in the mine at least you could have a good lunch with meat. And when there were no clothes for the kids, he'd say I should go ask the Housewives' Committee, that I should go ask the union. He suffered because he was also unhappy, you know?

Without meaning to, my children backed their father. They cried because they wanted a piece of meat, because they wanted chocolate on Sunday, because they wanted a mug of milk on Sunday. . . .

All of that made me suffer terribly because, since I wasn't as aware then as I am now, at moments I questioned everything I'd done. I almost gave in.

So then I went into the countryside to get some kind of work. And I worked till my hands bled, so I could forget my problems, to brutalize myself with work and also to earn a few pennies. At the end of the day I'd come home a wreck.

I felt like a criminal. In the DIC cells they'd convinced me that I was very guilty . . . and so I lived with an enormous feeling of guilt. I was sorry I'd ever gotten involved in the committee. Why had I spoken out? Why had I denounced injustice? Why had I gotten involved? I'd ask myself all that. I felt like this was the last straw, I was sorry for what I'd done. And at times I wished I had a stick of dynamite so I could blow myself up with my children and end it all. It was so painful!

After six months in Los Yungas, my father came to visit me. He was happy to see me healthy, working, and making friends.

The people of Los Yungas were good to me. When they saw me working in the fields alongside them, they were surprised. They knew that the people from the highlands, like us, don't work in the same way they do in the fields. They were surprised too that I, a woman, should work so much. They helped me and gave me whatever they could. They were very friendly. I also tried to be good to them. I tried to help them with the medicines I had. I tried to cure some of their pains. And the villagers began to like me a lot.

My father's visit was a great event. I could finally talk with someone. When my daddy asked me how my situation was, how

I was getting along with my compañero and the children, I began to cry.

"Daddy," I said. "You've had experience, you've worked politically. Why didn't you tell me that all that has its consequences? Why didn't you warn me that everything I was doing was bad?" In my anguish, I told my father everything I'd been thinking.

Then my father told me that when he was involved politically and saw that he had only daughters, he was very sad about not having a son. Because he wanted to have a son so that he could follow his ideals and continue his work, struggling until the people were free, until the working class took power. And that, seeing that I'd followed in his footsteps, seeing that I had his character, he'd felt happy and proud of me. And now, how could I possibly say all that?

"No, daughter. What you've done is wonderful!" he said. "Let's see, dear, what have you done? The only thing you did was protest against the injustices that the government committed against the people! That's no crime! On the contrary, it's a great truth. And because of the courage you've had, the people love you, the people ask for you. I travel a lot to Siglo XX and everyone there's waiting for you. One day this government will be toppled, it's not eternal. And then you'll go back with pride. But you've got to prepare for that, you can't go back the way you are now. You've got to learn more. You've got to live up to the trust that the people have placed in you. Being a leader doesn't only mean accepting a position, it's a big responsibility. You've got to prepare yourself, daughter."

"No, Daddy, no more! With all that happened to me, if I get out of this alive, if this regime changes, if I have the chance to go back, I'll never get involved in anything again. Never! How can I, after all that I've suffered?"

"Well. . . ." My daddy told me that he'd return next week. He was very sad.

My father went to the University of La Paz, he went to the University of Oruro, he went before the leaders. He told them the story and said that I needed to prepare myself for the future. And that, more than material help, I needed moral help, in order to find myself and understand that my cause was a just one. And he asked them to help me understand the situation.

My daddy came back and gave me a few books to read. They were books about the history of Bolivia and about socialism. And a professor from the University of Oruro had written comments in the margins. Those comments helped guide me in my readings. For example, if it was talking about the history of another people, there was a note like this: "Domitila, doesn't it seem to you that the problems that occurred in this country also happen in Bolivia? What happened to the agrarian reform? Don't you see that when there's a socialist revolution, the peasant has all the things described here, but that in Bolivia the agrarian reform was betrayed?"

Those books were very helpful to me. At the same time I was able to assure myself of something that I'd dreamed about ever since I was little: that there is a world where there are no poor people and where everyone can have enough food to eat and clothes to wear. I saw that those ideas that I'd had were there in those books. And that the exploitation of some people by others could be ended. And everyone who worked had the right to eat and dress well. And the state had to look after old people, the sick, everyone. That seemed very beautiful to me. It was as if my thoughts as a little girl, well, as if someone had gathered them together and written them in a book. In other words, I identified fully with what I read about Marxism.

That gave me strength to go on struggling. I thought, I've dreamed about this since I was little and now I have to work and begin to uphold this doctrine, base myself on this doctrine in order to go on, no?

Also, with everything I'd suffered in the arrests, in jail, and in Los Yungas, I'd acquired a political consciousness. In other words, I'd found myself.

The experience of being among the peasants was also very useful to me. Because, although my parents were peasants, I was brought up among miners. In Los Yungas, for the first time, I was able to see, personally, another reality of the countryside.

I realized that the workers, the miners, were already very organized, while in the countryside the government still had the people
very dominated.

For example, I could see how they build schools in the countryside. We set one up there. The people of the village made the plan.
We all got together, we talked, and we decided: "We've got to build
our little school."

We all got down to work: adobe brick by adobe brick, men and
women working collectively. We did it all, we put up the building
and the facade.

But it turned out that we didn't have roofing or paint. The government found out about the situation. A man came and said:

"Hurray! I've spoken with a minister of peasant affairs and he
said that he's going to help us, he's going to give us roofing and he's
going to give us paint!"

"That's wonderful! It's all set," said the people.

The roofing and the paint arrived. We grabbed the metal sheets
and "pah, pah," we nailed them up; the paint, "ta, ta," we brushed it
on. And the school was ready.

And on inauguration day the ministers came, the journalists
came, and the school was inaugurated with great fanfare "as one
more government construction." And, of course, the speeches
weren't lacking: "The government is fulfilling its duty to the
people. Barrientos's government thinks about the peasant first and
the Bolivian peasant will no longer be the ignorant peasant of the
past! Here's the proof: a school for the people!"

And everyone received them overjoyed, embraced them,
accepted everything. But we had done most of the work!

Even the roofing and the paint that the government sent were
products of the people themselves, right? Because everything you
take out of Los Yungas—a sack of coffee, a barrel of coca, a bag of
coal—you've got to pay taxes on everything. And from the taxes
we pay, they get the money for public works, isn't that so? What a
way to fool the people!

Another example of how they exploit the peasants which I could confirm with my own eyes is the "public highway bonds." There's a decree in Bolivia that everyone has to pay a certain amount each year to be used on road construction. In exchange for this payment, you get a document called a "public highway bond." Since sometimes the peasants don't have money to pay for the bond, they get it in exchange for work, see? Sometimes the local authorities themselves send the peasants to work in their fields, send them to fix the roads, for free, on collective labor days. After they do it, sometimes they give them the bond, sometimes they don't.

When the peasants get to the city to sell their produce, the guys from the office are already waiting:

"Public highway bond? . . . Don't you have one?"

And if they don't have it, they take their things away till they can pay for one. They have to pay, and to top it off, with a fine added. It's a terrible way of deceiving the peasants. But there are many more ways.

Everything I saw and understood in Los Yungas has been very useful to me in learning about many things, and it opened new horizons for me about Bolivian reality. Now I realize even more, that many people, even the revolutionaries and those who've had to leave the country because of political problems, have the totally wrong idea that the liberation of our country will come about only from the working class. But they've never left the city to go live in the countryside.

Ever since the time I lived in Los Yungas, that problem of the peasants has become a fundamental issue for me. And that's why I even had fights with some compañeros when I returned to the mine, because of the lack of solidarity in relation to the peasants. And it makes me mad when I see that we shout out against our exploitation, and at the same time we're exploiting the peasants.

For example, I've seen that in some miners' homes, when a peasant arrives, a little Indian, to sell his potatoes, they don't even let him sleep in their homes, they don't feed him on their regular plates, they don't give him the same food they prepare for the family. And when they have a peasant woman doing the housework for them, they hardly pay her anything and they don't treat her the way they should.

I could also see how, when harvest time comes, they leave the mine for the countryside in order to exchange foodstuffs, but in a very unfair way and the peasant always loses out, no? So I've often said: how can we expect to find an ally in the peasants if that's how we treat them? And if the peasants were to liberate themselves before us, they'd certainly be against us, if we continue this way. Besides, aren't almost all of us workers of peasant origin?

In Los Yungas I also had time to rethink what I'd heard and suffered among the army men who called me a communist, subversive, guerrilla liaison, and many other things. And that really gave me a clear idea that we did have to do something against those governments that were so unjust with the working class. And if, in the beginning, I wanted to find those hangmen in order to kill them one day, afterward I saw that the best way to fight and take revenge was to organize better, to make the people politically aware, and to struggle to free our country once and for all from the imperialist yoke. That's the only way to solve our problem.

So, with the experience I've had in Los Yungas, thinking over everything that I'd lived before in Siglo XX and that I'd suffered in prison, from all those things I'd become aware, I'd acquired a political consciousness.

So I already had a certain amount of preparation, which many people say can only be acquired in a party. For me it was the fruit of the people's experience, of my own experience, and of the few books I've been able to read. I want to emphasize that, because it seems there are people who say that they made me, their party made me. I don't owe my consciousness and my preparation to anything but the cries, the suffering, and the experiences of the people. I want to say that we have a lot to learn from the parties, but we shouldn't expect everything from them. Our development must come from our own clarity and awareness.

I don't mean to say that I'm against parties or that I'm apolitical. But there are several reasons why I've worked like I have until now, even though we have cooperated with leaders of the different parties.

In the first place, I think the Housewives' Committee is organized like the union and was founded to be right alongside the workers. It doesn't seem right to me, as a leader, to put the committee under the slogans of a party. Because that's even happened with the workers: at one time or another, the parties have used them. And I don't agree with that.

Also, I think that all the division we have among the parties in Bolivia is a great problem. It's a mess! There are so many parties!

Well, we have them pretty much classified, right? There's the left and the right. The people on the right are the rich, influential people, the people who exploit and massacre the poor. On the left are all the rest of us who want the people to be free from the capitalist system we live in. But on both sides, people are very divided.

So on the right is the *Falange Socialista Boliviano* [Bolivian Socialist Falange], known as the FSB; there's the MNR, which is the *Movimiento Nacionalista Revolucionario* [Revolutionary Nationalist Movement], which was the party that betrayed the revolution the people had made in 1952; the Barrientos government had its own party, which was called the *Movimiento Popular Cristiano* [Popular Christian Movement] and which, in the name of Christ, killed a whole lot of people; there's the *Democracia Cristiana* [Christian Democrats], which includes a right-wing group and a left-wing group; there's the PRA or *Partido Revolucionario Auténtico* [Authentic Revolutionary Party], which is a spin-off of the MNR. And there are others.

On the left, for example, there's the PRIN or *Partido Revolucionario de Izquierda Nacionalista* [Revolutionary Party of the Nationalist Left], which also split off from the MNR. There are the two communist parties, one that follows the Moscow line and the other the Peking line; there are the Trotskyists, who are organized in the POR, which is the *Partido Obrero Revolucionario* [Workers' Revolutionary Party]. There's the *Ejército de Liberación Nacional* or ELN [National Liberation Army], who are the people that went off to the guerrillas. There's the PS or *Partido Socialista* [Socialist Party]. So you can see that the left's really divided—into lots of groups.

And the worst thing is that there are times when one comes out against the other. And I think that by doing that, the parties really hurt the people a lot. And the enemy really knows how to take advantage of that, doesn't it?

Wouldn't it be good if all of them got together and, well, all struggled for what we know is the main thing? Because we know that the oppressors have very clear common goals. What are they? To earn more, to exploit more, to get richer and maintain repressive armies so that they can go on exploiting us more and getting more money. On the other hand, despite our situation of dependency, we go on being divided. And if by now we on the left aren't in power, you could say that it's partly because of that, don't you think?

I lived in Los Yungas for a year and a half. In 1969, Barrientos died and so I went back to Oruro. The climate in Los Yungas didn't agree with me and I was expecting again. In Oruro my daughter Rina was born. After she was born, I began to work. I cooked food to sell in the street. It was difficult at first, because people didn't know me. Little by little, I made some friends and, after a few months, we were able to survive better. My husband had gone back to Los Yungas to work.

BACK AT THE MINE

A few months after going to Oruro, we were able to go back to Siglo XX again.

It happened like this: after Barrientos died, Siles Salinas, who was his vice president, governed Bolivia. But that was only for a few months, because that same year, General Ovando kicked him out of the government in a coup.

So then the miners who'd been fired by Barrientos in 1965 asked Ovando to give them back their jobs in the mine. Ovando wouldn't listen to them. And so an important hunger strike was declared by the fired men along with their families. Because of that hunger strike, many of them were able to go back to work. Us, too. In the Oruro newspaper I read my husband's name on the list of those who could return to work, and I got in touch with him in Los Yungas. And that was how we went back to Siglo XX. It was a very special and important thing for us.

Ovando had worked with Barrientos in his government. He was even there as co-president for a while. When he came to power, he made out to be a leftist and called his government "nationalist revolutionary." And he did do some things. He even decreed the nationalization of the Gulf installations.[14] But he went on being what he'd been before, so some of his ministers left the government.

Well, back in Siglo XX my compañero told me that I shouldn't participate anymore in anything, that we'd suffered so much and had only been able to come back to the mine after much sacrifice, and that my obligation was to be with the kids and take care of our home. But I was already thinking differently. What I wanted to do was organize people better, participate better with the workers and be involved in all of that, you know?

And shortly after I arrived, they held the miners' congress in Siglo XX, which had been called by the Mine Workers' Federation.

My compañeras from the Housewives' Committee had already elected their leaders. But I was still secretary-general. They gave me back my position. So I participated in the congress. But after that, my compañero told me that he absolutely wouldn't allow me to go on participating. And that if I didn't go along with that, I could leave. Just like that, see?

So I told him that I only participated in the committee in order to help out at home, because I understood that all his sacrifice in the mine wasn't enough to meet our needs; that I even went

---

14. The Bolivian Gulf Oil Co., subsidiary of the North American company Gulf Oil, was the principal oil concessionary in Bolivia.

without lots of things in order not to bother him; that the work I did in the committee was to fight with him for a better situation, so that there could be a change and a better and happier life for us; and that, anyhow, I was going to the committee because I liked to talk with people and help them, just as he liked to have a couple with his pals, go to the movies, or go other places. And I told him that if he gave me everything I needed for the home, okay, then I wouldn't get involved anymore. And we reached an agreement: I'd leave the committee and he'd give up his pastimes.

But since he had to go out drinking with the boys, and go to the movies, the agreement didn't last. And so during the next few days, without telling him anything, I went to a Committee meeting. And so he asked me:

"What happened?"

"Well, what happened with you?" I answered. And I told him that my agreement was with him, and since he hadn't lived up to his side of the bargain, I could also do the same thing on my side. And finally my compañero understood that I had to go on doing what I was doing. His bosses had criticized him in the past and said that his compañera was a so-and-so, and at the beginning he'd suffered and couldn't answer them back; now he doesn't need to pay attention to their comments and he says: "That's my compañera's life and it's none of your business." So it seems like we've come a long way, don't you think?

In 1970 there was another guerrilla group in Bolivia, the Teoponte group. There were a lot of university students in it, about seventy, I think. And they were brutally wiped out.

We didn't participate in that second guerrilla group. We found out about it in the papers, but they didn't say anything to us about it.

I'm not knocking them, of course. People that go to the mountains to give their lives like that, knowing that death can come at any time, are people worthy of respect and admiration. What most of us say, we haven't got the courage to really do. That's why I do have a lot of respect for them.

But we've also got to realize that we won't get anywhere by just going up into the mountains if we don't have the people's support. That's the main thing.

It seems to me that that was the mistake those guerrillas made: they didn't get close enough to the people. No one can get anywhere if they aren't in tight with the people. That's the most important thing. We mustn't ever forget that the working class, the peasants, all of us, are the two basic pillars that socialism's going to be built on, right?

I'm not a *foquista*,[15] I believe that things shouldn't be improvised. The human being, in order to walk, first has to learn to crawl, then to stand up on two feet, then to take the first steps and bit by bit to walk, until finally he or she can compete in marathon races. A revolutionary movement isn't made from one day to the next either. That's why isolated movements aren't worth anything. I think that the people have to free themselves. And if a group carries on more radical action, the most important thing is to have the people's support.

The Teoponte guerrilla group showed who Ovando really was: he wanted to pass himself off as a leftist and, nevertheless, he had those young people mercilessly murdered, like he'd done before with the ones at Nancahuazu, remember?

THE PEOPLE AND THE ARMY

In 1970, there was another coup. And then the air force, the navy, and the army wanted to set up a troika to govern the country. But the people didn't accept that. A national strike was called. Representatives from the Central Obrera Boliviano went to Alto

---

15. A supporter of *foco,* a guerrilla tactic developed successfully in the Cuban Revolution based on spectacular demonstrations of military force, which at the same time is intended to accomplish the broader political goals of developing political (vanguard) leadership through the struggle as well as politicizing the masses and drawing the armed forces of the state into battle. Che attempted, unsuccessfully, to establish a *foco* in Bolivia.

de La Paz, where the air force is, to support General Torres so that he'd take over the government. And he accepted.

Torres wanted to do something for the people. And he did do something for them, even though he was only in power for a few months. For example, he kicked the Peace Corps out of Bolivia. He also nationalized the Matilde mine.[16]

Also, the mine workers told Torres about the wages that Barrientos had taken away from us in 1965, and he listened to them. It seems that he had even looked over the salaries that the managers and technical personnel of COMIBOL and *Yacimientos Petrolíferos Fiscales Bolivianos* [Bolivian Oil Deposits Corporation] earned. It was thousands and thousands of dollars, millions and millions of pesos that was much more than the salary of the president himself. So he made a decree and all those guys' salaries were lowered. And that money was used to replace part of the workers' wages. So that was a good thing he did.

General Torres also came to the mines to bring the news about the raise and to talk with the people. The miners wanted to carry him on their shoulders, which is the highest expression of honor that the working class can give a leader or someone they admire. But the general didn't want that. And he said: "How can I allow the workers to carry me on their shoulders? Actually, I'd like to carry the workers on my shoulders."

That time they had a dinner for him in Catavi. And he even sent a card with a personal invitation to us, the compañeras of the Housewives' Committee. I didn't want to go, because I still had something against the military after all they'd done to me in jail. But my compañeras made me go along with the others.

And we went to the banquet. The compañeras had prepared a little bunch of flowers with a red rose in the middle. When we got

---

16. Important mining complex—zinc, silver, lead, cadmium, etc.—exploited by the Phillips Minerals and Chemical Corporation and the U.S. Steel Corporation. In 1972, Banzer renegotiated the indemnification in favor of the transnational.

to the main offices, we saw a long line of people, of ladies with bouquets, who wanted to see the general, and the soldiers wouldn't let them in. "They aren't going to let us in," I thought. But we showed them the card and right away they let us in.

On reaching the table, a leader introduced us: "Here are the representatives of the Housewives' Committee of Siglo XX." The general greeted us and made us sit down in front of him.

Then I made a little greeting speech. I told him that we welcomed him, that we were grateful that he'd taken so much trouble to get us our wages back.

"So you've shown us that you want to be on our side," I said. "But it's very probable that just as there are good people, there are also bad people in the army. And if now you're our friend, then prove it by arming the people. Because we women are tired of seeing our compañeros die like flies in the streets, not for lack of bravery, but because they don't have weapons to defend themselves with. You say that you're a friend of the people, so arm us so that alongside you we can defend the people. Because the army is always a repressive tool of the current gorillas in power. And if now you're our friend, the army can be on our side. But when you're no longer in power, or are no longer our friend, the army will turn against us again. And to remind you of what I'm saying, I'm going to give you a bunch of flowers with a red rose in the center, representing the blood shed by our people in all the massacres that the army has carried out here."

And I gave him the bunch of flowers.

Then the general stood up and said:

"There's so much pain in the compañera's words. We're sure that she's suffered and been through a lot. But I want these massacres among Bolivians to end forever. The army will never again point its guns at you. The army will never again have the mentality it's had up to now. We're going to change the army's mentality completely. And you're going to help us. We even want the military people to come and live among you, at least to share two or three months of life with you, so that they can see your real situation and see if you're right or not."

But that was precisely his mistake, no? He trusted the army and didn't arm the people. We know that the army we've got is made up of lousy people, trained in the Pentagon, with bourgeois ideas, and ideas of domination. And it's just an illusion to think that these people, educated like they are, and sometimes already sold out, are going to change their mentality, isn't it?

That same year a group of university teachers came to Siglo XX to give some talks and show some movies on unionism and economics. Among them there were also some journalists and some movie directors who made up the group called "Ukhamau." They showed the movies *Ukhamau* and *Yawarmallku*. Then there was sort of a roundtable discussion where they talked about the movies. One of them told us that they were movies made from real life, because this group hadn't been formed in order to make money, but instead they were people with a lot of revolutionary consciousness and their mission was to place themselves at the service of the people. He asked us to help out by asking the government to lower the taxes on the movies they made.

We told them we wanted to help, as long as their movies didn't degenerate. Because once they got the license and all the authorization, they could make movies and organize them like others before, degenerating into purely commercial-type movies, New Wave, as we call them. They liked the way we talked.

We also suggested they make a movie about Siglo XX. So the director said he would. And not too much time went by, five months at most, and they came back to Siglo XX to film. And they made the movie called *El Coraje del Pueblo* [The Courage of the People]. We'd already agreed with them to open the picture in five different places on the same day. But Banzer's coup came and we lost sight of each other. No one in Bolivia, to this day, has been able to see that movie. I saw it for the first time in Mexico, and I like it, because at least we've documented there some accusations that are important to make. And the only thing I hope is that this group of artists keeps supporting the people.

During Torres's government, the Popular Assembly also took place; it was very well known, even abroad.

They said that the Popular Assembly meant that the workers were in power. All the federations which were affiliated with the *Central Obrera Boliviano* participated in it, the factory federations, the miners, construction, peasants, university federation, etc. The people's political parties also participated.

I heard comments about the assembly, but the Housewives' Committee wasn't invited to participate in it. So I wasn't there.

I think that the Popular Assembly helped to bring certain problems out into the open, like, for example, the miners presented their demands. But according to what I was told, there were too many differences among the participants. There were also people who wanted to make their ideology prevail and there were a lot of divisions, especially among the parties that were there.

Even though I don't know much about the history of the organization of the Popular Assembly, I think that if we'd been in power, we would have needed a mechanism that would back up that popular power. We have several examples to prove that. Vietnam has demonstrated it, the Cubans have demonstrated it by arming the people to the teeth—men and women—in order to force the "colossus" that's one step away from them to respect them. We can't go on being naive. We know that our enemy is very strong and has a lot of power, no? We have the bitter experience of the Chilean people. That's why I say: if the people are in power, they have to guarantee that power, right?

At the same time, if we'd been in power, the ministers and the other president's aides should have been workers and peasants. But it wasn't like that; instead, Juan Jose Torres's ministers continued to come from the bourgeoisie, even if they sympathized with the people's cause.

But we didn't have power in our hands. And the proof of that is that Torres fell right away. On August 21, 1971, General Banzer, with his army, took over.

THE WORKERS' STRENGTH

General Banzer didn't get into power through the people's will, but by force, machine-gunning the universities and arresting a whole lot of people. And once he was consolidated in power, he began to do a lot of things against us: first of all, there was the monetary devaluation, then the economic package, then the closing of our mine workers' radio stations. . . . Like that.

They've outlawed the unions, they've made a decree that says there can't be unions in Bolivia, not the Mine Workers' Federation, nor the Central Obrera Boliviano, the most important groups of the Bolivian workers' movement. They've made all of that illegal. And they think that that way they'll be able to do whatever they want to in Bolivia.

But, in reality, they've forgotten that the workers are united and organized and that the working class is a very large front, because not only men participate in it but also their wives and children. And the working-class movement hasn't ended, it hasn't died. Of course, we can't do things too openly. But we continue to move forward anyway, despite all the repression.

For example, when the decree on monetary devaluation came out, the dollar cost 12 Bolivian pesos, and from one day to the next it cost 20 pesos. And after that, the stores didn't open and there wasn't anything to buy so that the babies could eat. Also, the government said that it was giving us a voucher of 150 pesos a month or 5 pesos a day, something like that, but that was really nothing compared to how much the prices of things were going up.

So when we saw all that was happening, the first thing we women of the committee did was to ask for a hike in the cost of living allowance at the company grocery store. But they didn't pay any attention to us in the grocery store. That's why I had to call out a demonstration of the compañeras. I announced it over the radio and said that we were going to demonstrate to protest and that all the compañeras who didn't agree with the government's decree should come to the demonstration.

The subprefect of Uncía seized the radio station and insulted us in order to frighten us, so that no one would pay attention to our call.

"Only prostitutes, whores, lazy women, those who don't have anything better to do, are going to participate in the demonstration," he said.

When I heard that, I thought: after what he said, I'm sure no one's going to come.

I left my house feeling very sad. And in the street I bumped into a neighbor woman.

"Did you hear the subprefect's declaration last night, Señora?"

"Yes," I answered. "I think that this time we're going to fail."

"What do you mean, we're going to fail? We're going to the demonstration!"

And people went with even more enthusiasm and they wanted to hang that guy who'd insulted us over the radio.

There was no talking during the demonstration. But when we reached the Llallagua City Hall, some women vendors who sold meat in the street sharpened their knives and told people they didn't want to sell, that they weren't going to sell to them, that there wasn't any meat unless they paid them 50 pesos a kilo. Because, when the monetary devaluation was declared, the butcher shops were the first to raise prices from 9 to 50 or 60 pesos a kilo of meat. And so they only sold it to their steady customers who would buy it at that price. In other words, only the people with money could eat meat.

People attacked the butcher shop. The DIC agents arrived. When we reached the Plaza del Minero in Siglo XX, people were already grouped and were about to sing the national anthem as we always do.

Those of us who were going to address the crowd went up to the balcony of the union building, but the agents tear-gassed us and broke up the demonstration.

"Ay!" I said. "We've failed!"

But after a few minutes, when I could see again, the people were still there. And it was really hard calming the demonstrators down.

It was a pretty good demonstration, because we got something out of it, at least a limit was placed on the crazy way the prices of some articles were going up.

Another important demonstration we housewives organized was in favor of a higher cost of living allowance due to the "economic package."[17] The prices of staple goods had gone up so much that we didn't have enough money to buy anything.

We know that each month from 300 to 400 tons of tin come out of the mine at Siglo XX. It's the mining center in Bolivia that produces the most tin. So we think that we should have a corresponding cost of living allowance in the company grocery store. In other mines they get more goods and in other companies even the allowance that's fixed for each family takes into consideration the number of people in the family. But with us in Siglo XX, it's not like that. The allowance is the same for everyone.

Well, we women of the committee wrote a letter to the manager of COMIBOL saying that they should make our allowance the same as the highest one in the company, because our compañeros were the ones who mined the most tin. And we gave them a deadline for their answer. But we didn't get one. We went to the manager and gave them forty-eight hours more, but he didn't even answer us.

So then we got the women together. And since it had been in an assembly that we'd approved asking for the cost of living allowance hike, in that meeting I told them that the manager hadn't even had the decency to see me, he didn't even want to give us an answer because, according to him, he had no reason to talk with us. And since the manager didn't want to see me, we should all go to ask for the answer. We decided to go to Cataví and we went en masse, on foot. It was a pretty big demonstration.

When we got to Cataví, the manager wasn't there anymore. So

17. A group of economic measures, among which was a 100 percent increase in the price of food staples: bread, rice, sugar, oil, noodles.

LET ME SPEAK!

we asked the leaders, the secretaries-general of the company and of the unions who were in La Paz, to put us in contact with the manager of COMIBOL in La Paz by radio, so that we could talk directly with him.

It had been about a month since meat had been sent to Siglo XX, and meat's the basic staple we use to feed our compañeros so they can stand the hard work in the mine. We also wanted to tell him about that.

So the Cataví radio got hooked up with La Paz and, that way, we had a conversation with the COMIBOL manager. We spoke with him, we told him our point of view. And we asked for an immediate answer.

The general told us that it was something that should be done calmly and through legal channels. And he began trying to pretend. But we weren't happy with that, and in the end, we got really mad and said:

"Well, Mr. Colonel, it's obvious that you're a military man who can't know that there are problems in the mines. You know what kind of discipline is imposed in a barracks, how you lead an army, how you make it go. You know all about those things, don't you? But what it's like working in the mine, digging ore and being in totally lousy physical condition, that's something you know nothing about."

And we told him that he should try to understand our situation and send us the food for our compañeros right away and do something about our cost of living allowance. That's mainly what we were asking for, see?

He hung up on us. But we women didn't move.

So they connected us again with the gentleman. But he said:

"There's no law that says I have to talk with women. And I don't want to talk with you."

We took that as a joke and said:

"How terrible, Colonel, that you have to have a law so that you can talk to your wife!"

And our conversation got a little rough and once again he hung up. I was really stubborn and since I'm not very familiar with all those ranks and titles, I kept forgetting what rank the manager of COMIBOL had and sometimes I called him general, sometimes colonel, and sometimes sir. The workers enjoyed that step by step demotion.

Ah! And the COMIBOL people also wanted us to send a commission to La Paz to discuss the problem. So we women said that we didn't have either the money or the time to make so many trips. And that instead they should come to the mines to discuss it with us.

Then the leaders talked with the fellow over the radio and they told us that COMIBOL had agreed to study the question and give us an answer.

We didn't get the allowance hike that would have put us on the same level as the other mines; that discrimination is still going on. But they did increase it. Not as much as we asked for, but pretty much. They increased it by 30 kilos of meat a month, 20 kilos of sugar, 8 kilos of rice, and 80 rolls.

The next day we found a way to check up on the women who did or didn't go to the demonstration. Because what we had proposed was for everyone to go, but some women stayed calmly at home, washing, ironing. . . . And they laughed when they heard that we were going to have that demonstration. "You won't get anything," they said. And they even said that we were good-for-nothings wasting our time that way and that they had responsibilities at home. And all of us who went to the demonstration were waiting around for an answer till ten at night, even though they made so many problems for us and even cut off the connection so that we couldn't talk anymore.

At least four thousand of us women were there. We were plenty. The head of the demonstration was already in Cataví near the management offices and the tail was still in the Siglo XX cemetery. That's about two kilometers.

Then we decided to stamp the forearms of the people who were at the demonstration. We put on two stamps: the union's and the committee's. And only those women who were stamped had their names put down so that they'd benefit from the allowance hike we got.

Since 1973, we women in the committee have also tried to get in closer touch with the peasant women. Because we realize that the problem is that there still isn't as much worker-peasant unity as we need in order to be a group, a revolutionary force. Not only that, but the "worker-peasant pact" was signed by men, and women hardly took any part in it at all.

So we did some things, trying to get closer to the peasant women and talk together about our problems. We didn't get as far as forming an organization, because everything's really controlled and it's difficult to do anything, even if it's really, really important.

If it weren't like that, the present government wouldn't be working so hard to control all of the peasant organizations and win them over to their side, to serve their purposes, right?

Also, the government has really cracked down hard on the peasants on some occasions. For example, in January 1974, the army killed hundreds of peasants in Tolata, in the Cochabamba Valley. There were hundreds of peasants blocking the roads. Why? As a protest against the government's economic measures and especially the "economic package" that was terrible for them. So the peasants were asking for an answer, because they couldn't stand the price hikes of staple articles anymore. But the government answered by sending in the army to repress them. And in that massacre, hundreds of peasants died in the valley.

In Bolivia, the peasants still don't have as much strength as the working class to make themselves heard. Nevertheless, there are already various organizations and two fronts, apart from the *Confederación National de Campesinos* [National Peasants' Confederation], which is controlled by the government. These two fronts are the *Federación de Campesinos Independientes* [Federation of Independent Peasants] and the *Federación de Colonizadores* [Federation of Colonizers].

The colonizers or settlers are mostly ex-miners who agreed to go to unpopulated areas and begin to colonize certain parts of the jungle, mostly in the departments of Santa Cruz, Pando, and Beni.

The *Federación de Campesinos Independientes* unites all the peasants of the country. North of Potosi, for example, the peasants are grouped in five provinces. They were the ones who, in 1970, in the miners' congress of Siglo XX, signed the "worker-peasant pact" with us. Many of their leaders were arrested, beaten, and deported, along with union and university leaders, and others.

Another thing I'd like to clarify is the following: the working class and the governments of Bolivia have become famous for their confrontations in struggles, repression, and massacres. So a tactic that the present government tried to use was to change that image. And actually—at least in the first years he was in power— General Banzer didn't treat the miners the same way that previous governments had. Instead he began trying to win us over, offering to give us better opportunities.

For example, the government people know—because everything is in their hands—that my husband earned barely 1,500 pesos a month, added to the vouchers and subsidies. In other words, about 70 dollars a month.

So they said to me: "Señora, we admire you as a faithful defender of your class, and we, the military, want to be on your side. And look, because of the admiration we have for you and because we think you should prepare yourself more, we've decided to help you, with no strings attached." And they explained that they could give my husband a job, in other words, that they could give him a job as stock clerk in the COMIBOL warehouses in La Paz, and pay him 3,000 pesos a month. That's about three times my husband's present wage, no? They were going to give my children scholarships and I'd also get one so that I could get educated, so that I could prepare myself better.

This type of thing has been done with many compañeros.

But I turned it all down. My husband was pretty sad and he said:

"You say you love me, but you say no to one thing after another, you never think. You could have gotten me out of the mine which is so terrible. Besides, all you get are knocks and more knocks, and they say whatever they want to you and they hardly take into consideration what you really do. Why didn't you accept?"

So I answered:

"No, I live up to my word, I don't do favors for people or try to be liked by anybody, but I believe in what I do, I've got a conscience, because I've mapped out a road for myself. Ever since I was little, I've seen how important it is to be really convinced about something and to undertake it for all it's worth. I'm convinced that it's necessary to work toward liberation of the people and that, in order to do that, you've got to suffer. And so should I go now and ally myself with the ones who've massacred our people, who've filled the streets with blood, who even owe me a child? And just because they tell me now that they'll give me a job, should I ally myself with them? No. That would be betraying my principles, betraying the blood of our ancestors who have died for all this. I won't be their accomplice, wild horses couldn't drag me. Even though I have to die and my family too. We can't do what they want. We can't sell out."

You have to be upright, no? Because that's why you have an ideal. In order to make my situation better now, I'm not going to ruin forever what I've done with the people, right? I've got responsibilities as a leader. So it would be unpardonable, unthinkable, to team up with the ones who work against the people. I couldn't do that. After all, when I didn't have anything to eat, when my children were sick, I didn't accept. Why should I now? No! There are times when many have to die in order for the people to get ahead, no? I'm not happy anymore with short-range solutions. Any solution of that kind, little aspirins, little reforms, all of that no longer interests me.

Also, I couldn't accept being well off, knowing that my children and I are happy "through the goodness of our government," while the rest of the people are suffering. I can't do that as a real leader.

I said all this to my husband and he agreed with me that we had to do it my way.

There are people who say that if I'd accepted work with the Ministry of the Interior, I would have understood better how the government acts and I could have worked to change all that. But I think that you can do that when, let's say, the workers run the government, when it's our turn.

But in my case it's different. People already know where I stand, a lot of them trust me, and if they saw me in the Ministry of the Interior, they'd be let down. I represent a position; and it wouldn't be right for me to take on that role. People who aren't known can do that. You know, people are like that: they have a leader, they trust that leader. And the day he or she puts their foot in it, people don't trust them anymore.

And not only would they mistrust me, but the rest of the compañeras and the committee, too. And they'd say: "That organization that was supposedly on the people's side has betrayed us. . . .You can't trust women anymore." At least if they'd say: "Don't trust her anymore," but no, "Don't trust women, don't trust the committee. There's Domitila who suffered so much and who's betrayed us. Don't join the committee." It happens that way, no?

The year 1974 ended in a very dramatic way. On November 9 a government decree came out declaring Banzer dictator, outlawing all political parties, all unions, all workers' organizations, and even declaring that there wouldn't be elections until 1980. So he's wiped out all national laws with one stroke of his pen, no? And, just like that, he introduced the civil service law which is obligatory for all citizens.

As soon as these decrees came out, the workers immediately began to protest. In Siglo XX there was a demonstration and a work stoppage to repudiate the measures. In Huanuni they did the same thing and asked the compañeros of Siglo XX to participate, so our leaders went to Huanuni. But on returning to Siglo XX, they arrested Coca, leader of the Mine Workers' Federation, and Bernal, leader of the Siglo XX union. Bernal was in prison for several months. And Coca was exiled to Paraguay, to a very unhealthy and isolated place. His family stayed on in Siglo XX in great poverty, because they had no one to earn their bread for them.

That's always what happens with all the prisoners: they arrest our compañeros, knowing that they're the only support of the family, and the families stay behind, ruined and condemned to misery. In other words, the repression carried out by the Bolivian government against the men affects the whole family because of economic, health, and other problems, right? Because from the moment a miner is arrested, he's considered fired from the company and his family doesn't get any more medical attention, has no rights, nothing. So the repression not only affects him, but also his whole family.

Then another really important problem is the kids, you know? They're used to their daddy, their mommy. From one day to the next their father disappears, or their mother. That's a terrible moral suffering and it creates for the children special traumas that help to make them stubborn and feel hurt. This repression is pretty brutal.

Also in November 1974, immediately after those decrees came out annulling the constitution, the government appointed people called "grassroots coordinators." These coordinators have to be intermediaries between the boss and the worker, but with this idea: the government names these people and they have to see which workers are complaining the most, who makes the most problems, and then they denounce them. That's the job of the grassroots coordinators.

As soon as they did that, the workers really rejected the coordinators and said they wouldn't accept them. And they decided to elect their rank-and-file representatives, organized into what they called grassroots commissions. In Siglo XX they elected four representatives. In the beginning, the government didn't accept them and so they weren't accepted by the COMIBOL management. When we would go to present some issue, they'd say that they'd listen to the coordinators and not us. So there was a pretty big fight, until, finally, with pressure from the workers, the company had to recognize those compañeros who made up the grassroots commissions, the ones we'd chosen. But the fight still goes on.

The workers have a great strength: their unity. Now, the workers' unity plus strikes are practically the only weapons the working class has in order to confront the repression. Of course, first we always try to state our claims through demonstrations and protests. If they don't listen to us, then we resort to a strike.

I know in some countries that tactic is worn out. The workers go out on strike and no one pays attention to them. But in Bolivia, it so happens that tin is basic to the country's economy. And the government has signed agreements with the foreign capitalists and has to give them a certain amount of tin and other minerals.

If there's a strike, we lose, because they don't pay us our wage for the days we're striking. But the government also loses, and much more, because they're waiting for the tin in some foreign industry and the government has to live up to these contracts. So striking is one way to respond to so much repression and all the robbery that exists in our country.

Of course, the government has pretty strong allies and has the possibility of taking other measures against the workers in the future. For example, since we don't have funds, they might beat us through hunger. I really don't know how long we'll be able to go on this way. But for the time being, these are the weapons the workers have: their unity and their strikes.

"WHICH ONE OF YOU CAN ANSWER ME?"

The mine workers have three radio stations which are completely ours: "The Miner's Voice" of Siglo XX, the "21st of December" of Cataví, and "Radio Llallagua" of the town with the same name. We got them through our own efforts and sacrifices and we run them ourselves. The commentators are our own people, they speak our language and tell us about the situation in the whole country. That's the way we have of informing ourselves and communicating with one another.

That's why we took such good care of those station transmitters. They belong to the miners. And they're very important so that we can know what to do each time something happens. They also entertain and educate us.

That's why, each time there's a problem, we always try to defend our radios, so that communication among us isn't cut off. And every time the army enters the mines, the first thing it attacks are the transmitters, and we fight until they give them back to us.

There's also the "Pius XII Radio" which belongs to the priests. In the beginning, Pius XII Radio didn't do its job, because it was in the hands of people who had a "special mission" and who were priests with special training. Since Pope Pius XII was alive and the Vatican had given orders to fight communism throughout the world, all those priests who came that time openly fought against communism. And since in Siglo XX we had leaders who declared openly that they were communists, there was a constant battle against the leaders, against the union.

Now all that's different, ever since a few years ago, and Pius XII Radio works pretty much in our favor. And if before they didn't bother the priests, now they beat them up like they do us, they send them to prison and kick them out of the country.

Until 1974, we knew about radios but we'd never had a television in the mine; many of us didn't even know what a television set was.

It turns out that "thanks to the generosity" of Banzer's government, five thousand TV sets appeared in Siglo XX that year. The government distributed them to each house as if they were going out of style. They handed out lottery tickets, they gave out sets with easy payment plans; in other words, COMIBOL buys them and then takes some money each month out of the miners' wages until the set's completely paid for, see?

But what happens is that Bolivian TV has channels that only have government-controlled programs, which shows the present government as "very good" and also programs with lots of foreign influence, very heavy imperialist influence.

And so my son went to a neighbor's house and saw a TV set, watched a program that showed him a marvelous world where there were mice that spoke and beautiful parks and things. That was the world of Disneyland. And my little son came back home and said to me:

"Mommy, I'm going to be a good boy. Why don't you send me to Disneyland? I want to play with the little bear, with the little mouse. You're going to take me to Disneyland, aren't you? I also want that little train, Mommy."

And for a week my son didn't want to play with his toys anymore, with his sardine cans and milk cans. He didn't want to go out in the street, he wanted to go to Disneyland. He dreamed about Disneyland.

"I want to go to see the children's park," he'd say to me. "I want those balloons."

I want this and I want that, and so on and so forth. And so I got annoyed and said:

"You're not going to watch any more TV. We don't have any of those things here in the mine."

Two or three days later I met my compañeras in the grocery store.

"Have you watched TV, Señora?"

"No, I don't have a TV."

"Ay! Last night there was a fashion show. It was beautiful, just beautiful! And to think that we, who work from four in the morning washing, ironing, cooking, taking care of the kids, coming to the grocery store, will never, never be able to have one of those suits, one of those hairstyles, one of those jewels you see on TV. How sad that we married miners!"

Imagine that! I thought: this TV isn't good for my people! Our children don't want to play with their toys anymore. The women are beginning to complain about their lives. But they shouldn't be complaining about those things! TV is doing bad things to us. It's bad.

What does television do for the working class? On TV the government shows the programs it wants. Whenever it wants to, it uses the television to insult us and call us agitators, saying that the people of Siglo XX are extremists, or whatever. The government puts us down on TV. And we can't even answer back, because we don't have a people's television.

We do have our radio programs. And precisely so that we can't answer what the government says, one morning in January 1975 the army came in and destroyed our transmitters. They broke them to bits. Left them in pieces. It made you furious just to see it. They didn't leave one single nail in place.

And they took everything: radios, equipment, records, records that were real folkloric jewels, ancient music, contemporary music, recordings that we had of our leaders . . . they took everything.

They also arrested a whole bunch of people: people who worked at the radio station, union leaders, and others.

And so the army caused all that damage that morning and thought that since we no longer had an officially recognized union organization and our union leader was in jail, we'd shut up, we wouldn't say anything.

But what happened? The workers stood united and said: "Until you give us back our transmitters, we won't go to work." And they declared a strike.

And since there was no answer from the government, the strike was called indefinitely. And one strike committee was formed among the five strongest unions of the region.

They tried to destroy that unity every way they could. For example, the "20th of October" union, which is the *locatarios'* union, had been asking for another area to mine for a year, because the place where they were didn't have any more ore, it had run out.

Another area means that the company should show them other places where there's ore so that they can work there. And the company didn't want to give them that area. But when all the unions began the strike, they sent an emissary to find the compañeros of the 20th of October union and tell them that the government was going to let them work another area for one more year, but only if they went back to work and broke the strike. So there was some doubt among the compañeros. And they said: "If we've been waiting for this for so long, we'd better go back to work, right?"

But the revolutionary ideas and the unity of the working class were difficult to break down. And though to start off with we asked them to return our transmitters and free the political prisoners, now we added a new point: "Bigger mining areas for the workers of the 20th of October union with the support of the five unions after the strike is over." That was pretty good.

They also tried to buy people off by offering them higher wages and scholarships and other things. And they were able to organize about a hundred people who went back to work. But then their names went up on a blackboard which said: "Worker so-and-so is a traitor to his class, because he's lent himself to this maneuver." And the workers were furious and would look for him. And so they stopped working, because it wasn't worth it. Very few of them sold out to the government, which has carte blanche to do anything it wants.

Facing the workers' strength, the government people said: "Okay, let them starve to death, then."

And the army surrounded us. They wouldn't let us in or out. No one. And they thought that right there they'd stifle the thing by surrounding us. They didn't let vegetables or other foods in. Nothing. They didn't allow us any kind of communication. After all, they had the radios.

But—and this is why I say the participation of young people is important—a kid whose father had been killed in the massacre came to talk to me about this problem.

"Señora, I've really studied the situation. The soldiers are placed one every five meters, but they sleep at a certain time at night. I've seen them. I could maybe get out, through there, while they're sleeping. I could crawl on my stomach and slip out."

"Don't be silly," I said. "How can you do that?"

The boy didn't answer, but later I found out that he'd gotten out with three other boys. They went to get in contact with other places and they said: "This is what's happening in Siglo XX: they've surrounded us. . . ."

So public interest in the rest of the country was aroused about us. And the university students, the factory workers, and other miners began to support us. And the strike began to spread across the nation.

So the government, which was saying that even if they were backed into a corner they wouldn't give us back the transmitters, immediately had to send a commission to "talk things over, because this thing must be settled one way or another."

So the commission came. The DIC agents told them that there were about fifty of us agitating in there. So the commission wanted to speak with those fifty people only.

The workers who were there said what they really thought. One of them said:

"You've shut down our transmitters which are very important to us. You want to make us go back to the Middle Ages when there weren't radios or anything. You want to drown us in ignorance."

So then one member of the commission answered:

"Ah, compañero. But you've got television! We've given you the most modern equipment! Soon we'll have several channels in Bolivia and you'll be free to choose the program you want. With time, you'll have all that: radios and record players are going to disappear because new inventions are coming in. It's important that you understand that the TVs have been sent to you so that you can get ahead."

And they wanted us to settle for that, see? They also said:

"You've got to realize that you exaggerate things. There's an anti-militarist psychosis here, there's an anti-militarist sickness here. It's true that in the past the army had to take some drastic measures against the working class. But now we want to talk, we want to discuss, we want to guide the nation forward."

And he continued talking at us. They also made it look as if we were the ones responsible for closing down the radio stations, because we'd dared to say that we weren't happy with the sell-out measures of Banzer's government, especially when they handed over the oil and iron of El Mutún to Brazil.

The Housewives' Committee also participated in that meeting. I had a few concrete points to make, and so I took the floor: "If you would just let me speak . . ." I said.

"Yes, all right, yes. In a time like this, maybe a woman's ideas can clarify something," said one of them, laughing a bit.

First, like always, they'd shown us a bunch of numbers saying that the country is nearly bankrupt, that only so much comes in and that there's so much going out, and that if we can't make enough to cover that, then the country will go bankrupt, and that if we go on having strikes this and that will happen, and that we've lost this much from this strike . . . and so on and so forth.

So then I said: "I'm here representing the Housewives' Committee of Siglo XX, which has organized the majority of the worker's wives.

"We women, like the workers, repudiate this attempt against our culture and our people. Because you've destroyed four of our transmitters, stomping on them like thugs, you came here and destroyed all that's ours. We won't stand for this treatment. And we demand that you immediately return our property which has cost us so much to get.

"Now I'm going to talk about what you said. For example, you say, reading from your book and putting your numbers on the blackboard, that Banzer's government is doing marvelously and that we're the ones who are doing damage. Well, we don't live off of numbers; and right from the start we're going to tell you, Señor, that we don't live off of numbers. We live from reality.

"If you've found this government so good, please help me to understand which of the government measures is good for us.

"In the first place, General Banzer has taken office in a country where no one elected him. He came in through the force of arms, he killed a whole lot of people and among them our children and our compañeros. He machine-gunned the university, he repressed and goes on repressing a lot of people. Our resources are being turned over to foreigners, especially to Brazil.

"Now I ask you, which measure has been in favor of the working class? First he decreed the monetary devaluation. Then the 'economic package.' He intervened in the university. He ended the academic year. He massacred the peasants in Tolata. He dissolved the unions and political parties. And now he's raided union headquarters to shut the transmitters down. All of that's true, isn't it?

"So, I'd like you to answer me, please, which of these measures taken by the government favors the working class? Which one of you can answer me?"

They were all silent.

"Now, let's continue: you've said that we suffer from an anti-military psychosis, a sickness against the military. That's also false. You don't seem to appreciate what the people are worth and what the people know.

"I'll just give you one example of how that theory of yours is false: a military, fascist-type government, the Barrientos government, took away the working class's wages. Another government, also military, returned them to us, and that was Juan José Torres's government. Our husbands were willing to give their lives for that government. And they proved it. Each time there was the threat of a coup against Torres, the miners didn't mind leaving their wives and children, and together they'd all go to La Paz in trucks. They weren't armed. But if they had a knife, they took it with them; if they had a machete, they took it; if they had dynamite, they went with dynamite to La Paz to defend General Torres's government, and he was also a military man, no? So you see that the workers showed they don't have that anti-militarist sickness. Because of one thing that Torres did to help the working class, the miners were willing to give their lives for him. You've got to be fair with the people.

"Now, you've distributed five thousand TV sets. We aren't against progress. Yes, we want progress for our country. But, what happens with TV? What good is it to us at this moment? TV is run by the state. And the government says terrible things about us on TV. It says about the miners: 'They're crazy, they're lazy, they're reds,' they're this, that, and the other. And we don't have a TV station where we can answer back. We only had our radios. And, in order to silence that last voice, they wrecked them.

"Now look: what's happened to the people who've got a TV? What good is the TV to them? Our radios, even though they used rough language—uncivilized is what you call it—spoke about us, about our problems, our situation. But the TV they give us, where they tell us about and show us worlds that aren't ours, worlds we'll never reach . . . what good is that TV? To make us more frustrated and unhappy.

"Of course it's nice to have a TV, to see other countries and all that. But . . . what a misfortune, what a misfortune to see other countries that don't produce tin and yet are getting rich from it, they have fantasy-like worlds for their children and we don't have anything! How painful it is to see that our compañeros are wrecking their lungs in the mines only to make the foreigners wealthy. And how painful it is for us women who have to be cook, washerwoman, babysitter, and everything, without ever having any of those comforts they show us on TV. Aren't we also women like the ones we see there? Don't we work as much as they do? And they can have everything and wear everything, while we're drowning in poverty.

"So, what happens with the TV? Instead of being useful in our education, or as entertainment, it only makes us more miserable. Yes, on those very same TV sets you brought in, we see that and we realize all that. It's not that we're against civilization. How nice it would be to have a television channel for ourselves, in our hands! In that case, yes, it would be beautiful. Yes, we'd like to have a TV channel, but one that talks about our situation, our problems, one that educates us. How nice it would be if the mine workers, instead of our radios, had a TV channel that could transmit the reality of the miners all across the country! Then everyone would understand who we are, because a lot of people in this country don't understand us because they don't know us. There are a lot of Bolivians who say: what do you know about the *khoya locos*?

Don't you know that they chew coca, that they're drug addicts, that you shouldn't support them? But for us the miners aren't *khoya locos,* they aren't ignorant men, they're men who are supporting the country's economy."

I said all that to them. And I asked them to answer me. But none of them wanted to.

And the only thing they said was that we were agitators and that they wanted to talk to the masses.

In the afternoon they met with the masses. But it was something! The workers were very rough with them. They made them see that, above all else, they wanted their transmitters back. And that the government people were savages who brutally destroy everything.

The guys from the commission got up and left. They were scared. And on May 1, they gave us back our transmitters. But Pius XII Radio was silenced for several months more. And they went on distributing TV sets in the mines.

"AN UNFORTUNATE ACCIDENT!"

In Bolivia all young men have to go into the army at eighteen; some of them are already there at seventeen. Why? Because they can't get a job if they don't have their draft cards. And if they don't serve in the armed forces, they pay a heavy price; they go through hell, sometimes they're even killed.

And the parents, when their sons go away to the barracks, have nothing to say in the matter. And in the army they have to kill their own people sometimes. That's happened more than once in Bolivia. For example, in the San Juan Massacre in 1967, more than ten young men died because they didn't want to shoot. And they didn't want to shoot because their families, their parents, their brothers and sisters, their relatives were in Siglo XX. And the officers said to them: "Let's see! Who's from Siglo XX, from Cataví? Step forward!" And since the boys didn't want to shoot, they fired on them right there. But how could they shoot at their families, in a terrible situation like a massacre?

In May 1975, something happened that we still don't understand to this day. That was the killing of some conscript soldiers.

Right near Siglo XX, in Uncia, there's a swimming spot where we used to go every Saturday and Sunday to spend a pleasant time, have a picnic with the kids, swim. Now we don't even have that, because the army's taken it over. The barracks are there now. The soldiers come at night to Siglo XX-Cataví, to Llallagua, and they go to the taverns and if anyone contradicts them in something, they grab him and beat him up. They come on market day, for example, and walk around arrogantly, pushing people around, elbowing them aside, armed with two pistols, like cowboys. And they think they're hot stuff.

What we know is that in May 1975, a contingent of conscripts was sent to the barracks. They'd enlisted in La Paz and some thirty or forty of them went to Uncía. They'd been stationed there.

They say that as soon as they got there, they were subjected to a "chocolate" [18] that lasted six hours, before they received their uniforms, when they'd barely had their heads shaved. And that they'd been put in the pool and there they'd suffered a "collective cramp" and the poor guys had drowned. According to Major Adolfo, who worked there, "Those Indians . . . they don't even know how to swim . . . the fools got scared and drowned."

Imagine that! What do you suppose a "collective cramp" is? Had an electric current cramped every one of them? That's not possible, because the pool isn't so deep and if one of them was standing he could have been saved. The fact is that nine young soldiers died in the Uncía swimming pool.

So then the union called us and said:

"Let's see, señoras, find out if those kids really drowned."

We went to the barracks at Uncía and asked for a hearing. And Colonel Ramallo told us:

"My God, ladies! Come in. What a tragedy has just occurred. An unfortunate accident! All those young boys got a collective cramp.

---

18. Military punishment: trotting for hours.

It's that they're Indians and can't swim, they don't know how, and so they got scared and they died stupidly in the swimming pool. But we're going to have problems now, the extremists are going to take advantage of this matter."

More or less wanting to believe it a little, we women said to him:

"Maybe that did happen . . . couldn't we see the bodies?"

"How unfortunate, ladies!" said the Colonel. "We've just shipped them off to Cataví, to the hospital, so they can do an autopsy, so there aren't any uncalled-for comments."

"Well, then, we'll go there," we said. And immediately we went to Cataví to see if the boys had really drowned.

We got to Cataví and asked the doctors if the bodies were there.

"No, no bodies have been brought here. Yes, there's a wounded man who's been here for three days. He's got a bullet wound, but he's a big fish there, they've given him blood and he's guarded by soldiers. But people who've died by drowning? No, there aren't any here," they told us.

We went to Siglo XX immediately and informed the secretary-general of the union. The leader went to the Cataví hospital and asked for three doctors to accompany him to the Uncia barracks to perform the autopsy. But the hospital director said:

"I'm sorry, compañero. We've gotten a memo from the Cataví Mining Company that says we shouldn't get mixed up in this problem of the autopsy. Go to Llallagua and get the coroner there."

But the coroner said:

"Who'll guarantee my personal safety? I can't perform the autopsy."

Then we were sure that something had happened and had to be cleared up.

The secretary-general of the union decided to write letters to La Paz, asking for a special commission from the medical school, the Commission of Justice and Peace, and the press, to come and investigate.

Three days had gone by since we found out about the matter. The military had already buried the bodies. When they found out that the commission was coming from La Paz, they wanted to take the bodies out of the Uncía cemetery and make them disappear. That was at eleven at night, and about twenty soldiers, well armed, were putting the bodies into two trucks. They'd put four of them into one truck and five in the other.

But the people were alert. They saw there were lights in the cemetery. Word got around. And some women went and surrounded the soldiers. The compañeras did it so well that the soldiers didn't have time for anything. They couldn't even shoot.

So then the soldiers began to get angry with the women, to ask them what they were doing, why they were troubling the dead, things like that.

The truck with the four coffins left at once. But the other one, with five coffins, couldn't leave, because the driver wasn't at the wheel. So while one group of women argued with the soldiers, another group was unloading the bodies. The compañeras spread out their shawls and put the coffins on them. And they took the bodies to the church in Uncía.

Another compañera telephoned us from the main gate and said:

"We're asking for help from the compañeros of Siglo XX. They're taking away the bodies of the young soldiers and we've rescued the coffins. Please come."

The miners mobilized and went to the church. There they stayed on guard with the other people all night long. And everyone could see that, when we pressed on the stomachs of the dead soldiers, no water came out, but a whole lot of blood gushed from their mouths and noses. Their abdomens were completely black and blue. Some had skull fractures, some had fractured sternums. You could see that the boys had been very mistreated, it wasn't that they'd drowned.

Besides, they were almost naked, with really lousy clothes. So the union bought some clothes for the boys. They gave me the clothes and the job of going to Uncía to dress the compañeros, because their clothing was so poor that their trousers were completely ripped, their sweaters too. We could even see that one of the boys had a pair of filthy old underpants on his head, put there as a joke.

In spite of all this, the army declared over the radio that they'd been buried with all military honors. So then we saw what "military honors" are for the sons of workers and peasants.

All of that made the people very angry.

Now what good did the death of those young soldier boys in Uncía do for our country? Why did they kill them? To this day it's still a mystery to us. But we do know that we saw those boys bleeding from the mouth.

How much we've seen! Imagine what must be happening in the rest of the country! Because the radio, the press, the television, all of that's controlled by the government and most of the news doesn't even get to us. But we do know that, today, there's also division in the Bolivian army, there are aware people who criticize the military regime we live under and who show their discontent in one way or another. And so the army makes these people disappear secretly, deports them to some place, relieves them of their duties. Frequently you hear about soldiers who've been discharged, imprisoned, deported. Things like that.

AT THE INTERNATIONAL WOMEN'S YEAR TRIBUNAL

In 1974, a Brazilian movie director came to Bolivia, commissioned by the United Nations. She was traveling through Latin America looking for women leaders, to find out their opinions about women's conditions, how much and in what way they participate in bettering their situation.

With regard to Bolivia, she was very intrigued by the "housewives' front" which she'd heard about abroad and, also, she'd seen the women of Siglo XX acting in the movie *El Coraje del Pueblo* [The Courage of the People]. So, after asking for permission from the government, she went into the mines. And she came to visit me. She liked what I said and she said it was important that everything I knew should be told to the rest of the world. She asked me if I could travel. I said I couldn't, that I didn't have money to even travel in my own country.

So she asked me if I'd agree to participate in a women's congress that was going to take place in Mexico, if she was able to get money for me. I had just found out that there was an International Women's Year.

Although I didn't really believe it much, I said yes, in that case I could go. But I thought it was just a promise like so many others and I didn't pay much attention to it.

When I got the telegram saying that I was invited by the United Nations, I was quite surprised and disconcerted. I called a meeting of the committee and all the compañeras agreed that it would be good for me to travel, along with one more compañera. But there wasn't enough for two of us to go. The next day I went before a meeting of union leaders and rank-and-file delegates and gave them my report and they agreed that I should particpate in the event and they even helped me economically so that I could begin making the arrangements.

So with some other compañeras I went to La Paz and we looked into the details, we got guarantees, and I stayed there alone to finish the arrangements. Several days went by. It got to look like I wouldn't be able to make the trip because they didn't want to give me the travel permit.

And it turns out that some Siglo XX leaders arrived in La Paz and were surprised to see I hadn't left. So they went with me to the secretariat of the Ministry of the Interior. And they asked:

"What's happening with the compañera? Why isn't she in Mexico already? The International Women's Year Conference opens today. What's happened here? Is it or isn't it International Women's Year? Do our wives have the right to participate in this conference, or can only your wives go there?"

And they told me:

"Well, compañera, since they don't want to let you go, let's leave. Even though you have an invitation from the United Nations, they don't want to let you go to that conference. So we're going to complain to the United Nations. And not only that: we're going to have a work stoppage in protest. Come with us, compañera."

They were all set to take me out of the ministry when the guys there reacted:

"But . . . why didn't we start there in the first place! One moment, one moment, don't get so hot and bothered. If the lady has an invitation from the United Nations, we should have started there. Where's the invitation?"

The invitation! Every single day, at every turn, I was asked for the copy. And with the experience the miners have, they'd made lots of copies of it. So of course, one copy would get lost and I'd make another. And so on. And the original, well, the leaders themselves had it, because if the first copies got used up, they could make others.

I gave them one more copy; and after an hour, more or less, they gave me my documents. Everything was okay, everything was ready. The plane left the next day at nine in the morning.

When I was about to board the plane, a young lady from the Ministry of the Interior came over to me. I'd seen her there on various occasions, hanging on to her papers. She came over and said:

"Ay, Señora! So, you got your pass? I'm so happy! You deserve it. I congratulate you! How I'd like to be in your shoes, so I could see Mexico! Congratulations!"

But then, very mysterious, she went on:

"Ay, but Señora, your return to the country depends a lot on what you say there. So it's not a question of talking about any old thing—you've got to think it out well. Above all, you've got to think of your children who you're leaving behind. I'm giving you good advice. Have a good time."

I thought about my responsibility as a mother and as a leader and so my role in Mexico seemed very difficult to me, thinking of what that young lady had said to me. I felt I was between the devil and the deep blue sea, as we say. But I was determined to carry out the mission the compañeros and compañeras had entrusted me with.

From La Paz we went to Lima, then to Bogotá, and finally to Mexico.

During the trip I thought . . . I thought that I'd never imagined I'd be traveling in a plane, and even less to such a far-off country as Mexico. Never, for we were so poor that sometimes we hardly had anything to eat and we couldn't even travel around our own country. I thought about how I'd always wanted to know my homeland from corner to corner . . . and now I was going so far away. This made me feel happy and sad at the same time. How I would have liked other compañeras and compañeros to have the same opportunity!

In the plane, everyone was speaking in other languages, chatting, laughing, drinking, playing. I couldn't talk to anyone. It was as if I wasn't even there. When we changed planes in Bogotá, I met a Uruguayan woman who was also going to Mexico to participate in the Tribunal and so then I had someone to talk to.

When we got to Mexico, I was impressed by the fact that there was a bunch of young people talking all different languages and they were there to meet all of us who were arriving. And they asked who was coming to the International Women's Year Conference. They made it easy for all of us to get through customs. Then I went to the hotel they told me to go to.

In Bolivia I'd read in the papers that for International Women's Year there'd be two places: one, the "Conference," was for the official representatives of the governments of all the countries, another, the "Tribunal," was for the representatives of the non-governmental organizations.

The Bolivian government sent its delegates to the conference. And these women traveled making fancy statements, saying that in Bolivia more than in any other place, women had achieved equality with men. And they went to the conference to say that. I was the only Bolivian woman invited for the Tribunal. There I met other Bolivian compañeras, but they were living in Mexico.

So I had this idea that there'd be two groups: one, on the government level, where those upper-class ladies would be; and the other, on the non-government level, where people like me would be, people with similar problems, you know, poor people. It was like a dream for me! Goodness, I said to myself, I'll be meeting peasant women and working women from all over the world. All of them are going to be just like us, oppressed and persecuted.

That's what I thought, see, because of what it said in the papers.

In the hotel I made friends with an Ecuadorian woman and went with her to the place where the Tribunal was being held. But I couldn't go till Monday. The sessions had already begun on Friday.

We went to a very big hall where there were four or five hundred women. The Ecuadorian said:

"Come on, compañera. Here's where they talk about the most important problems women have. So here's where we should make our voices heard."

There were no more seats. So we sat on some steps. We were very enthusiastic. We'd already missed a day of the Tribunal and we wanted to catch up, get up-to-date on what had been happening, find out what so many women were thinking, what they were saying about International Women's Year, what problems most concerned them.

It was my first experience and I imagined I'd hear things that would make me get ahead in life, in the struggle, in my work.

Well, at that moment a *gringa* went over to the microphone with her blond hair and with some things around her neck and her hands in her pockets, and she said to the assembly:

"I've asked for the microphone so I can tell you about my experience. Men should give us a thousand and one medals because we, the prostitutes, have the courage to go to bed with so many men."

A lot of women shouted "Bravo!" and applauded.

Well, my friend and I left because there were hundreds of prostitutes in there talking about their problems. And we went into another room. There were the lesbians. And there, also, their discussion was about how "they feel happy and proud to love another woman . . . that they should fight for their rights. . . ." Like that.

Those weren't my interests. And for me it was incompre-
hensible that so much money should be spent to discuss those
things in the Tribunal. Because I'd left my compañero with the
seven kids and him having to work in the mine every day. I'd
left my country to let people know what my homeland's like,
how it suffers, how in Bolivia the charter of the United Nations
isn't upheld. I wanted to tell people all that and hear what they
would say to me about other exploited countries and the other
groups that have already liberated themselves. And to run into
those other kinds of problems . . . I felt a bit lost. In other rooms,
some women stood up and said: men are the enemy . . . men
create wars, men create nuclear weapons, men beat women . . .
and so what's the first battle to be carried out to get equal rights
for women? First you have to declare war against men. If a man
has ten mistresses, well, the woman should have ten lovers also.
If a man spends all his money at the bar, partying, the women
have to do the same thing. And when we've reached that level,
then men and women can link arms and start struggling for the
liberation of their country, to improve the living conditions in
their country.

That was the mentality and the concern of several groups, and
for me it was a really rude shock. We spoke very different languages, no? And that made it difficult to work in the Tribunal.
Also, there was a lot of control over the microphone.

So a group of Latin American women got together and we
changed all that. And we made our common problems known,
what we thought women's progress was all about, how the majority of women live. We also said that for us the first and main task
isn't to fight against our compañeros, but with them to change the
system we live in for another, in which men and women will have
the right to live, to work, to organize.

At first you couldn't really notice how much control there was
in the Tribunal. But as the speeches and statements were made,
things started to change. For example, the women who defended
prostitution, birth control, and all those things, wanted to impose

their ideas as basic problems to be discussed in the Tribunal. For us they were real problems, but not the main ones.

For example, when they spoke of birth control, they said that we shouldn't have so many children living in such poverty, because we didn't even have enough to feed them. And they wanted to see birth control as something which would solve all the problems of humanity and malnutrition.

But, in reality, birth control, as those women presented it, can't be applied in my country. There are so few Bolivians by now that if we limited birth even more, Bolivia would end up without people. And then the wealth of our country would remain as a gift for those who want to control us completely, no? It's not that we ought to be living like we are, in miserable conditions. All that could be different, because Bolivia's a country with lots of natural resources. But our government prefers to see things their way, to justify the low level of life of the Bolivian people and the very low wages it pays the workers. And so they resort to indiscriminate birth control.

In one way or another, they tried to distract the Tribunal with problems that weren't basic. So we had to let the people know what was fundamental for us in all of that. Personally, I spoke several times. Short speeches, because we could only use the microphone for two minutes.

The movie *La Doble Jornada* [The Double Day], filmed by the Brazilian compañera who invited me to the Tribunal, was also useful in orienting people who didn't have any idea of what the life of a peasant woman or working woman is like in Latin America. In *La Doble Jornada* they show the women's lives, especially in relation to work. There you see how women live in the United States, in Mexico, in Argentina. There's a big contrast. But even more so when you see the part about Bolivia, because the compañera interviewed a worker in Las Lamas who was pregnant. In the interview she asked her: "Why aren't you taking it easy since you're expecting a baby?" The working woman said that she couldn't because she had to earn a living for her children and her husband too, because he's retired[19] and his pension is very small. "And the pension?" asked the Brazilian woman. Then the miner's wife explained that her husband had left the mine absolutely ruined physically and that all the money from the pension was spent trying to cure him. And that's why now she had to work, her children too, in order to support her husband.

Well, that was pretty strong stuff, and dramatic, no? And the compañeras at the Tribunal realized that I hadn't lied when I spoke about our situation.

When the movie was over, since I'd also been in it, they asked me to speak. So I said the situation was due to the fact that no government had bothered to create jobs for poor women. That the only work women do that's recognized is housework and, in any case, housework is done for free. Because, for example, they give me 14 pesos a month, in other words, two-thirds of a dollar a month, which is the family subsidy that's added to my husband's wage. What are 14 Bolivian pesos worth? With 14 pesos you can buy two bottles of milk or half a box of tea. . . .

That's why, I told them, you have to understand that we won't be able to find any solution to our problems as long as the capitalist system in which we live isn't changed.

Many of those women said that they'd only just begun to agree with me. Several of them wept.

The day the women spoke out against imperialism, I spoke too. And I said how we live totally dependent on foreigners for everything, how they impose what they want on us, economically as well as culturally.

In the Tribunal I learned a lot also. In the first place, I learned to value the wisdom of my people even more. There, everyone who went up to the microphone said: "I'm a professional person, I represent such and such organization. . . ." And blah-blah-blah, she gave her speech. "I'm a teacher," "I'm a lawyer," "I'm a journalist,"

---

19. Retired as an invalid. For the majority of miners, the invalid condition is caused by silicosis.

said the others. And blah-blah-blah, they'd begin to give their opinion.

Then I'd say to myself: "Here there are professionals, lawyers, teachers, journalists who are going to speak. And me ... what am I doing in this?" And I felt a bit insecure, unsure of myself. I couldn't work up the guts to speak. When I went up to the microphone for the first time, standing before so many "titled" people, I introduced myself, feeling like a nothing, and I said: "Well, I'm the wife of a mine worker from Bolivia." I was still afraid, see?

I worked up the courage to tell them about the problems that were being discussed there. Because that was my obligation. And I stated my ideas so that everyone in the world could hear us, through the Tribunal.

That led to my having a discussion with Betty Friedan, who is the great feminist leader in the United States. She and her group had proposed some points to amend the "World Plan of Action." But these were mainly feminist points and we didn't agree with them because they didn't touch on some problems that are basic for Latin American women.

Betty Friedan invited us to join them. She asked us to stop our "warlike activity" and said that we were being "manipulated by men," that "we only thought about politics," and that we'd completely ignored women's problems, "like the Bolivian delegation does, for example," she said.

So I asked for the floor. But they wouldn't give it to me. And so I stood up and said:

"Please forgive me for turning this Tribunal into a marketplace. But I was mentioned and I have to defend myself. I was invited to the Tribunal to talk about women's rights and in the invitation they sent me there was also the document approved by the United Nations which is its charter, where women's right to participate, to organize, is recognized. And Bolivia signed that charter, but in reality it's only applied there to the bourgeoisie."

I went on speaking that way. And a lady, who was the president of the Mexican delegation, came up to me. She wanted to give me her own interpretation of the International Women's Year Tribunal's slogan, which was "Equality, development, and peace." And she said:

"Let's speak about us, Señora. We're women. Look, Señora, forget the suffering of your people. For a moment, forget the massacres. We've talked enough about that. We've heard you enough. Let's talk about us . . . about you and me . . . well, about women."

So I said:

"All right, let's talk about the two of us. But if you'll let me, I'll begin. Señora, I've known you for a week. Every morning you show up in a different outfit and on the other hand, I don't. Every day you show up all made up and combed like someone who has time to spend in an elegant beauty parlor and who can spend money on that, and yet I don't. I see that each afternoon you have a chauffeur in a car waiting at the door of this place to take you home, and yet I don't. And in order to show up here like you do, I'm sure you live in a really elegant home, in an elegant neighborhood, no? And yet we miners' wives only have a small house on loan to us, and when our husbands die or get sick or are fired from the company, we have ninety days to leave the house and then we're in the street.

"Now, Señora, tell me: is your situation at all similar to mine? Is my situation at all similar to yours? So what equality are we going to speak of between the two of us? If you and I aren't alike, if you and I are so different? We can't, at this moment, be equal, even as women, don't you think?"

But at that moment, another Mexican woman came up and said:

"Listen, you, what do you want? She's the head of the Mexican delegation and she has the right to speak first. Besides, we've been very tolerant here with you, we've heard you over the radio, on the television, in the papers, in the Tribunal. I'm tired of applauding you."

It made me mad that she said that, because it seemed to me that the problems I presented were being used then just to turn me into some kind of play character who should be applauded. I felt they were treating me like a clown.

"Listen, Señora," I said to her. "Who asked for your applause? If problems could be solved that way, I wouldn't have enough hands to applaud and I certainly wouldn't have had to come from Bolivia to Mexico, leaving my children behind, to speak here about our problems. Keep your applause to yourself, because I've received the most beautiful applause of my life, and that was from the calloused hands of the miners."

And we had a pretty strong exchange of words.

In the end they said to me:

"Well, you think you're so important. Get up there and speak."

So I went up and spoke. I made them see that they don't live in our world. I made them see that in Bolivia human rights aren't respected and they apply what we call "the law of the funnel": broad for some, narrow for others. That those ladies who got together to play canasta and applaud the government have full guarantees, full support. But women like us, housewives, who get organized to better our people, well, they beat us up and persecute us. They couldn't see all those things. They couldn't see the suffering of my people, they couldn't see how our compañeros are vomiting their lungs bit by bit, in pools of blood. They didn't see how underfed our children are. And, of course, they didn't know, as we do, what it's like to get up at four in the morning and go to bed at eleven or twelve at night, just to be able to get all the housework done, because of the lousy conditions we live in.

"You," I said, "what can you possibly understand about all that? For you, the solution is fighting with men. And that's it. But for us it isn't that way, that isn't the basic solution."

When I finished saying all that, moved by the anger I felt, I left the platform. And many women came up to me, and at the exit from the hall, many were happy and said I should go back to the Tribunal and represent the Latin American women who were there.

I felt ashamed to think I hadn't been able to evaluate the wisdom of the people well enough. Because, look: I, who hadn't studied in the university, or even gone to school, I, who wasn't a teacher or a professional or a lawyer or a professor, what had I done in the Tribunal? What I'd said was only what I'd heard my people say ever since I was little, my parents, my compañeros, the leaders, and I saw that the people's experience is the best schooling there is. What I learned from the people's life was the best teaching. And I wept to think: how great is my people!

We Latin American women issued a document about the way we see the role of women in underdeveloped countries, with everything we felt was important to say on that occasion. And the press published it.

Another thing that I got out of the Tribunal was meeting compañeras from other countries, especially the Bolivians, Argentines, Uruguayans, Chileans, who'd been in similar situations to those I'd experienced in prisons, jails, and all those problems. I learned a lot from them.

I think I fulfilled the mission that the compañeras and companeros from Siglo XX gave me. In the Tribunal we were with a lot of women from all over the world, and we made everyone who was represented there aware of my country.

It was also a great experience being with so many women and seeing how many, many people are dedicated to the struggle for the liberation of their oppressed peoples.

I also think it was important for me to see once again—and on that occasion in contact with more than five thousand women from all over—how the interests of the bourgeoisie really aren't our interests.

MEETINGS WITH EXILES

During my stay in Mexico, I had the opportunity to meet several Bolivians and spend time with them. Some were exiles who'd left the country in 1971. Many of them had been in prison and then expelled from the country, others had fled, others had sought asylum in the embassies. Of the ones I met there, I only knew one from before, who had come with some students to the mine.

I was impressed to see all those professionals there. I didn't find workers or peasants. Of course, I know there are some exiled in other countries, but, really, the people who leave the country are mostly professionals, no?

I noticed in the exiles very good intentions; they act in solidarity with the people of Bolivia, they don't forget their people.

Personally, they treated me very well, they gave me their help, they made me very comfortable, they had my knee operated on, they even helped me get my teeth fixed which had been broken the second time I was in jail. There wasn't a single compañero or compañera who didn't show me solidarity.

The Bolivians also helped me get in touch with the people I had to see. In Mexico I had all the comforts I don't have here. I had a bed with a mattress, I had a bathroom to myself, I had water and electricity in the house, I had my meals cooked.

But despite all the comfort I found in Mexico, I never felt the desire to stay and have all that, as long as the people in Bolivia are suffering so much. Instead of feeling happy, I thought about how in the mine the people have to walk, how the women, even when they're pregnant, have to carry such heavy loads along such long roads. I thought about the miners of San Florencio who have to go all the way to Siglo XX to buy things. I thought about the women who have to travel several kilometers to reach home after having sold something in the market, and only then start to get some food ready. All that made me feel uncomfortable; me, who'd come to Mexico as a leader invited to the International Women's Year Conference, to speak as a representative of poor and working women.

Of course, I dream of the day when I'll have all those comforts. Yes, I like comfort, but I want it for everyone, for all my people. I don't want it for me alone. I'd like to have all that comfort, but I can't accept it while my people are dying of hunger, living in misery, working so hard. I can't. When we all have comfort, good living, then we'll all be happy, because we won't have to think maybe the neighbor isn't eating today or can't get over a sickness.

No longer will we feel ashamed of having a nice new outfit while the rest can't.

That's why in Mexico I missed my people and my environment so much, and I wanted to get back home soon.

A man told us we are like fish who need to be in the water and that die out of the water. And the day that we, the leaders, the ones who are on our way, aren't in the heart of the masses, then that day we'll die. And I really believe that it's easy to die apart from them. Because if a leader isn't with his or her people, that person can't feel happy. And I believe that all who call themselves revolutionaries or are so called, have the obligation to return to the people and fight by their side.

And while they're outside the country, the revolutionaries who've fought for their country shouldn't forget the people who continue fighting in Bolivia in the mines, in the countryside, in the factories, facing the repression which still goes on. They shouldn't forget this and instead should try to prepare themselves as much as possible for their return, in order to respond to the demands the people will make on them.

Those who remain outside calmly, without doing anything, waiting for us to win the victory, those are really traitors to the people, aren't they?

And it's always possible to do something during the time one can't return home. I mean that we, the revolutionaries, shouldn't believe in borders, and wherever a revolutionary is, he or she should transmit the experience of our people to others who are interested in it, especially to the working class and peasants.

1976

WHAT MY PEOPLE WANT

After the Tribunal I stayed in Mexico for two months more, because of my health. I wrote to my family several times, but it seems the letters were lost. And that caused many rumors about my delay; some compañeros even went to La Paz to protest, thinking that the Ministry of the Interior was making problems for me. But it wasn't so.

On returning here, I informed the workers and the committee about what I'd done in Mexico. I also spoke over the radio. It wasn't as much as I would have liked, but I did tell everything they allowed me to.

During my stay in Mexico, several leaders of the Central Obrera Boliviano had been imprisoned, about twenty-nine I think. They grabbed them during a clandestine meeting they were having in Oruro and jailed them, held them incommunicado. When I returned, I found out that in Cochabamba the workers of La Manaco had called a strike. La Manaco is a shoe factory of the Bata Company, from Canada. That factory's pretty big, they have about eighty workers. They're the workers with the longest tradition of revolutionary struggle in Bolivia.

The Siglo XX leaders supported the La Manaco workers in their speeches. The workers showed their solidarity by giving over one day's pay. A commission went to give them food. It was a great strike, because others also joined in, especially the university students and several peasant groups. The La Manaco workers were able to win several of their demands.

In Siglo XX, I also found several changes. For example, the leader, Bernal, with whom the committee had worked pretty well, had resigned from the union, and there were new elections.

In January of that year there was a meeting of the Housewives' Committee in front of the grocery store to protest the raising of prices of some articles, and also the poor quality of the milk for infants.

In that meeting I was reelected as secretary-general of the committee, and they also chose me to represent the committee in the miners' congress in Corocoro.

The miners had a lot of things to work out. We had a lot of things to discuss. But since the company didn't want to recognize our rank-and-file commissions, they'd decided to discuss matters with delegations from each section. For example, from the workshop section, the extraction section, the factory, each one went on its own to present its case. The company promised several things, more to some of them and less to others. And, in the end, they fooled everyone.

So, we decided to meet in a congress at Corocoro to present our problems once and for all in a general way.

At first the government opposed the congress. They tried to say we wanted to overthrow the government, that we were in a subversive plot. But later on they didn't say anything.

On May 1 of that year, the congress at Corocoro began. Representatives of all the miners' unions participated. There were also four representatives of the Housewives' Committee: two from Siglo XX and two from Cataví.

Many things were discussed in that congress. For example, whether unions are useful or not, the rejection of the measures adopted by the government in November 1974, solidarity with political prisoners and exiles. Things like that.

But the first goal was a wage increase in proportion to the cost of living. Another problem that was pointed out was the pension, which is so low it's not enough to live on, and there are thousands of workers who are sick with mine sickness and who now survive on a pension. The widows also have a serious problem, that is, they receive a pension for only five years after their husband's death. And if they remarry, the pension is immediately withdrawn. And many other problems that affect us were brought up in the congress so that we could look for a solution.

There were several commissions set up to touch on the different problems. We housewives insisted on the economic question. For that reason, we analyzed our situation in the last six months, in other words, since Banzer took power.

"The economic situation throughout the country," we said, "has become more and more difficult. With the measures adopted by the government, such as the monetary devaluation and the economic package, the cost of living has risen terribly. As if that weren't enough, years ago our children were very small and therefore our needs were smaller; with the years, they've grown and increased in number, and the cost of clothing and food has also gone up.

"Our husbands' strength gets used up day by day and they're getting older, because work is hard and the low wages they earn don't allow them to replace all the energy they use up, and we're condemned to be widowed at any moment, either because of the mine sickness which affects them, or because of some kind of accident, because industrial safety is very bad; almost nothing's done to guarantee the safety and life of our companeros.

"The worst thing is that we don't even have a roof over our heads, because with the low wages that our compañeros earn, we can't even get a small dwelling. We can't even get one from the 'housing cooperatives' anymore, because in the past years they've been offering houses that cost up to 100,000 pesos. And when would we be able to pay that? Everyone wants to get rich off the workers.

"In some ways, the peasants' situation is still enviable in comparison with the miners'. It's said that the 'land belongs to those who work it,' and if a peasant has tilled a hectare of land [hectare =2.74 acres], when he dies his children continue to till it, they go on having the land. On the other hand, the miners, despite the fact that they've worked and removed tons and tons of earth and given the country so much wealth, benefiting everyone by their sacrifice, it turns out that when they die, their families have ninety days to get out of the small house that the company loaned them during the miner's life: the widow's thrown out into the street, without being able to get work, neither she nor her children, on the pretext that they're going to enjoy the small pension which isn't even enough to pay the rent on a room; and in other cases they don't even get that small pension, because the worker has died before having paid up all his dues to the social security fund.

"The lack of jobs also means that our older children can't work at anything, despite the fact that the sons have already done their military service.

"And what can be said about their education? Many workers' children are studying in different schools in the country, where they have to send tuition, food, clothing, supplies, the cost of renting living quarters, transportation, and other necessities. The other children stay behind and they have to be dressed, fed, educated; and even though they say that education in the mines is free, we always have to buy uniforms, books, school supplies, different kinds of paints, and other materials that they need. The worst thing is when the people in charge decide to end the school year without caring about the bad effects of this on our children."

That was our analysis of the situation. And we explained that that was why we supported the demands of the workers for a wage increase.

In Corocoro our participation was pretty good. In the first presentation, we told the workers that we were happy they were able to have the congress in spite of its being banned. And that the men should realize that they weren't alone in their struggle because in each and every home we're exploited by the boss, COMIBOL, because everything we do in the home isn't considered as work and it would be wrong to think that only the paid worker is exploited: his family is also. And that in the congress we should write up a good document that would be useful for the working-class movement.

Our speech was heard over the radio and then they invited us to give a talk in the school during our stay in Corocoro. And after that talk, the students decided that I should speak to their mothers. We accepted, fixed the day and the time, and when we got there, they were there with their mothers and fathers. It was a pretty good meeting and the Housewives' Committee of Corocoro was organized. And that committee was seated in the congress, and the president was a young *mestizo or cholita* who spoke very well about women's interests in struggling side by side with the workers. In the papers I read that they'd begun to work. But now I don't know what's going on, because there was a lot of repression in Corocoro, the army went inside the mine, they arrested men and women, and we lost contact with those compañeras.

In the congress we also made the following motion: Housewives' committees should be organized in all the mines and a congress of women should be called as soon as possible in order to immediately form the National Housewives' Federation, affiliated with the Central Obrera Boliviano, just as we women of Siglo XX are affiliated right now. The motion was approved. But because of the events which followed we couldn't carry out our plan. Since then, I've found out that the "nationalist women," in other words, the women who support the present government, are going to hold a national congress in the mines.

Despite the maneuvers on the part of government agents who'd infiltrated the congress, the position of the workers' representatives won out. And a document asking for a wage increase was approved.

Before the discussion and approval of the document, we saw a chart that showed how much a general earns, how much a colonel earns, etc., etc. There were incomes of 20,000 to 25,000 pesos a month,[20] while the workers here only earn up to 2,000 pesos. A study was also done on how many calories a worker needs to live on, how much he has to eat to get them, and how much he has to earn in order to cover all his personal necessities and those of his family. They added some basic human necessities, such as clothing, shoes, entertainment—not even that—but, for example, a newspaper so that they can be informed. They arrived at an average of 170 pesos a day which the worker would have to earn in order to live normally. Well, since they give us cheap groceries, we get from those expenses an average of 40 pesos a day contributed by the worker in order to have price-frozen items, which reduces to 130 pesos a day the minimum wage he should earn. The Miners' Federation said that they'd asked for 80 pesos a day and that it was better to stick to that. So we accepted.

We also said that the workday of the inner-mine workers should be reduced to six hours, because of the situation they live in, so that they'd have time to rest up properly.

The problem is that we proposed all that and we gave the government thirty days to answer us. If they didn't, the working class would declare an indefinite strike.

The government's answer came before our cut-off date. First they arrested the members of the Mine Workers' Federation; then there was military intervention in the mines, they raided our transmitters, even Pius XII Radio was raided, they declared military zones, they arrested and persecuted all the leaders and many other workers.

On June 9 the army sneaked into the inner mine when the workers were there and they began the persecution, especially of those

---

20. In Bolivia, the high military hierarchy receives, in addition to their salaries, other sums from para-state institutions or from the administration, in which the officers hold important posts. These are supplemented by vouchers, honoraria, travel fees, expense accounts, food, uniforms, tax-free imports, and so on.

who'd taken part in the congress at Corocoro. The workers they took were terribly beaten in the Uncia barracks and taken to the cells in La Paz. Many were deported to Chile, turned over to Pinochet.

They made us listen to a whole lot of slanderous statements. Among other things, that we were plotting against the government. And so they took advantage of the fact that the miners had had a demonstration to protest the assassination of General Torres in Argentina and the fact that Banzer's government wouldn't accept the repatriation of his remains. That day the workers only had a demonstration, because they wanted to save their strength for a strike if it were necessary. The army took advantage of that, too, in order to shut down our transmitters, raid our homes, pressure and mistreat us in all kinds of ways.

It was noon. We were having lunch, as usual. After lunch, my little child said: "Mommy, take me to the bathroom." So I took him to the bank of the river.[21] Suddenly I noticed a special kind of silence in Llallagua, which isn't usually like that at noon, because there's always the sound of radios, music, etc. And I asked myself: Why is it so quiet in Llallagua? I began looking around . . . and I realized that along the main street the soldiers were going from door to door.

"The army! The army's coming in!"

I ran toward the radio station and there I found two compañeros and I told them that the army was coming in. But right there on the corner the soldiers showed up.

The soldiers took over the transmitter and then we women asked ourselves: "What shall we do? What shall we do? How can we let the workers inside the mine know?" Because they didn't know.

Someone was able to inform the compañeros inside the mine that the mine had been occupied, that the radio stations had been taken over.

Then, on leaving work, in the entrance to the mine, the miners held a meeting and called an indefinite strike.

That night they called us. They said to my husband: "The leaders

---

21. The Ch'aqui Mayo, the Dry River, which separates Siglo XX from Llallagua.

have to go into the mine. We're going to organize a strike committee, we're going to resist from inside, because they'll be safer there.
There's no way to escape from the houses."

Inside the mine one can hide, because it's like a city. There are
some 800 kilometers of underground tunnels and different mine
entrances which only those who know the mine very well are able
to use, see?

We went into the mine and organized the strike committee.
And the first instructions were sent out: we must maintain unity
among the workers. We must only trust the real leaders and not
accept instructions from others who use the union for other purposes that don't benefit the working class. We must collect food in
order to last out the strike. We must share everything we have with
the soldiers, because we have to understand that they're our sons
and are forced to take a position against us. The housewives must
organize and, if the company grocery store is closed down, have a
protest demonstration. These were the first mandates.

All night long we took turns standing guard. The next day, too.
Without eating. Pretty late, some workers brought us food and
told us that the night before the army had raided almost all the
homes and had arrested a lot of people.

And some agents infiltrated and were with us in the mine. When
we discovered that, we had to go much deeper into the shaft.

My husband and I and another compañero were taken to a place
called San Miguel. They got me a slab of tarboard and they put
it on the floor so I could rest, because I was expecting and was
already in my ninth month. That situation was too much for me. I
couldn't stand the stench in the inner mine because of the gas and
the lack of air. I was thirsty, hungry, I was really too tired.

That's how we were all day Thursday. On Friday at dawn, I
couldn't take it any longer. I was suffocating. I couldn't breathe.

"I don't feel well," I told my husband. "I can't take any more."

"What shall we do?" he asked.

"Let's get out," I answered. "Even if they arrest me, it doesn't
matter. I can't take any more."

"I'll find out if we can leave by Cancaniri," he said.

He left and found out that we could.

So he took me out through the Cancañiri mine entrance. There a compañero helped us to get out. We went to the drugstore and they gave me medicine. That way I was able to get home.

On the way we passed hundreds of soldiers:

"Halt! Where are you going?" they'd shout at us.

"I'm taking my wife. She's about to give birth," my compañero would say.

"Go ahead," they answered.

So that way we were able to get home, always going by special shortcuts. I was trembling with cold, because it was six or seven in the morning. My sister gave me something hot to drink and I rested a while.

But right away some women came to the house and told me that the army was occupying the grocery store. They asked me to go and talk to the army people so that they'd keep it open at least one day more.

When we reached the grocery store, there were some high-ranking officers who insulted us arrogantly, with that sick hatred they have for the working class. One of them shouted: "Come on, fast! Close it up! These lazy good-for-nothings. You had your little strike all prepared, eh? Lazy good-for-nothings, we'll see if you stay out of work. You'll have to starve to death. You can eat your shit, you lousy bitches! Today we'll take away your groceries, tomorrow we'll cut the water, day after tomorrow we'll cut your electricity off. We'll see who's going to win. If you want a hit over the head, we'll give you a hit over the head; if you want bullets, we'll give you bullets."

The hands of the grocery store manager were trembling and he couldn't put the padlock on. I turned to speak with the compañeras in order to see what we'd do, but they weren't there anymore. They'd left because they were scared.

And my son arrived, he grabbed my hand and said:

"Mommy! What are you doing here? The agents are on their way to grab you."

My son had seen some agents informing the colonel:

"That Chungara woman has gone with a group of women who are armed with sticks and rocks to attack the grocery store. . . ."

So the commander said:

"Didn't they say that woman's pregnant? And she's doing that?"

"Yes, she went with them a little while ago."

"And what do they want? Go get her. Bring her here to me, and we'll kick that brat out of her."

The officer had said that. Luckily my son heard him and came running to warn me. I was just barely able to save myself.

The streets were so full of soldiers that it was very difficult to escape. Along each row of houses there were four soldiers walking up and down, passing each other, two on each corner.

Since I knew they were going to arrest me, I spoke to my family; I told them that I was going to leave the house and not come back. And that they shouldn't look for me, because I didn't even know where I'd go.

I went out with no fixed destination. And, well, just like that, I knocked on any old door and asked them to let me at least spend the night. The workers showed a lot of solidarity: "Of course, Señora, come in and rest." For ten days I hid like that, from one house to another.

On that same night, the agents went into my house. My children had locked themselves in. They knocked on the door and the kids didn't open. That happened three or four times, until the agents entered over the yard wall. And they began to ask the kids arrogantly:

"Where's your mother?"

"She's not here."

"Where is she?"

"We don't know."

"You mean you, her very own children, don't know? Now we'll teach you to answer. Get up, God dammit!"

So my eleven-year-old daughter began to laugh. And she said to them laughing:

"Do you really think my mommy's so dumb? Knowing that you'd look for her, do you really think she'd tell us where she is? My mommy isn't so dumb and hasn't told us where she went."

One of the agents got really tough. But the other one said:

"She's right. Their mother wasn't stupid enough to tell them. Let's go. And you, lock the door. The bird has flown the coop."

But before leaving, they searched the house, under the beds, everywhere. When they saw that my children didn't cry, they said: "These kids are well trained."

According to what some families told me, the army raided houses every day and every night, thinking they'd find me.

During those days, President Banzer came to Catavi. He arrived without warning, after landing in Uncía. But he didn't want to talk with the real workers' leaders. He absolutely refused to. Instead, he said he was going to appoint other rank-and-file coordinators.

The repression by the agents from the DOP (Department of Political Order) began. Then some really sad things happened.

For example, they began grabbing the kids in the street and beating them to make them sign documents written by the DOP agents. Then they'd show these signed documents to the parents. And in order to get the kids out of jail, they made the parents sign something saying they'd end the strike and go back to work. Some of them, in order to get their kids back, wept as they did it.

Apart from that, the agents grabbed the kids in the streets and told their parents: "Your child's a subversive. Now, if you don't want him or her taken to La Paz, you've got to pay 500 pesos, 800 pesos." I know one woman whose two kids weren't involved in anything, but she had to pay 2,000 pesos to free them. Many parents were in that situation, looking for money, selling their things to free their children.

They pressured us in many ways. On the radio, which was no longer "The Miner's Voice" but the voice of the military, they said that anywhere between 50 percent and 80 percent of the workers had gone back to work. And they incited other strikers to do the same. But it was a pack of lies, no one had gone back to work.

They got back at us in so many ways. The last rank-and-file delegates they arrested were brutally beaten and with a gun to their heads were made to turn in the leaders and to say: "They're being paid by foreigners, we don't want to be fooled by them anymore, and we're going back to work for the good of the country."

Some families were already beginning to suffer from real hunger. And so the women began to organize "people's soup kitchens" so that no one would go hungry. In the mining camps they collected food. Everyone gave what they could: a bit of flour, rice, noodles. And that was distributed to those who needed it most.

They also sent food and clothing from La Paz and Cochabamba, but all of that remained at the main gate of Playa Verde. The army wouldn't let it through.

During the whole strike, which was really long, news of the solidarity of other sectors in the country reached the workers. The university students, the factory workers, the peasants, the workers in the privately owned mines, all showed their solidarity. But the press and the radio didn't say anything about that, because everything was well controlled by the government.

A woman came in saying she was from the Red Cross and she got all the women of Cataví together. And she said to them:

"My daughters, tell your husbands to go back to work. Do you want another massacre here? You've got to get them to agree and break the strike. They shouldn't lend themselves to working for people who are paid from abroad."

She was very dramatic, she wept as she spoke.

Then a woman said:

"But I can't even ask my husband to go back to work because he's in jail. And the only thing he did was to ask for a wage increase, because we don't have enough to live on. I myself have had to sell my clothes, I've sold my jewelry, even my wedding ring, to buy food. Who's going to fix this situation? Who do we work for? Why do our husbands have to kill themselves?"

And the woman said:

"Everything will be fixed through dialogue, my child."

Then they began to distrust her and one of them said:

"You came here as a Red Cross worker. Well, show us your credentials."

The woman answered then that she wasn't with the Red Cross, that she was a leader of the nationalist women.

The compañeras got upset and asked her:

"How can you say that you're on our side and then you treat our leaders so badly?" According to what a friend told me, another woman said:

"You're persecuting our compañera Domitila de Chungara so much, and she's expecting a baby."

"Ay! . . . Don't even talk to me about that woman. That woman is paid by foreigners, by the Cubans, the Russians, the Chinese, and now she's paying 30 pesos a day so that the workers stay on strike."

They say that they got furious and the woman had to leave.

Well, they couldn't break the strike, not even by saying to people, "You're all fired as of tomorrow," because no one went back to work; so then they closed down the grocery store. They just closed it down, for a whole week.

Then they changed their minds. "Let them have their grocery store again, because they'll get back into debt with everything they buy and then they'll have to go back to work." And so, at the crack of dawn, the wives of the local agents went to stock up. But the other women said: "Since they took away our grocery store, let them keep it." They closed the store and stoned the other women. The agents broke it up, they tear-gassed them and they even arrested some of them.

Since they couldn't break the strike with threats or punishment, the agents began to gather the unemployed to go work. They even went to the countryside and distributed food to the peasants, and told them that they'd pay them to work in the mine. They even dressed the soldier boys in civilian clothes so they could begin working.

The peasants accepted the food, but they didn't come. Because they knew that they live off what we buy from them, and also the miners are mostly of peasant origin. I myself was able to speak with some peasants. And they said: "How could we go into the mine, if it's our sons, our godchildren, who work there? Besides, we don't know how to work in the mine, we're afraid of the dynamite."

So none of that worked out, because very few people came. The unemployed who the agents were able to convince did go in to work, but it turns out that, since they didn't know how to work in the mines, several of them died in accidents or other ways.

The agents reported over our radios that 55 percent had gone back to work. And in the papers they showed people working. But in reality it wasn't the company's workers, it was the scabs who'd been sent to break the strike.

The women organized themselves into shock groups against the strikebreakers. One day, at about six in the morning, some women stoned several trucks in the Salvadora camp, because they were transporting the scabs.

Since the men couldn't do anything anymore because they'd be arrested and imprisoned, the women organized spontaneously with their children and stood in front of the mine entrances.

Very early in the morning, they were at the mine entrances. They put children on the rails so that the convoy couldn't go in. And they said that if they wanted the train to go forward, it would have to go over the children. And the people who went into the mine to work were treated really badly by the women: "Cowards! We have seven, eight children and we're sticking with the strike; how can you sell out and go back to work?" They stoned them and made them get out.

So they sent the army to drag the women away. When they got there and saw that it was just women and children, the soldiers didn't dare do anything. The officers wanted to force them and they shouted: "These women are communists and we've got to destroy them! Those aren't women, those aren't children, nothing like that!"

And they made them sing a marching song and move forward. But the mothers with their children began to sing: "Long live my country, Bolivia." And the scene was so impressive, they tell me, that the army couldn't do anything. And because even that had failed, the officers called the agents out to tear-gas and disperse everyone.

Well, since there hadn't been a real clash between the army and the women and children, they brought in policewomen from La Paz. Early the next day, they were at the mine entrance. They're strong women, all of them trained in karate. And our women, when they heard the policewomen had arrived, didn't go to the mine entrance. So the policewomen couldn't pull it off.

But anyway they began to carry out the other task they'd been given: to raid houses and kick out the families of the men who'd been imprisoned.

Those families were given a notice, like in 1965, saying they had twenty-four hours to get out of their houses. But how can someone get up and leave in twenty-four hours, especially if they have nowhere to go? So the women ignored the notices. Then the army commissioner and the management sent the policewomen to take the families off in a truck.

They told me that fairly early, at about seven in the morning, the policewomen arrived at the house of compañero Severo Torres, who'd been arrested and exiled. His wife was pretty sick and they have a "staircase" of eight children.

The most moving scene was when the policewomen made the woman and her children get out of bed and began to load the truck with all their things and to make the children get into it. A little boy came out clutching his bottle of tea, because in the mines they drink very little milk. Another little one came out with his bottle too, but with only sugar water in it. Another with a piece of bread, and like that, all naked and trembling with cold. That's how they came, one by one, out of the house.

One of the policewomen couldn't contain herself any longer. She went behind the house and began crying. She was very nervous and sobbed loudly.

A worker saw her and asked:

"Why are you crying? Why are you crying? Do you know who those children's father is? He's a worker who went to the miners' congress and proposed a wage hike so he could bring more bread home, so he could buy milk and fill those bottles you see full of water or tea. That was the crime committed by the father of those children. And that's why they're sending you now to kick out his whole family."

The policewoman cried and said that she didn't understand, that they'd told them one thing at La Paz and she was seeing something else in the mine. And she continued crying.

Then the neighbor woman said:

"Why get upset? We'll finish your job."

And they put the children into the truck. The whole family was taken to La Paz. To this day we don't know what happened to them.

We don't know the exact number of people in prison, either, or those who are fugitives, those who were exiled. Well, in Siglo XX alone, more than sixty families are in that situation. That's happened in several parts of the country. Many, many workers were fired by the company.

They told me there's a government plan to take those evicted families to San Julián. Some women thought that San Julián was another mine. But no. It's a tropical place in the department of Santa Cruz. Well, I know that a human being has the capacity to adapt and to develop mechanisms to protect himself or herself. For example, we're used to the cold of the highlands and we have reserves to protect ourselves from it. But the same doesn't hold true for the heat. And since almost all the workers have mine sickness, the tropical climate is fatal and speeds up their death. Since those are virgin regions, they haven't been worked yet. They have to begin from scratch, from cutting down the trees and killing the insects. The miners who go there don't have the necessary material, they don't have conditions to start their lives again there, so they end up as peons of other people who come with more money and more possibilities, see?

On June 22—we'd been on strike thirteen days—I realized that

I was about to give birth. So I called for my husband and asked him to go speak with the Red Cross to ask for guarantees, so that I wouldn't be bothered in the hospital.

My arrival at the hospital was a surprise, because over the radio they'd announced that I'd had twins and that I'd had them inside the mine, and that I could leave, that there were full guarantees for me. Another rumor was that Banzer's wife had come and had been touched by my condition, and that, weeping, she'd taken me to La Paz with my little children and that I was being well taken care of in a clinic. They told people not to worry about me anymore, that the government had been good to me and that the president's wife herself had taken charge of me.

I don't know why they spread such ridiculous stories. Maybe it was a weapon so that I would show up as I was and they could grab me? Or maybe it was so that the compañeros and compañeras would believe that I'd sold out to the government? I don't know. But it was a surprise for everyone when they saw me arrive in an ambulance. There I found out everything that they'd said about me.

In the hospital I was well taken care of, by the director and the midwife and nurses. And I had my two children. My little daughter Paola was born well. But the other one, a little boy, had smothered to death, the doctor told me, and was already beginning to rot inside me. The placenta was also rotting. That's why it was so hard for me that time getting better. I stayed in the hospital till August 6.

My husband went to the Red Cross as soon as he got the company ambulance and had left me in the hospital.

The people from the Red Cross arrived and said they'd been very worried about me, that there'd been a lot of rumors and that they had spoken with the government on my behalf, because of my condition. From that moment on, I was under the protection of the Red Cross and they told me I shouldn't be afraid, that I should rest like a mother deserves. They told the director of the hospital not to allow anyone to mistreat me.

I was in the ward where we workers' wives are put. Then the director sent me to the ward for employees, which is smaller and safer.

In the hospital I got news from the people who came to visit me. The only way I participated there was in the hunger strike that all the people in the hospital carried out one day.

A compañera came to the hospital badly wounded: the agents had beaten her badly and she had to be operated on. Some women came over and said: "How can we accept being so well taken care of here, eating several times a day, while our compañeros are suffering so much?" So that day we didn't eat a bite.

I wasn't bothered at all by government agents. Neither before nor after my little girl was born. First, because I'd been in hiding before the birth and then, because I'd gotten the Red Cross's protection. But they looked for me all over the place, and several families really suffered because of me, because they raided their houses looking for me. One day, before I went to the hospital, the agents came in, searched every bed, even in the maternity ward. Some of them spent the night in the hospital because they knew I was going to give birth and they wanted to be sure to get me.

Aside from that, the nationalist women sent out documents in the name of the Housewives' Committee and had them read over the radio. It was all meant to confuse people, wasn't it?

So then we wrote up a manifesto, explaining the committee's real position. In that manifesto we repeated the proposals we'd made in the congress at Corocoro and we spoke out against what was happening in the mines then. And we asked:

"Officers, when have we workers ransacked your homes the way you're doing to ours? Do you know what it's like to work in the mines? Do you know of the miseries and sadness of the working class? No, señores! You only know how to kill the people and you don't know how to contribute economically to the country. While you have good things, cars, homes, servants, the workers have their misery, their malnutrition, their lungs punctured by silicosis, and now they have a gun pointing at their heads. You don't know what it is to start out working as a healthy person and soon end up dead, smashed to bits, leaving your family in absolute misery."

We said more:

"The people in the government forget that we're no longer in the Spanish colonial period and that we won't work with a gun pointed at our heads; we're workers and not slaves, and we aren't going to allow the mercenaries to do whatever lousy thing occurs to them while we can't even open our mouths. If the government keeps up like this, we'll be forced to emigrate to other countries, where they treat us as human beings and we promise to work and bring greatness to those countries which open their doors to us. Let the military work in the mines."

And in the end we came out in support of everything the unions had agreed on.

It was important to clear up our situation, wasn't it? Because another Housewives' Committee had been organized here. A woman came from La Paz to elect new leaders and offer seventeen scholarships to study. Well, there were women who sold out, they allied themselves with some women workers and were their representatives. Even some of the secretaries of our committee have collaborated with that group, according to what I read and heard.

Now it's not safe to do anything. For example, after the strike we wanted to make some proposals to the company but they answered us: "The Housewives' Committee has disappeared. There are no more housewives."

At this moment I think that if the union—which is the maximum authority of the working class here—doesn't have guarantees of being able to function, then our committee—which was organized to work alongside the union—won't be able to work either, right? To make our committee into a nationalist organization which helps the government would be to betray the ideals of the working class. That's why I think we're outlawed also. But we can't collaborate with this government.

I don't think that the majority on the grassroots level is confused by the creation of the new committee. When I left the hospital, several women came up and said: "Rest for a while, take care of yourself, because right now we can't do anything." I think that it will be the rank and file who, at the right moment, will judge us.

So many things have happened that one doesn't even know what to say. For example, given that some leaders are in prison, others underground, others sold out, and that the workers are silent right now, there are people who say that we leaders only manipulate the masses, that there isn't really any strength in the working class.

I remember that in the past, there were also periods when we had problems and they arrested and even killed the leaders. Nevertheless, others sprang up. So I think that now once again we're in a period of recession. It's only been a few months that we've been living like this. I hope that this situation will be temporary and that we'll continue like we have at other times. Because if it weren't so, the government would have been able to simply wipe out the leaders, and put an end to the working class of Bolivia a while ago, no?

Of course, the problem we're facing now is quite serious. Because since August 4, after twenty-nine days on strike, the workers returned to their workplaces, but without getting what they'd demanded. Now we're living in a military zone, almost in slavery. Even though the government agreed to raise the workers' wages a few pesos, this is taken out somewhere else.

For example, they've eliminated overtime pay. And if the worker misses a day, they don't pay him his "*mite*" like they used to, and not only that but they take half of what is due him in the grocery store. In my family, for example, every other day we have the right to two kilos of meat and thirty rolls for the nine of us. My husband missed a day of work and they only gave us one kilo of meat and fifteen rolls. Like that.

As for the increase we got out of the government, at first they said it would be 35 percent. But it turns out that that too was a fraud. Each worker only got a 5 pesos per day increase. Last year, my husband earned 17 pesos a day: when he began to work as a *lamero* they increased it to 23 pesos and now, after the strike, he's getting 28 pesos a day, in other words not even a dollar and a half, despite the fact that his work is harder than before. So our situation hasn't improved even in that respect.

I'd also like to say something about our political parties. What I see is that many of those who speak nice during peaceful times don't know how to work with us when a difficult moment like this comes along. I think that many of them are giving their lives "for the party" and maybe not "for the people." And that's why, I think, they get more and more divided. I also see that they have cadres, but few of them really reach the masses. That's how it was in this last strike.

I think it's vital for us to learn to organize in other ways so that we can defend ourselves better. Because we have a very strong tradition of struggle. How many people have already given their lives for our cause! But the measures we took are no longer sufficient to confront our oppressors who come well armed and who walk all over us each time. We need to think about that and find a better way to work things out.

Short-range solutions no longer interest us. We've already had all kinds of governments, "nationalist," "revolutionary," "Christian," with all kinds of labels. Since 1952, when the MNR government began to betray the people's revolution, so many governments have come and gone and none of them has done what the people really want. This government, for example, isn't doing anything for us, but instead, those who benefit are first the foreigners, who continue stealing our wealth, and then the private businesses, the state companies, the military, and not the working class or the peasants, who get poorer every day. And it's going to go on that way so long as we have a capitalist system. Because of everything I've been through and read, I can see that we identify with socialism. Because only a socialist system will bring more justice and everyone will have the benefits that today are in the hands of only a few.

Look how it was the very government and the way they treated us that started us on that road. For example, in my case, when they beat me in the DIC cells for being a "communist" and an "extremist" and all that, they awoke a great curiosity in me: "What is communism? What is socialism?" Every day they beat me over the head with that. And I began to ask myself: "What's a socialist country? How are problems solved there? How do people live there? Are the miners massacred there?" And then I began to analyze: "What have I done? What do I want? What do I think? Why am I here? I only asked for justice for the people, I only asked that everyone have enough to eat, I asked for education to be better, I asked that there be no more massacres like the terrible San Juan massacre. Is that socialism? Is that communism?"

In books I've read and from lots of people I've talked with, we know that in such-and-such a socialist country the population has better living conditions, health conditions, housing, and education. The workers are treated better. The peasants aren't left out. Women have the opportunity to do productive work, because there are new jobs so that the people can better themselves collectively. Women no longer have to suffer so much because of their condition as women, like we do when we ruin our bodies with so much work, we ruin our nerves with so much worry about our children's future and about the health of our husbands who are workers and who we know from the start are going to end up with mine sickness. And so many other things that do us in.

We know that in a socialist regime all that changes, because there have to be equal opportunities for everyone, jobs for women and day-care centers where their kids will be well taken care of while they work. And that the government itself has to take care of old people, of widows, and all that.

So, those are aspirations we have, we want all that to happen to us, right? Also, as far as I understand it, in a socialist system the people have to participate so that they don't once again fall into exploitation of some people by others, right?

I know that in all the countries that have reached socialism, there's still a lot to be won. But I realize that they've already gotten a lot of what we still want.

That's why I think that we, the Bolivian people, should watch the experiences of those countries carefully, their mistakes and their advances, and together look for a solution that has to do with what Bolivia is, with our people, our situation. And not waste time fighting among ourselves to see what Russia, China, or Cuba says and distracting ourselves in the defense of one of them over the other. Marxism, as far as I understand it, should be applied to the reality of each country.

My people are not struggling for a small victory, for a small wage increase here, a small answer there. No. My people are preparing themselves to get capitalism out of their country forever, and its domestic and foreign servants, too. My people are struggling to reach socialism.

I say this, but it's no invention of mine. This was upheld in the congress of the Central Obrera Boliviano: "Bolivia will only be free when it becomes a socialist country."

And whoever doubts that should take the opportunity to come to Bolivia someday, and here they'll be convinced that that is what my people want.

Postscript, 1978

AN INTERVIEW BETWEEN DOMITILA AND MOEMA

Moema: Domitila, you've said you'd like to clear up some things regarding certain interpretations of your statements. What would you like to say?

Domitila: Well, in the first place, what I think is that the book is a personal account and should be read from beginning to end without seizing on a single paragraph and interpreting it according to one's own opinion or way of seeing things, but that the book is all related, and it has to be read by understanding it from the beginning to the end. I also think that this account can be a textbook for analysis and criticism, but it's not a question of looking in it for a theoretical position in and of itself. It's an account of my experiences.

For example, regarding political parties, even though I've mostly talked about the union, I think that the people's liberation struggle should be run by a party that really is of the oppressed and exploited, of the workers. In other words, that we have to have our own party and we have to guide it, right? Now, with the little I know of Bolivian reality, not because I don't want to know more, but because the means to that aren't open to me, I think that it's necessary for the intellectuals to work with us. Because we don't want to carry out our struggle separately, just workers and peasants, but the intellectuals also have to be there. But they have to be close to our reality always, applying Marxist-Leninist theory correctly to the country's reality. And the party has to be led by the working class and the peasants. And the other popular sectors also have to participate. It was pointed out that in my testimony I don't mention, for example, the slum areas. It's true that I don't know much about the reality of our country. I sometimes imagine what the situation of the slums must be like. But I haven't lived there. I know that their situation is much worse than ours, and so I think: if the miners have such bad living conditions, what must the situation of the peasants, of the slum people, and all those I've never gotten to know be like? But I don't want to speak in a purely theoretical way about my people. That's why, maybe, I didn't mention some groups, because I don't know much about them. What can I say about the slum dwellers, about the peasant women, if I don't know them? I don't only want to speak theoretically. I want to know them.

Moema: Some people say that you imply that with socialism all the problems of women's liberation will be solved.

Domitila: What I think is that socialism, in Bolivia, like in any country, will be the tool which will create the conditions for women to reach their level. And they'll do so through their struggle, through their participation. And their liberation will be their own work.

But I think that at this moment it's much more important to fight for the liberation of our people alongside the men. It's not that I accept machismo, no. But I think that machismo is a weapon of imperialism just like feminism is. Therefore, I think that the basic fight isn't between the sexes; it's a struggle of the couple. And when I say couple, I also include children and grandchildren, who have to join the struggle for liberation from a class position. I think that's fundamental now.

Moema: Would you like to say something about the methodology used in the elaboration and application of *Let Me Speak*?

Domitila: Yes. I'd like to underline that. I've been interviewed by hundreds of journalists, historians, many people who've come from different countries with television cameras, with movie cameras, to interview me. And I also know that a lot of anthropologists, sociologists, economists come to visit the rest of the country, to study it. But of all those materials they take away with them, very few are returned to the working class, to the people, no? So I'd like to ask all those people who think they want to help us, that all the material they've taken with them be returned to us, like you've done with this problem of the methodology you use, you know? So that we can use it to study our own reality. *Let Me Speak* has to serve the people because it's being returned to them. In the same way I think that the movies, documents, and studies that are produced about the reality of the Bolivian people should also get back to them to be analyzed and criticized. Because, if not, we'll stay in the same condition and there's no contribution which can help us to understand our reality better and to solve our problems. There haven't been many studies which have been useful to us.

That's why I want to say that I'm happy with the work method we've used. I think it's correct that you've understood and not changed what I wanted to say and interpret. I hope that in Bolivia and in other countries the people's experiences are gathered up not only to elaborate theories on an intellectual level, alien theories, but to be used, as the title you gave this book says, so that the people can be allowed to speak.

And regarding the work method used, I especially want to refer to the following: that after transcribing and organizing the recordings, this testimony now returns to the working class so that together—workers, peasants, housewives, everyone, even the young people and the intellectuals who want to be with us—can learn from the experiences, analyze and also learn from the mistakes we've committed in the past, so that through correcting these errors we'll be able to do better things in the future, guide ourselves better, direct ourselves better, to see the reality of our country and create our own instruments to improve our struggle and free ourselves definitively from imperialism and establish socialism in Bolivia. I believe that that's the main object of a work such as this.

— DOMITILA BARRIOS DE CHUNGARA
— MOEMA VIEZZER
LA PAZ, BOLIVIA, MARCH 10, 1978

Where Is Domitila?

A HUNGER STRIKE FOR DEMOCRACY

In 1977, we did a hunger strike in Bolivia lasting twenty-one days. It was a very special strike and undoubtedly a historic event in the country; it was also well publicized internationally. We had been under Banzer's dictatorship since 1971 and he had dismantled the country. The Constitution was no longer being applied, there was no parliament, and all our organizations had been destroyed. For example, in the mines, to control the workers, they had replaced the union leaders with their own agents, called coordinators. Our leaders had to carry out all their work in secrecy. There was no freedom whatsoever. The dictatorship was so harsh that governments of many countries, including the Carter administration in the United States, began pressuring for an end to that reign of terror.

The only kind of organization that managed to do anything publicly was [the Permanent Assembly on] Human Rights. That's why human rights committees were established throughout Bolivia. They were initially driven by the Catholic Church, but open to anyone who wanted to participate. I helped initiate human rights work where I lived, and I was elected president of the Comité de Siglo XX. I also helped organize human rights committees in other mining centers, such as Villoco.

It wasn't easy to do this because people were very afraid, you see. In the assembly we held in Villoco to create the committee, the military was present, threatening people. That's why people didn't want to enter and stayed outside, circling the place. That was when I grabbed the microphone and said to them: "Well then, people. Let's ask ourselves, who is our main enemy? We might say it's Banzer . . . we might say it's the military, or the agents and informants among our people, or the ones who torture us. Or we might say it's imperialism. But that's not true, comrades. Our main enemy is our fear! And the day we manage to overcome our fear, on that day neither imperialism nor anyone else will be able to stop us, and we'll triumph." It was on that day that the Villoco Human Rights Committee was created.

In 1977, faced with all the pressure both inside the country and internationally, Banzer decided to call for elections. But he did so in his own way, meaning without popular participation. So, with the COB and particularly the Miners' Federation, we decided to do a general strike. It was quite a long process, and everything was done very carefully, in secrecy, you see, to ensure the strike's success and prevent it from turning against us. In Oruro, for example, the leaders started appearing on market days, and people were delighted to know that they were not dead but still looking for ways to organize and restore democracy. The federation had told me that I needed to get involved in human rights work, because it would be a chance to take a stand and be with the people.

When Banzer called his special breed of elections, we went to La Paz and began organizing the strike. Some suggested that it should be done during the Christmas season, while others said that wasn't a good time to attract attention and that we should wait until after the holidays. We started communicating with the clandestine leaders and organizing everything to ensure our success. Finally, it was decided: we would start after Christmas.

Initially, our idea was to begin the hunger strike at San Calixto School. But when we entered the school and explained the situation, the priests got scared. They said it couldn't be done there, that it wasn't safe, and that it didn't behoove us. They talked and talked ... In the end, we decided to initiate the strike at the Archbishop's Palace. But then I said to the comrades, "I'm not leaving here until it's confirmed that the strike has begun. We need a signal." A white handkerchief raised in the window of the Archbishop's Palace would be the signal that the strike had started. That's what we agreed upon.

I'd noticed that there was a telephone in the room, and I thought, "If we all leave, then the priests can call the Archbishop's Palace, and they could block the entrance, right?" So I stayed there, more or less holding the priests hostage. Then Father Gustavo arrived with the white handkerchief. That was it! The hunger strike had begun. It was December 28th.

So I stayed two more days among the leaders from the COB, the Miners' Federation, and those in student, political, and human rights organizations, to coordinate everything and ensure that news of the strike didn't just stay among us. It makes a big difference if someone communicates with the entire country, for example, if the BBC in London reports the news. It was necessary to see to all of that, wasn't it?

Meanwhile, the other four comrades were already doing the hunger strike. On the third day, we organized a second hunger strike committee at the headquarters of the newspaper *Diario Presencia*. There, I worked with Luis Espinal and Xavier Albó from [the Permanent Assembly on] Human Rights, members of the Union of Women of Bolivia, university students, journalists, and others.

Strike committees began to be organized throughout the country, and more people decided to join the hunger strike. Then the reprisals began. Banzer ordered the places where hunger strikers were present to be broken into and those of us on strike to be removed. They took us out of *Diario Presencia*, they removed the members of the Cochabamba committee, and those of Santa Cruz. They even removed people from the United Nations building. Then, at that moment, despite being in clandestinity, the COB and the Miners' Federation declared an indefinite general strike.

Every day, more and more people joined the strike. The strike, you see, was planned to unfold in a staggered way. For example, we said: "Today, the workers in Siglo XX will stop work." The army would go there, and then they would start working again. But there would be another place where the strike was also being carried out, and when the army tried to return, the *campesinos* had blocked the road. That meant the army couldn't move, and they had to attempt to clear the entire road. Then, while that strike was suppressed, the strike would begin in another place. . . . And so it went on in every department, and in every province. Throughout Bolivia, factories stopped, mines stopped, oil production stopped. And you know what? Tin and oil were at their highest prices at that time. Moreover, international pressure had intensified. Hundreds of exiled people in other countries had joined the hunger strike. There was also a lot of pressure from the international press. Chaos was setting in!

So Bánzer had to back down. We had sent Bánzer a proposal with four points that he would have to accept for us to end the strike: unrestricted general amnesty for all people who had been persecuted or were exiled for political and union causes; return to work for people forced to retire for reasons that were political or related to labor organizing; approval of all political and union organizations; and withdrawal of the army from our camps. Bánzer agreed to the first three points, and we accepted it. That's how the strike ended, on January 17, 1978, with unrestricted amnesty being decreed, and the possibility of elections with everyone's participation. It was truly a great victory! Anyone who knows what a military dictatorship is like can appreciate what that victory meant for the country.

On January 17, 2002, a tribute was paid to us, the five women who initiated the hunger strike against Banzer's dictatorship. A plaque was placed on the door of the Miners' Federation with our names: Angélica de Flores, Aurora de Lora, Domitila Barrios de Chungara, Luzmila de Pimentel, and Nelly de Paniagua. They also gave us a plaque for what we had done.

It's true that we headed up that strike, and that should be acknowledged, right? But when I talk about the general strike that we started with five women, I always try to emphasize this: it was the people's support, the indefinite general strike of the entire working class that the COB called for, along with all the international solidarity and pressure that allowed us—those who initiated the strike—to achieve what we wanted and what the people wanted. And that also needs to be recognized.

It's important, you see, to recover the real history. Because many people don't know it. And there are even those who are not interested in the truth, and who present the hunger strike as something that just sprang up overnight like a mushroom, as if it were a miracle, instead of showing how people know how to organize themselves. There are people who say, "How brave those women were to conceive the strike! It's great that they did that and defeated dictator Banzer!" But when they say that five women defeated him, it's important to add "with the entire people who joined them in the strike." The Miners' Federation was there, the COB was there, and the *campesinos* and the students. No isolated individual or group could have achieved it. It was a victory of the whole people and of international solidarity.

So, that's how another process got going: the long road to democracy. The truth is, we thought it would be faster. After more than twenty years, it must be said that things didn't turn out as we wanted in Bolivia. In the first place, that is because we had to keep struggling to prevent the military from seizing power again. Then, alliances were formed among several parties to create the Popular Democratic Union, the UDP, to enter the elections. In the 1978 elections, another alliance was formed: the Revolutionary Left Front, the FRI, which invited me to be the vice presidential candidate. But democracy is not built only with elections, that is, only by seeking the popular vote. It's necessary to create conditions for responding to the trust people put in you, right? And many of those who ran as candidates in those alliances focused solely on gaining power for the sake of power and even accepted pacts with our enemies. I don't agree with that.

Can you imagine what it's meant to those of us who helped remove General Banzer from the Government Palace through the hunger strike, to see him become president again in 1997 by popular vote? It's Banzer himself who's responsible for the massacre that started in La Paz when he seized power with his tanks in the 1971 military coup. If the University of La Paz could speak, it would tell the story of what happened when the military entered its campus, where they even murdered Father Mauricio Lefebre. It shouldn't be forgotten that it was Banzer who militarized the country. But the years went by, and Banzer now appeared to be a "nice old man." And what's more, it seemed like he had even gone on a hunger strike with us to achieve democracy! Many people who didn't see him as he truly was—the head of a bloodthirsty government—voted for him.

Yet he was a general who remained the same as before, without any sensitivity. Can it be that people didn't realize how much money was stolen by those who had been in power? When the results of the 1997 elections came in, it felt as if the population had lost its memory in voting for a person who had caused the majority of Bolivians to suffer. But in truth, it's not that the people had forgotten. In fact, the IMF pressured the parties in power, such as the UCS [Solidarity Civic Unity] and CONDEPA [Conscience of the Fatherland], into bringing Banzer into power through those elections.

I still seek to understand the working-class people who supported him with their votes because—in their desperation, faced with lack of work and opportunities in life—they trust the promises of politicians without thinking too much. But what I don't understand are the former left-wing leaders, socialists, and even communists who jumped on the government's bandwagon, even awarding medals to President Banzer on his birthday. Among them were people who had participated in the Revolutionary Left Front in 1978 and had supported me as a vice presidential candidate after the hunger strike and Banzer's departure. How can that be understood? It seems like we are going backward in time. Many of them seem to have just entered power for themselves and not for the people.

What people sought was a democracy where they would have the right to freely express their opinions and the right to work. But no one has job security now. Every day more and more workers are thrown out onto the streets. In the villages, there is poverty that's hidden behind adobe walls. However, every day a few take advantage of this quote-unquote democracy. Millions are embezzled and stolen. There are the thieves in plain sight, and the government does nothing about it, nor has it created the jobs people need.

When I lived in Europe, I realized that people there are accustomed to seeing violations of human rights only in connection with dictatorships. But that's not true. The system imposes two forms of governance on us: dictatorships—in which there are massacres, bloodshed, and pain—but also pseudo-democracies, which serve as a kind of smokescreen to cover up human rights abuses and are often more cruel than dictatorships. I say that they are crueler, because they undermine health and education; there is hunger, unemployment, no work, and a lack of care for women and the elderly. That's also cruel, wouldn't you agree? With that model, they also condemned the people to death. The tortures of the dictators are cruel and painful, and they hurt and kill people. But what hurts most is knowing that there are children on the streets, without food, sleeping on sidewalks, mistreated, without education or clothes, without parents, and forgotten by the governments. Isn't that more painful than physical pain? Unfortunately, that kind of repression is not seen or recognized abroad. People don't want to talk about it, because they think it doesn't happen under democratic governments.

I feel sorry, and sometimes ashamed, when I see the type of

democracy that was built on the backs of our struggle. That's why this year, when comrade Don Felipe Quispe, of the Pachacuti Indigenous Movement, the MIP, invited me to run as a vice presidential candidate, I declined, in light of the current situation. And when I am asked who would be suitable for president, I honestly say that, right now, I don't see anyone. That is because we would be a minority in parliament. If we were organized, educated, united, it would be different.

At this moment, those who rule the country are agents of neoliberalism and imperialism. And the others—the few who defend the people—they can speak, shout, and tear their garments, claiming "this world is unjust" and so on, but when it comes to voting, the majority [in parliament] will always win. We have to stare reality in the face, don't we? The way our parliament works: even if we participate, even if we were president, when there is a protest for work, for example, we won't be able to prevent the police from using tear gas and beating and killing people.

So, precisely because people have placed their hopes in us and see us as their leadership—but we would still be the minority in parliament—it's quite possible that people would be disappointed and say: "Did you see? Felipe is in power, but the police keep beating and tear gassing us. There's Don Evo, there's Chungara . . . and so what? It's all the same, nothing has changed." So, I ask myself, why should I encourage false hopes in the people?

For example, look at what happened with Comrade Evo Morales, who was an Indigenous parliamentarian here for the Chapare region and tried to address the issues of peasants living in the coca-growing area. When there were protests here because of the water issue, and later because they didn't live up to their agreements to provide assistance to the coca growers and help them with alternative kinds of production, people took to the streets in protest. There were confrontations and even deaths. Evo Morales's parliamentary immunity was revoked. He went on a hunger strike and presented evidence to explain the accusations against him, but nobody paid any attention. He lost his parliamentary seat; that is, they have parliamentary immunity, but the law is only respected when they want to and for whom they want. When it comes to condemning or silencing the people, they do it without any problem. But would they apply the same laws to the parliamentarians who are stealing millions and collaborating with smugglers?

It's clear that with this political system—which has already failed but is still very entrenched—nothing can be achieved through elections alone. It's necessary to do a great deal of work so that the people get organized and have conditions to really act. I have a lot of respect for Comrade Evo and Comrade Felipe and for what they believe in. And many people have placed their hopes in them. If Don Felipe wants to fight that way, he should do so. And Don Evo as well. It's their right. All individuals and communities have that right. However, I'm currently focused on what I consider important for me at this moment: the project of educating people to organize themselves politically.

I've made some decisions about my participation in politics. In that sense, the meeting I had with Comandante Tomás Borge when I went to Nicaragua in 1979 has helped me a lot. Tomás asked me about the situation in Bolivia and what had happened, because he knew that workers and *campesinos* together had managed to defeat the army in Bolivia in 1952. They had taken power, and yet had not advanced for many reasons. He wanted to know when it would be done again. I told him that I didn't know, because there wasn't enough unity among the people, and it's difficult to bring them together because the parties are very divided. He asked me, "Half are on the right and half on the left?" "More or less," I said. Then he asked me, "But on the left, what is the correct position?" "I don't know," I said, "because when the time comes to unite, there isn't agreement about who should be the leader that we should follow."

Then he said that they themselves didn't have a leader, and that was good because it wasn't just one person. It was a team, and that was very positive. "If it were like that in Bolivia, and if we were to do that," I told him, "we would always be arguing about the methods we should apply, with each person defending their own side: the *foquistas*, the guerrillas, those who go to the countryside, those who want popular insurrection or prolonged war—in the end, there's no agreement." Then he asked me, "Is Bolivia at war, perhaps? Do you have guerrillas?" "No," I said, "we have elections. But it's the same; people are arguing about those things."

Then he said, "How can you argue when you haven't achieved anything yet? That's something to debate after you are organized for it! And it has to be worked on by experts who will devise the strategy, and all that it implies." So I told him I was disappointed with politics. He asked me, "Were you a candidate?" "I was, and I don't want anything more to do with it." Then he said, "You have to ask yourself: when you were a candidate, what did you hope to achieve? To be there in parliament on the same level as the others, enjoying the privileges that power offers? Or did you want to be with the people, working with them for better living conditions?" "What I wanted was for the people to be in power," I said. "But what have you done?" he asked me. "If you want the people to be in power, you have to go down to them and, from there, hand in hand with the people, push the process forward." That meeting has greatly influenced my decision to continue working in politics, but in a different way.

I believe that the electoral reforms that are now being carried out will ultimately benefit the bourgeoisie, the rich, and not the poor. I am concerned about the unemployment and inequality that there is. We believed in having a more just democracy, one that is less caught up in cold numbers and the market. But, with such an insipid democracy, a semi-democracy, who's going to defend that?

To me, this pseudo-democracy is just the prelude to human misery. The situation has gone so far that we, the poor, are killing each other. Here in Cochabamba, children have already been killed by others of the same class. Can you imagine? Children have been burned for stealing a bicycle. Every day, in the market, children are beaten for stealing a loaf of bread to eat, since they are hungry and their parents, who are without work, can't offer them anything. Taking away the people's right to work is like condemning them to death. Why does life have to be so harsh? Could it be that there's no alternative to work turning into exploitation?

Definitely, the democracy that we've lived under here these days is very different from what we imagined during the long days of the hunger strike. Those of us who fought for democracy always wanted a democracy with freedom of expression and action, where there is food, justice, and equal conditions for all. There should be work, too, which is essential for human beings to survive and the nation to progress.

BOLIVIA'S SPOKESPERSON IN COPENHAGEN

After the hunger strike and the fall of Banzer in 1978, we went through a difficult electoral process. There were three consecutive elections, and they staged a coup in all three. The will of the people was not respected. There was fraud, you see. Despite the alliance of the left-wing parties, known as the Democratic and Popular Union (UDP), winning three times in a row, the elections came to nothing each time due to the coups that took place.

Then, in 1980, came the coup by General García Meza. At that time, I was once again attending a United Nations conference. I had received an invitation to the NGO Tribune of the World Conference on Women in Denmark. When the COB's leadership found out about it, they called me and said: "You have to leave, there's going to be a coup, and you have to go and denounce it." I didn't want to go because my children were still young, and I wanted to look out for their safety, at least by hiding them in neighbors' houses. But the COB assigned me the task of being their spokesperson, to explain what was happening here, among the women gathered there at the conference. They gave me a letter from the COB denouncing the cruel coup that was being plotted in Bolivia. They told me that once I got set up in Denmark, I should get in touch with one contact in Venezuela, another in Mexico, and a third in Peru, to inform them of the hotel where I was staying and my phone number there, so they could update me about what was happening.

Since it was a World Conference—and it was believed that I'd be heard, as before in the Mexico Conference—the leaders thought that we could use the opportunity to avoid being isolated during the coup d'état that was going to take place. They knew it was a well-planned coup with the collaboration of the Brazilian and Argentine governments. The Brazilian army was here, as were representatives of the Argentine army. That's why they sent me to Denmark with the very important task of being an initial liaison there to denounce the coup, convene press conferences, and so on.

I left Bolivia on June 12th and arrived in Copenhagen on the 14th. On the 15th, when I arrived at the venue of the World Conference, I saw that there was a room with journalists from all around the world, and I asked for an interview, a press conference. They gave me a room, and I denounced that a coup d'état of the cruelest kind was being plotted in Bolivia, explaining what that meant, how dictatorships are in Bolivia, how many coups we have already had, and so on. It was published on June 16 in Denmark: "Bolivian delegate denounces that there will be a coup in Bolivia . . ." along with everything else I had said.

On the 17th, the coup took place. That day, the session of the conference went on until late. I went to have dinner where I was staying, and there were already numerous phone calls that had come in. They were giving me the messages, when, at that very moment, the phone rang. When I answered, they told me, "There has been a coup d'état, the Miners' Federation has been occupied, many people have been killed, the army has taken control of the mines, there's a curfew . . . " So I did what I had been told: I called Mexico, Peru, and Venezuela to let them know where I was staying.

From that moment on, I became the COB's mouthpiece to the world at the conference. That meant I no longer had the opportunity to really participate in the conference as initially planned. Instead, I asked if I could please be given the floor to denounce what was happening in my country. And, indeed, they granted it to me. On the night of the 18th, just before the session started, I told them what was happening and asked for their solidarity. I asked to be excused from participating, because I had to be free to try to mobilize a lot of support since it was an extremely bloody coup. Then the press from various places called me and there were press conferences.

All this led to a march being organized the following day. The organizers had requested permission from the police, and we all went out to protest against the coup. The march started from the NGO Tribune site. The idea was to go to the location of the official conference and ask women from the various governments to condemn the coup d'état in Bolivia; that UNHCR commissions be sent to prevent further crimes; and secure places that would be off-limits to the army and repressive groups, where people could seek refuge.

I didn't know that the Danish police was going to march ahead of the protesters! There were police officers with horses and dogs, and they were the ones who started the Women's March. We had to walk behind them. I said, "If I were to tell this to people in my country, no one would believe that the Danish police led the protest march against the usurping regime in Bolivia!" It was a very large march. There were thousands of people! Everyone in the NGO Tribune expressed their solidarity. I don't think anyone was missing. They all had signs in their own language, and banners filled the street.

We reached the area where representatives from all the governments of the world were gathered. However, what happened was that, when we were asking the Official Conference to receive a commission to inform them about what was happening in Bolivia, the doors opened, people rushed out, and they started beating us. The police did the same: they started to turn against us. Think of it! They beat a great many people. Some women were dragged by their hair, others were seized by their hands. They broke the arm of a Chilean comrade.

Women and men from the government, the Danish police, and people from the Official Conference—all came out to fight with us. I started crying and asked myself, "How is it possible that here, at a United Nations conference, a protest against a military coup is being repressed?" They wanted to arrest me. A policewoman who first beckoned to me, suddenly grabbed me by the neck. I wanted to break free, but she had an iron grip. I couldn't get away. She held on to me and pulled me back. Other police officers were pushing me. That's when the women reacted forcefully. A Dutch woman went over the police line, and, taking hold of my arm, pulled me out of there.

Since it was a World Conference, the international press was there. So the journalists started getting into vehicles and taking photos of us, with a flash here and another flash there. Suddenly, I remembered: "It's true, we're at an international conference!" I saw a young man with a megaphone and asked him to lend it to me. I told him, "Please, I want two translators, one in English, and one in Danish." The translators appeared, and then, with the megaphone in hand, I spoke: "Is this the Danish Police? Is this how a democratic government treats its visitors, its guests? Mr. Prime Minister of Denmark, I am not here to unseat you. I am not here to disturb your country. What I want to do is inform people at this World Conference that in Bolivia, my country, a very cruel, bloody military coup has taken place. But by preventing us from denouncing this before world public opinion, I believe that you gentlemen are acting like accomplices of the regime, are you not?"

Of course, they didn't want us to speak about how they were beating us. So when we spoke and it was translated, the police started to stand still, to retreat. Then we all sat down on the ground. It began raining. We started to sing and chant slogans, hoping to be received by the conference: to be allowed to send a commission to inform them about the coup and ask for their solidarity. After a while, they said yes, that a commission of ten people could enter.

As soon as we entered the conference venue, Bolivia's delegate came out. At that time the president was a woman, Lidia Gueiler. The official delegate representing Ms. Lidia, who had been overthrown by the coup, said to me, "Well, Domitila, I congratulate you on organizing this mobilization. But you know that you cannot speak here, because this is a congress of government representatives. So, since I am representing the Bolivian government that has suffered the coup, they decided to let me speak today, even though I was scheduled to speak fifteen days from now. In about half an hour or fifteen minutes, I'm going to speak. What do you propose?"

I said that all countries should condemn the coup d'état, break diplomatic relations with García Meza's government, and no one should give moral or economic support to the new government. I said that the United Nations should send international organizations to observe what was happening and also provide tents, or whatever is necessary to prevent the massacre and murder of the many people who have to go into exile. Also, governments remaining silent should be criticized because anyone who doesn't speak out is an accomplice to all the crimes being committed right now in Bolivia. I had everything written down on a paper, carefully written out, so as not to forget anything.

Then she said to me, "Okay, I'll do that." And I told her, "Yes, you are the one who has to do it because if you don't, I'll take the floor anyway and say everything." "Don't worry," she said to me. And she was indeed given the floor. That is, the woman who coordinated the session gave the floor to the Bolivian delegate, and she explained very diplomatically that Ms. Gueiler was the real president of Bolivia, that a coup had occurred against her, that it was an outrage committed against a woman during the World Conference on Women. She also mentioned everything that was in the note that we, the commission of ten, had given to her. The president of the session put it to a vote, and in the end, the delegate said, "All those in favor of what we propose, show your support and move to my side."

Those of us from the commission were standing on one side of the room. Quite a few people stood up. And they started to pass by: those from Nicaragua, those from Cuba . . . from many countries. Even some Arab women with their dresses and veils passed over to our side to express their solidarity. They supported us, saying that they would consider our request, reflect on the matter, and then give us the response later, informing us of the conclusions they had reached. Further, they congratulated us on the support we had obtained: "Great job, what a mobilization!" they said.

The next day, we were invited to a street festival in a square in the Danish city. We went there to denounce the coup. But it turned out that the Danish government sent someone to look for us. "What's happened?" I asked. Since I had accused them of beating us and asked if that was how Danish democracy works, claiming that he [Prime Minister Anker Jørgensen] was an accomplice to the dictatorship, and the press had talked about it, he found himself in a bad situation. Now he wanted to make amends. That's why the government sent for the Bolivian delegation. First, they got to our Official Delegate, but the government envoy said, "She's not the Bolivian who made the accusation. It's someone else. We must find her and bring her here. Let's talk."

So, when the police and the Danish government's envoy arrived to the square—with a special guard and motorcycles and everything—and told me that I had to go, because the Prime Minister was inviting me to a meeting, people of course became agitated and worried. Those who had invited me to the festival didn't want to let me go. Finally, they said they would wait there until I returned, but the government would have to guarantee that I wouldn't suffer any reprisals. The man who came on behalf of the government said, "The Danish Government just wants to be informed about the situation in Bolivia, and that's why they want to talk with her."

So I went. They took me to the Missions Hotel, a first-class hotel, and there the Prime Minister was waiting for me. When I entered, cameras and journalists quickly showed up, and asked me, "Are you a representative of the government?" "No," I said, "I'm a housewife, I'm from the mines of Bolivia." "What are you going to ask for from the Minister?" "The same thing I asked for yesterday: to sever diplomatic relations with the García Meza government." The assistant of the official delegate appeared and told me: "Please, don't make any statements to the press; you should speak with the Prime Minister. We have already talked to him, and he's agreed to support us."

The Latin Americans who were there had sent me a translator. So I went inside. There, on the stairs, the Danish Prime Minister was waiting for me. He welcomed me with a hug and said, "Yes, I want to talk with you. I was not informed about the situation. There was a mistake, because we were told that a terrorist wanted to blow up the hall of the Women's Conference, so we had to take precautions. But we weren't aware of your problems. Please accept my apologies on behalf of my government and on behalf of my people." "Thank you very much, Mr. President," I said. "But apologies mean nothing if no measures are taken against the García Meza government."

We entered the other room and started to talk. I recounted Bolivia's history up through the coups that brought in the Barrientos and Banzer dictatorships. Finally, I explained our desire to live in a democracy, how there had been three consecutive elections, but each was drowned in blood, concluding with coups d'état. I ended by saying, "That's why we insist that diplomatic relations be severed with the Bolivian government."

The woman next to me said, "Listen, control yourself, you're an audacious one. You're talking to a Head of State, not to your younger brother. You can't *insist*, you can only *ask*. Besides, you are not addressing him as 'Excellency,' even though he's a representative appointed by the people." "Yes," I said, "that's true, but we're also representatives of a people. What happened to our march here is not only an offense to Bolivia but also to the various countries represented in the World Conference. He also needs to apologize." The minister was looking at us, but since he didn't understand Spanish, he asked the secretary what we were saying. She told him, "It's their problem," but a friend who could translate and spoke Danish explained to him what it was about.

Then the Prime Minister said that, yes, he could apologize and that he had decided to do so. He added that in Denmark, democracy is respected. But he asked me, "How do you want relations to be broken? Okay, maybe we sever diplomatic relations. But should there be no economic aid? For example, we have the PIL milk project in Bolivia. How could we withdraw the millions in aid that we've committed to sending to your country?" I didn't know about that project, which was in El Alto. So I told him, "We don't consume milk, Mr. Minister. Our children get only breast milk. We don't know anything about PIL milk. Moreover, that money, if given, will probably not be used for the children's milk, but to maintain their dictatorial regime." The minister said he would take that into account.

The press in Germany, Holland, Switzerland, and many other countries had heard about what happened in the march. I began to be invited everywhere. So the mistake they made and what the Danish police had done opened the doors much wider, allowing us to make Bolivia's situation known to the world.

After that, I began traveling everywhere, always accepting invitations to denounce the coup and the situation in Bolivia and call on everybody to support our people. I wasn't able to participate in the Women's Conference I'd been invited to. I asked for permission and left. Right away, I began traveling to different countries to explain what was happening in Bolivia and ask for solidarity, just as I had done at the conference in Copenhagen.

There was a lot of support from the women at the conference, which was crucial. So was the solidarity I received from Bolivians exiled in the countries that I visited in the following months. They took care of travel, lodging, meals, and translation. They also took charge of promoting the events and inviting people to them. And it wasn't only Bolivians, but also other Latin American men and women who were in exile, such as Chileans, Argentinians, and Uruguayans. They provided me with a great deal of support and solidarity, so that I could carry out all that work for my country and my people.

After going to Denmark, I never attended any other United Nations conferences. However, I was invited several times to Ecuador, Bolivia, and other places in Europe to participate in events that addressed the topic of women, especially the subject of "Women and Democracy." And here too [in Cochabamba] we always try to talk about the situation of women and women's participation, whenever we're invited to speak to groups as part of the Mobile School project.

In Bolivia, as in many parts of the world, women have become machines for producing human capital, don't you think? They make workers who toil in the mines, peasants who produce, and also soldiers who later go on to kill their own brothers.

In the past, workers spoke about the exploited worker but forgot about the family, and about women, who are also exploited. Ultimately, ignoring half of the population—women—helps the powerful and it reinforces the exploitation of men, women, and children.

I'll never forget what happened with my cousin Rosa. Her husband was a union leader and he always said, "One revolutionary in the house is enough!" He didn't want her to get involved in or participate in anything. He wouldn't tell her about anything. Well, one day when the army went to the mine with their officers and he had to go into hiding, his wife, thinking she was helping him, unwittingly gave the officers all the information they needed. And, of course, he was arrested. When he came out of prison, he said, "I'm going to beat her, I'm going to kill my wife." But I grabbed him by the arm and said, "No, comrade, you are responsible for what happened. You always said that one revolutionary in the house was enough. . . . Well, that's the result!"

In our country, discrimination exists, and there's a lot of machismo. The violence against women, for example, is a violence that's institutionalized, both at home and outside of it. This practice, which is very reprehensible, is carried out by all kinds of men, including husbands, employers, members of government, and military personnel. Bolivia has not yet freed itself from it.

Why does the exploitation of women and discrimination against them exist? There are many explanations. Some say that discrimination against women got even worse after the Inca Empire, with the arrival of European culture, especially because of their religion. I respect everyone who believes in something—I do too. But I've read a great deal about religion, and it's said that it was Eve who led Adam to sin, and that is why there is discrimination against women. I also read a religious text that taught men to say, "Lord, I thank you for not making me a woman." You get the picture?

Even women from the bourgeoisie and petty bourgeoisie suffer from violence against women. Recently, the press talked a lot about a woman from the bourgeoisie—a mother, in fact—who was murdered by her own partner. In the past, these things were hardly ever made public. And now it seems that this is also happening in our own class.

What can be done to reduce violence against women? I think that, first of all, women have to learn to value themselves. The problem is that they are beaten from the time they are children. So the problem starts, you see, with the parents. It begins with the education provided by parents, who never trust their daughters. Their daughters are not raised to make decisions, but are taught to be always fearful, so that they depend on men and remain under their authority. And they also learn that women don't do anything!

Therefore, it's necessary to get women to value themselves. Because once a woman values herself, she's stronger, and not a dependent who has to constantly ask for things. Additionally, women need to be in good shape in terms of self-esteem, so they don't go on putting up with just anything, as in the saying here that goes, "He hits me because he loves me."

We may have made progress in political terms by building organizations in which many women participate, both women who are housewives, and those who are workers and *campesinos*. However, if we look at the list of leaders, there are still very few women. Quite often, I am invited to speak to women, and I always talk about that: about the importance of women's consciousness and organization.

I also like to talk about the importance of women in educating their sons and daughters. On Mother's Day, for example, I always take the opportunity to reflect on that. As I said to a group that had invited me to speak in Santa Cruz, Mother's Day has become so commercialized that it seems to have lost all meaning. Although we all like to receive gifts, the best gift a woman can get from her children is their effort and desire for improvement. And precisely because we are mothers, what we have to do on Mother's Day is reflect on our country, which is also the future country of our children. We live in a country burdened with debt and suffocated by the neoliberal system, while the government keeps the majority of the people, especially women, in ignorance. It is we who, as mothers, pass on values and customs. We are the ones who spend the most time with our children when they are young and to whom they always turn for everything and at all times. For all those reasons, if we are ignorant, if we don't have education, and if we don't know what our rights are, it's very difficult for things to change.

Before, you know, these things were not talked about. Even in the mines, when we started organizing, the nuns wanted to throw stones at us and the bishops wanted to excommunicate us. They said, "What are these women getting themselves into? They should go home and cook, take care of their children and husbands." Today, there are many programs for women everywhere, even in the churches: programs to combat violence against women, for women's health, for women to have their documents, and be able to vote. All of that's important, but we can never forget the root causes, the sources of violence against women, of women's health problems, and of everything else.

In terms of health, for example, we need to ask: Why, if there is so much land and wealth in Bolivia but so few Bolivians, the only thing some health programs do is advise women and men to be sterilized and not have any more children? We can't forget that everything is organized according to the interests of those in power. When I was invited to the International Congress on Women and Mining in Oruro, I told the comrades, "During the colonial times, if a scientist had invented a drug to make Bolivian women—women of the Incan Empire—give birth, they would have made us give birth to ten children at a time. They would have done it because they needed labor for the mines, they needed labor for sugar and coffee, and to produce all the wealth we have. Nowadays, science has advanced, and they are removing us from work. They no longer need 'human capital.' But the solution to our problems will not come just because women simply stop having children, right?"

I always ask: While they are developing training courses on women's health, why don't they improve the conditions and facilities for women to actually live in good health? And why do they bring medicines from outside to cure us, while taking away the natural remedies that we know how to use to maintain our health? Why don't we use what exists in nature and the millenarian wisdom that women and men in this country have, which is already recognized worldwide? Moreover, why are they trying to patent our plants, herbs, and everything that women and men have known about for millennia, so that they'll have all the rights, while we won't even be able to use what is ours and what we know how to use to heal ourselves? When it comes to health, all of that also needs to be explained, don't you think?

In our country, discrimination exists on all levels: racial discrimination, religious discrimination . . . all kinds of discrimination. There is discrimination against women due to the patriarchal system established in our society. That's why we need to educate and organize ourselves. Here, we have seen how once a woman breaks free from what religion imposes, breaks free from the customs society imposes, frees herself from concerns about "What will people say?" and starts fighting for her rights, then the consequences start to rain down on her. It doesn't matter who you are or where you come from.

But in the midst of all this, there is also the economic issue, you see. That defines relationships. It's like that all over the world. For example, when the Bolivian government started to discuss the issue of gender in the country, the First Lady was Ximena, Sánchez de Lozada's wife, and the Second Lady was the wife of

Hugo Cárdenas, who was then vice president. Here in the Chapare region, there was an intervention by the DEA. There were deaths, injuries, and arrests. So, the women from here in the Chapare went by foot to the city of La Paz, trusting that among women, "as members of the same gender," there could be understanding. They went to La Paz to make their grievances known. Only the First and Second Ladies of the nation would meet and talk with them.

I was sick and bedridden, but I saw on television the *campesina* women who came from here to La Paz carrying their babies. They were in a terrible state, with their feet all bruised and full of blisters, perhaps even without having eaten or slept. You get the picture, don't you? These women dressed in rags, completely malnourished, and the others receiving them were elegantly clad. Then one of them said, "Mrs. First Lady of the nation, I come to talk woman to woman. What would you think if the army entered your home and mistreated your family, looting everything, raping your daughters, killing your partner, arresting, sacking, and so on. What would you do?" The woman said it with so much feeling and so much pain, but the other woman didn't even move! She didn't even blink! After listening, at a certain moment, she said, "I don't understand!"

Of course, efforts are being made to change things, and that's why there is a lot of talk about women being in power. There is even a law establishing a quota: 30 percent of the candidates from each party in parliament must be women. That's all well and good: 30 percent women. But with the economic problems we face, it's very difficult to achieve. Think about it: how many working-class, *campesina*, and Indigenous women, how many women committed to the struggles in the poor barrios, have the preparation and calling to make up that 30 percent minimum? These women are sometimes invited just to put their names on the ballot so that the 30 percent quota is fulfilled. Eventually, however, the very comrades from the party tell them that they are not capable and that it would be good for the women to resign so that a man can take their place.

So, are things going to go on like this? Before, they said we had to organize as "women." Now it's "gender." Honestly, the label doesn't matter to me. In a feminist or gender issue, it all depends on who is running it. To be in solidarity with and help each other, to end the marginalization of women, we need to organize and unite. But if there is no education, organization, and unity, women of the people like us will always remain in the same situation. Because nowadays, to hold any position, you have to be a graduate, have to have a degree, and have to have money, right?

I believe that women who are intellectuals, who are affluent, should think about how women can unite to change this society. There are women's associations that are better able to organize and educate themselves. For example, there are associations of professionals that organize among themselves and from their perspective try to fight for women, for their rights, and for everything. Yet I see that they are more focused on their own small groups, and separated from the world of the majority of women. They could achieve a great deal, because of their economic situation and intellectual abilities, if they united with us. But will they do so, if they need us to be their servants, employees, housekeepers, and laundresses?

But it's not only women who have to learn to organize. If women alone cannot free themselves, neither can men do it alone. That's why in my talks I always say that, beginning with the family and our class condition, all of us—women and men, fathers and mothers, children, grandchildren, and grandparents—we all need to learn to respect each other, unite, and organize, to change everything that needs to be changed in society.

EXILED IN SWEDEN

After the Copenhagen conference was over, I wanted to return to Bolivia. I went early to the airport with one of the women who had invited me. She was, I believe, a United Nations representative and was there with the translators. She said to me, "Look, Domitila, everything is already set up here. You stay and wait. When they call, you board and return to your country. I'm going to leave here one hour before."

So, I stayed there, waiting. When I went to board the plane, a man checked my passport at immigration and saw the word "Bolivia." Then he looked at his computer and said, "Wait a second. Do you speak Spanish?" I said yes. He called over a woman who spoke Spanish, who asked me, "What are you doing here in Denmark?" I said, "I was invited to a World Women's Conference, and I'm returning to my country." Then she explained, "Look, it says here that you can't return to your country unless you have a visa from the Bolivian Consulate. You have to get a visa from the consulate." Then I asked, "But when can I do that? My plane leaves at seven, and the consulate surely opens at nine, so I'll miss my flight. I can't do it." "Well," she said, "they told me to translate, and that's what I'm doing. You will not board the plane if you don't have a visa from your consulate." "But what can I do?" I asked. "I don't know, you will have to speak with your consulate. That's what you must do. They'll explain how to solve your problem."

That was the saddest thing for me: needing a visa to return to my own country because the government was punishing me for discrediting it. There were newspaper articles about that. During a rally in Bolivia, García Meza and Arce Gómez said that I was "a traitor to the homeland, and traitors to the homeland had to have their wills in hand."[1] So, they made me step back from the counter. I sat there, not knowing what to do or who I could explain things to. I couldn't think of anything except: "I'm going to miss my flight. . . . It's an issue for the consulate . . . how do I ask where the consulate is? . . . how do I get to the Bolivian Consulate in Copenhagen?"

I spent all day ruminating, thinking, and weeping at the airport. At the end of the day, they started cleaning, and I was still there, sitting all alone. Then the cleaning person came up and said something to me, in Danish, of course, and I couldn't understand it. In the end, she opened the door, took my suitcase, and put it outside. I grabbed my suitcase again and reentered the airport. Finally, a police officer arrived and spoke to me in Danish. He was probably telling me that I had to leave and go home—what could I know?—I didn't understand anything.

Then a man arrived and told me, now in Spanish, that I had to leave, and that people couldn't stay there because they had to close the airport. I told him that I'd been invited to the World Conference, but I'd missed my flight because they told me I had to go to the Bolivian Consulate, but I had no contacts in the country. So they talked among themselves, and then a chubby older guy, who was also a police officer, came up to me, laughing. I asked him, "Why are you laughing like that?" He said, "It's because they're saying that I'm chubby like you. Are you in contact with any Bolivians here?" I told him no.

Then the man asked me if I had the addresses of anybody from Bolivia in Denmark. Only then did I remember that I had a little notebook with addresses of Bolivians who were exiled in Germany and Sweden that I'd met at the conference—people who had come from many cities to show their solidarity with Bolivia and with me. The old guy took the notebook and called someone on the phone. On the line was a Bolivian who asked me, "Where are you, Domitila?" I explained everything that had happened. Then he said, "If in Bolivia they say that you have your will in hand, it's because they're very upset about everything you have done here, having gotten wind of it. So, it's better for you to stay here for a while." "But where?" I asked. "You can live with us, you'll stay at our house," he said. "Oh, well, then come pick me up, please!" However, he told me, "No, go to the place where you were staying; I'll call the hotel." "I don't have money to stay in a hotel in Copenhagen," I replied. "We'll pay for it. But go to the place where you were staying. It's late, but tomorrow we will have breakfast together and go to our house."

I didn't even know who I was talking to and wondered, "Why don't they want to receive me today? Why do I have to wait until tomorrow? Why go back to the hotel instead of going straight to their home?" In any case, the policeman took me to the hotel.

When I arrived, the hotel manager was waiting for me and gave me the same room I'd stayed in during the conference. That night was something. Being in a country where you don't speak the language, not knowing when I could return to Bolivia, or what was happening in the country after the coup, where my family was, and all of that. . . . I think I've never felt so bad in my life. I wept until almost dawn. Finally, I fell asleep.

When the phone rang, they were already there. I sped downstairs with my things, so they could take me "before they changed their minds" (I thought this to myself because, you see, I had nowhere else to go). When I got downstairs, several *compañeros* were already there, and we all went inside the hotel to have breakfast. While we were eating, one of them asked me, "Did you come with a visa or a passport?" I responded, "With a passport, why?" He said to me, "We're going to Sweden." I told him, "No, I don't want to go to Sweden, I want to resolve this here in Denmark. Please help me with the paperwork here so that I can return to Bolivia." That's when I realized why they hadn't come to pick me up the previous night. These *compañeros* were from Sweden, and I had thought they were from Denmark. Then they told me, "When the man at the airport called us and we told him you would come to live with us, we left Sweden, traveling all night. We're just arriving now to have breakfast with you." They had done all that to come and find me! That's when I asked, "But don't we have compatriots here in Denmark?" They said, "No, there's no one here. You have to go to Sweden and live with us."

That's how I ended up in Sweden. The *compañeros* suggested that I seek asylum, but I didn't want to—staying in Europe would be a big change for me. I insisted, "I'm going back to Bolivia, no matter what." I asked them to find out if I could change my ticket, so that I could at least go to Mexico, Peru, or Venezuela, and bring my family somewhere where they speak our own language and where it would be similar to what we were used to. In effect, the shock of cultures, customs, and languages was really hard for me. Yet it turned out that changing the ticket wasn't possible; it had already expired. So I went to Sweden and stayed there, staying in the homes of different Bolivian exiles.

Then I started traveling and giving talks, over and over again. The press from countries that had attended the conference, but especially the Bolivian exiles from CONADE [a Bolivian organization in defense of democracy that operated both inside and outside the country] took care of most of it. Everywhere I went, they had already prepared a schedule, with visits to unions, political parties, and women's organizations, along with interviews for newspapers and television. And in the end, there was always a speech in a large venue, before representatives from civil society organizations and governments. The aim was for them to support the Bolivian people and not the military government that had taken power. During most of my time there, I was constantly traveling from one place to another.

For seven months, I traveled like that, without seeing my family. Communication with Bolivia wasn't easy, and from July to October, I had no news. But in October, when I was giving a talk in Spain at a labor union, a priest called me over and told me that a nun had brought me a letter. That's how I got in touch with my younger sister, Marina, who had written a letter saying that all my children were with her in Cochabamba and that the father of my children had stayed at the mine. She said she was going to Chapare to live with my children and told me to come back home, however possible. "Finally, I got news from my family!" I was happy and decided to return.

That year the organizing committee of the Fourth Russell Tribunal had invited me to participate as a jury member. In November, the Russell Tribunal was going to be held in the Netherlands and was going to focus on the violation of human rights of First Nations and Indigenous communities of the Americas. So I proposed to the committee that they pay for my return flight to Peru instead of Sweden. Since I was a member of the jury, they agreed.

So, I was waiting to return, but one day, when I was in England visiting coal miners, I was told that my sister Marina was seriously ill. The next day, when I was about to enter the press conference, they told me that she had died. It was a shock for me! "Marina is gone. What did my sister die of? Was she killed by the army? Since she was with my children, what happened to them?" I lost consciousness. I didn't know where or who I was anymore and was totally lost. When I regained consciousness, I saw that they were rubbing me, putting something on my face and nose. Then they said, "There's the press conference, Domitila. The press is waiting for you, hurry up."

I felt lost thinking about my children. I wanted to cry and to know where they were. It felt like I had lost them. I was very afraid because we had heard a lot about what was happening in Chapare. The army was killing a lot of people! My sister was a leader in the coca-growing region. She was the female liaison of the coca farmers union in that area. So anything could occur to me, right? My mind was spinning: "My children were with her. . . . Maybe they were killed. . . . Maybe my daughters had been raped. . . . What had happened?" I was suffering a great deal. Then I picked myself up a bit and went to the press conference, but I kept thinking about my sister, my children, and my family all the time.

After the press conference, they told me I'd gotten a message from Sweden. It turned out the Bolivian exiles there had requested that the Swedish government grant political asylum to my children and my entire family. That was because I'd told them, "If my whole family was there with my sister, what will happen to my children now?" A *compañera* informed me: "The entire Bolivian community in Sweden got together and is requesting political asylum for your family from the Swedish government. That's why you have to give us their names, information, and whereabouts. A special commission from the Swedish Consulate will find them." I had provided the names and all the information they asked for.

Later, I was informed that UNHCR, the United Nations High Commissioner for Refugees, was moving things along in Cochabamba to bring my children here, and the asylum papers for them were ready, authorizing them to go to Sweden as political refugees. Then I learned that they were in the custody of UNHCR, and they had taken my children to a refuge in La Paz. They were looking for the father of my children, whose whereabouts were unknown. "You have to go back to Sweden," they told me. "Your children are going to come there, and you can no longer go back to Peru." So, I had to change my plane ticket and go back to Sweden again.

The people who were hosting me in Sweden were very support-ive, but my situation was still quite precarious. Every time I went out, I didn't know if I'd be returning to the same house or going to another one. I was ashamed about being a burden on the host families.

They told me that my children would be arriving around Christmas. I went three different times to the airport to wait for them. Yet they only arrived on January 15. They came without any notice, because it would have been too much to send word and risk my being let down at the airport. A family reunification request had been made for me, and the government granted politi-cal asylum to my children. Then, I began living in Sweden as a political refugee with my children under the family reunification agreement. Their father, who was being persecuted, first hid inside the mine, then in another place. After a month, he was located, got asylum, and came to live with us.

So we got set up to live in Sweden, in the city of Västerås. Yet even once we were all together there, I kept on traveling, accept-ing invitations to speak all over. I went to Paris four times, Austria three times, Spain twice, the Netherlands three times, Brazil twice, Denmark four times, Canada twice, Italy once, and so on. I partici-pated in Women's Festivals, Trade Union Congresses, etc., always talking about the situation in Bolivia and asking for solidarity with our people. I would go from airport to conference, and from con-ference to airport. They paid for my plane tickets and food, and gave me lodging; but I did all that as a union activist, as a spokes-person for the COB. However, I didn't have a salary as a union activist, since I was a woman, you see? Only men who had held jobs got that, but not the housewives. We women always worked like that in the committee: as volunteers. That was the custom. So, that was my work during the exile, up until the end of 1982, when we could finally return to Bolivia.

That's why I didn't devote much time to my children during that period. It was a really big change for my whole family. When they arrived and saw themselves in such a large house, with five rooms, a living room, a kitchen, a television, and a fridge full of food, my children didn't know what to do. They ran from one room to another, trying everything in the fridge. It seemed like something from a movie. Life in Sweden was much more comfortable—with amenities we had never had—than when we lived in our small house in Llallagua. Later on, the children started going to school, to learn Swedish.

Of course, we experienced culture shock too, related to their ways of learning things, behaving in the family and society, issues of sexuality and sex education, and all of that. But the children gradually got used to it, much more so than I did.

Another new thing for me was the "Social Assistance" that is given in Sweden for those who don't work. Since I had arrived as a refugee and wasn't working, I had to ask for assistance for rent and all our expenses. I wasn't used to that. So I went looking for work. They told me to go to social services. I was so embarrassed! I didn't know what it was going to be like, you know. I was also worried that they would question me because I was traveling: *How was it that I had money to travel all over Europe but didn't have money to bring food home and pay off my debts? Why did I need to travel? Since I was there as a refugee, I shouldn't be traveling.* . . . That's how they would see it.

"Well," I told them, "I don't want to live off social services. I don't want assistance, I want to be given work. Even if it's sweeping the streets, doing cleaning. I believe I can do that, and I'll do it well." The woman said, "Send her to do cleaning." "To clean the streets?" the instructor there asked. I said yes. Then he explained to me that I would have to go to school to learn how to clean the streets, because everything was done with machines. And I would have to know Swedish to read the texts. Moreover, he said, there were many people applying, so I would have to compete with them. If I could get good grades in the exams, well, they would give me the job of sweeping the streets.

So, yes, I had to turn to social services. The first time I went, they asked me how many children I had, and why my children lived with me. They told me children over sixteen were considered adults, and should live in a separate apartment. At least three of them would have to leave. I told them that, no, they were used to being with me. Social services gave me assistance for the first month, and I was able to pay off my debts. When I went the next month, it turned out that I had to account with receipts, down to the last penny, for everything I'd spent. However, I didn't know I had to keep all my receipts that way. Also, when I was traveling—since I was the exiled person responsible for family reunification—they would cut half the assistance for my family. From the 4,500 kronor in social assistance I got for all of us, they would cut it back to 2,000 while I was traveling. So, I stopped going to social services, and the father of my children took care of that. But every time I returned from a trip, he would argue with me, saying that there was not enough money, that we owed rent, telephone bills, payments for the television. . . . In short, there was not enough to cover our monthly expenses.

As a refugee, I had the right to study Swedish. I must have studied it for about fifteen days, but then came an invitation to Canada, which I accepted. When I returned one month later, my classmates were already speaking and writing Swedish. Yet I didn't know a word, and my mind was full of the English and French that I'd heard in Canada, because there are English- and French-speaking regions there. You see, I had almost forgotten the Swedish I had studied in the first few weeks. The teacher told me she would help me catch up, but then came an invitation to Austria, and when I came back, I'd forgotten even more. So, I didn't want to continue attending school and told the teacher, "Swedish won't be of much use to me because I don't plan to stay here. I want to go to Bolivia."

I always missed my country. One night, while we were having dinner, my youngest daughter asked me, "Mommy, why do we have everything here in Sweden, and children like us in Bolivia have so little?" Seeing my daughter, so young, already wondering about that—maybe that was the final thing that made me decide to return to Bolivia and continue fighting so that all children could have what they need, because their parents have jobs and are able to provide for them. So we stayed there in Sweden until the dictatorship of García Meza ended, and then returned.

In Sweden, I learned about many new things, many modern conveniences, and met many caring people, too. However, amid so much comfort, I noticed that many important aspects of human life were disappearing.

Consumerism is part of that. I noticed it mainly in my youngest son. When we arrived, it was such a major change: the food, clothes, toys—it was marvelous! But after a year of being there, one day I was with a journalist who came to visit me, and my son came over and said, "Mom, can you give me a hundred kroners because I need to go buy a toy?" Since I was busy, I gave him the hundred kronors and said, "Okay, you can go." My son went to school in the afternoon and when he came back, he asked me: "Mom, can you give me three hundred kronors?" I asked, "And why?" He replied, "To buy another toy." I said, "But you already bought a toy this morning." He said, "Yes, but I don't like that toy anymore." I asked, "What do you mean, my dear, you don't like it?" He replied, "There's a bigger, better one."

When I saw his toy, it was the size of a cassette recorder, with a little man holding a fishing rod and a river, and some small buttons that he had to press over and over. He found it boring. I said, "Look, son, at how many toys you've got in your room!" There were really a lot: he'd received gifts, won prizes, and stuff had been bought for him. "In Bolivia, you didn't have so many toys, only one or two." "Oh, of course! There, I had my little cart!" In Llallagua, he'd made a cart out of a sardine can and a spool of thread, and would transport dirt, stones, and all kinds of things in it. He played all day with it. And he said to me, "Do you know, Mom, why I wanted to play with my cart every day in Bolivia? It's because I was playing with my friends. But here, Mom, I still don't have friends, only toys. And I only enjoy them for a while; then I don't like them anymore."

I could see that: every house I went to was always full of toys—baskets of dolls, shelves of toys . . . they looked like toy stores! Those Barbie dolls . . . they would have dozens of them in the house. However, that made children more consumerist, always wanting to buy another toy and then another. When you looked around you realized that the society was like that. People felt compelled to quickly adopt any new product, and then another and another and yet another. It was a consumerist society. However, consuming itself didn't make children happier; on the contrary, you see, it made them very eager to consume more and very individualistic.

Another thing that struck me was the loneliness of many people. I never understood that kind of Swedish person who sits in front of the television, spending their afternoons with a can of beer, alone for so long. I also noticed that among many exiles, communication—that human warmth that is our essence—was disappearing. When we arrived in Sweden, people there thought we would be without motivation and on the brink of despair. They thought our approach to life was odd, and said, "How can you still go on wanting to be happy after having suffered so much?" But we're used to it: if today we suffer a massacre, we cry for our dead, we bury them, then we pull ourselves together again to go on living.

And what about old age in those countries? There are good public services for the elderly in Sweden. However, I got the sense that many people just wanted the elderly to die because they are a nuisance. By contrast, we would love to be able to bring our elderly back to life so they could always be with us. I remember my father, when I went one time to visit him to ask for support when my husband had been laid off. On seeing me, he said, "I'm an old tree, but even though I'm old, I still have branches that you can lean on. My room is small, but you can come and live with me, and we'll live huddled up here." Then, when I began living in Sweden, I saw trees that had their branches laden with snow for the first time. All of a sudden, I saw one big tree, with its fallen branches, and I remembered my father. Amid the loneliness and silence of exile, I wanted to be with him once more, to lean on his branches. But I never saw him again; he died while I was in Sweden.

While I was in exile, there were many surprises with the book. We never imagined the success that *Let Me Speak!* would have, both as an exposé of the situation in Bolivia and an inspiration for many people to reflect on their situation and compare it with ours. In my travels throughout Europe and in Latin American countries, I became aware of that, you see. Lots of people would come over to ask for autographs. Even here in Bolivia, when I go to schools, there are always people who come and ask me to sign their books.

The book also helped garner more support from people against Garcia Meza's dictatorship, because, through the book, they already knew me, and I could make myself better understood than when they only saw me on television or heard me speak. They had, you see, already read it in their own language.

Furthermore, I could see its impact on various important figures, who showed their solidarity with Bolivia. For example, there was Mr. Böll, who had won the Nobel Prize in Literature, or Eduardo Galeano, a great Latin American writer. The writer Elena Poniatowska, who wrote novels based on testimonies she collected in Mexico, asked to speak with me when she came to Bolivia to receive an award. We had lunch together at the Mexican Embassy. She was surprised that the book was an account of my real life.

The book brought me closer to comrade Rigoberta Menchú from Guatemala, who had received the Nobel Peace Prize. For a long time, we had wanted to meet—she was also traveling a lot in Europe at that time—but what usually happened is that when she was leaving a place, I would be arriving. But I had a day off during a trip to the Netherlands, and a German friend who knew where Rigoberta was going to speak about her country took me to meet her. We could only talk during lunch, since they didn't let us into the meeting. "Domitila," she said to me, "you are just like me: short, chubby, and that's why people who read your book ask if I'm Domitila when they see me."

We talked about various topics related to Bolivia and Guatemala. At the end, since they were always at war there, I asked her, "Rigoberta, when the army attacks and you have to escape, what is the most important thing you should take?" She replied, "The pot! The first thing you have to grab is the pot. If you don't have a pot, you can't cook your food, and you can starve to death before the army kills you."

During my exile, I also met Salvadoran, Guatemalan, and Nicaraguan women who had been involved in their countries' liberation movements. Some of them told me that the book was required reading in their organizations. One of them confided to me that she treated the book like a "bible" that she would reread whenever she had to go back to the mountains.

There's no doubt that the work we did together helped the country quite a bit, even if there has been criticism, and people who disagree. For we can see the results. On the one hand, the book's denunciation about what was happening in Bolivia had an impact and helped build solidarity with our people and our country. On the other hand, there are so many people in our condition who identified with the book's testimony, and whom it helped to reflect on their own situation! It was so important to do the work we did: after redacting it, you came back and went over the text with me, to make sure that I agreed with the written testimony and verified it.

How wonderful it would be if many more writers, journalists, and researchers devoted themselves to that kind of work and collected the stories of *campesina* women, women who are workers or domestic employees, and many other kinds of people—including men who might be unknown to the world but have a lot of knowledge in diverse areas. Hearing from many more people could contribute to a better understanding of our reality and to the realization that history does not belong to just a few, don't you think?

In late 1982, after much had happened in Bolivia, the military returned power to the UDP, which handed the government back to Hernán Siles Suazo. So, we decided to return. There were planes leaving Europe full of returning Bolivians—"On our way to our own country," they said, "poor, but happy." The Swedes would ask us, "But why are you leaving?" They didn't understand why we wanted to go back if we had nothing there and had all those comforts here. It was true, but Sweden wasn't our country; the customs, the way of seeing things, and the organization of life were all different. At least for me, I couldn't adapt. Also, I missed my people and wanted to be with them.

But the whole family didn't return. Most of my sons and daughters had already made their lives in Sweden and stayed there. It was difficult for me to leave my children in Europe, and I still miss them a lot. I think we, Bolivian mothers, are very attached to our children. In Europe, that didn't seem to be the case because there, children are almost always in daycare, raised outside the home, far from their mothers. So neither do the children seem to miss their mothers much, nor, I think, do mothers miss their children very much.

For the father of my children, returning to Bolivia was very difficult. Besides, even among the union comrades and committee members, there was this idea that, because we had been in Sweden, we'd returned with bags of dollars. They didn't know what life was like there, you see. We even had to confront many slanderous accusations. Additionally, many people turned their back on my husband because I continued to be involved in union organizing. René couldn't handle the pressure, and one day he presented me with an ultimatum: "Either you give up everything you're involved in, or I'm leaving." I tried to talk to him, to get him to consider everything in the life we had made, our children, and everything we had shared. But he left. He married another woman and had two children with her. He passed away three years ago, while we were settling the divorce. But there was so much that took place, mainly in front of the judge! I couldn't believe what they told me. They blamed me for everything.

Thus, because of García Meza's dictatorship, our home was practically destroyed. Even though my sons and daughters live in Sweden, they haven't forgotten about me, and whenever possible, they come to visit along with their little ones. I now have thirteen grandchildren. Furthermore, they provide me with a small pension so that I can maintain myself, mainly for the medications that I have to take for the rest of my life to control my diabetes and thyroid issues.

It's always so wonderful to see them! When your children are living in the same country with you, you see them once a year. But when they're living so far away, it's not that easy. I have a son and a daughter living in Cochabamba. They are married and have their families here. They like being in Bolivia but, of course, they also suffer from the problems of employment that we have here. In Bolivia, it's no longer enough for only the man to work to support the family: both husband and wife always have to work. And many things are lacking, even for children. So there is always that difficult situation, you see.

When I thought about my grandchildren living in Europe and those living in Bolivia, since I always wanted there to be equality and fairness among them, I also felt the differences due to their living situations. Thinking about how things were in Sweden versus here in Bolivia, I devoted myself for some time to helping out my children who had stayed here, even using my savings to do so. Now each one takes care of their own household, and I think it's good that it's like that. We help each other when needed; they are always close to me, constantly visiting, sending the grandchildren to see me, giving me a hand when I need help around the house or with transportation. I have a lot of love for all of them: those who are here and those who are far away.

Many people ask me if my sons and daughters are following

the same path as I did. As it is, some of my daughters tell me, "Yes, Mom, what you're doing is good. Everything you've done is very valuable." But others say, "I don't even want to know… It brings back very sad memories." You see, my home was always being raided. During García Meza's coup, while I was in Europe, our house was also occupied. So, they went through that suffering many times, fleeing from here to there. They had to leave school, and move from one city to another. All of that must have affected them a lot, even if they don't talk about it much. I won't deny that I would like to see my sons and daughters following the same path as I do, working to emancipate our people. But it has to be their decision. They have to choose.

You know, you don't have to be crazy to do the things we did. We weren't crazy. We love our sons and daughters so much. And it is precisely because of that love that we did everything we did, side by side with the people, to obtain a better life for ourselves and our children. If all women had thought like that, we would certainly have achieved more.

I have been living here in Cochabamba for thirteen years with my new partner, Felix. On May 7th, I turned sixty-five, and my partner is the same age as my eldest son. When he suggested living together, I said, "You've got to be crazy! You're old enough to be my son. I'm old, look at me, look at how I am." And he laughed! He has a lot of respect for women, and is very compassionate and supportive. With him, I feel young once more. I started taking care of myself again, wearing new clothes, and doing my hair. He is very affectionate, and that helps me overcome my insecurities. We talk a lot about how to relate to each other as a couple, how we must not mistreat one another. How can a man say he loves his partner and then hit her, and afterward approach her to make love? Of course, sometimes a person is in a bad mood. So you have to go outside for a while, out on the street, and wait for the bad mood to pass. Later, you talk again. Even to make love, you need to talk to know what each person likes and all that, don't you think?

When a man is all alone in the struggle, or a woman is all alone, it's hard and many things do not go well. However, when a woman and man are both involved in the same thing, they both feel supported, protected, and helped. That's true for both the man and the woman. My partner and I have the same ideals, and we do the work together. He won the trust of people around him and was elected Director of the Mobile School. He devotes himself to popular education, translating political texts, condensing them into shorter versions, and so on.

For example, when I travel to give my talks or for other matters, my partner helps me with what I have to prepare, and when he accompanies me, he's always there, taking notes, reminding me of things we agreed upon. I do the same when he travels. He never tells me, "As a woman, you have to do this or that." We share everything between the two of us—in the house too. Sometimes we do the wash together. Sometimes I do it myself. If I'm feeling unwell, he helps me in the kitchen, peeling potatoes, and so on, and he also cooks. He enjoys cooking for my family when we have them over. Of course, there's always a process of adjustment when such a big change occurs in a family, and we went through that too.

My children living in Sweden wanted to bring me there to live with them. They would tell me, "Mom, you've already done so much! Come live in peace with us here." But my life is here. This little house, in this working-class neighborhood of Cochabamba, is "my castle."

"RELOCATED" FROM THE MINES TO COCHABAMBA

To continue the story of those years after I came back from exile: in 1984, the head of government was Siles Suazo, who had been elected by popular vote in 1980. But between that year and 1982, there had been three elections, followed by three coups. Then Siles, who had been overthrown by the military coups, was put back in the Presidential Palace by the UDP in 1982. That happened thanks to popular resistance and international pressure. That pressure,

you see, included some countries' non-recognition of the governments put in place by military coups, which affected the country's
economy.

In Bolivia, the economic crisis at that time was serious. There
had been a terrible devaluation of our currency!! At least we were
all millionaires then, since with one million pesos, you could buy
five loaves of bread. The price of everything was increasing by the
minute.

Siles had promised that he would solve the crisis within the first
hundred days of his government. But not only did he not solve it,
things actually got worse. Food disappeared from the market, just
as had happened with Salvador Allende in Chile. Do you recall
how food disappeared from the market there? It was just the same
here. Yet we knew there was food, and so the miners wanted that
issue to be resolved.

Further, we'd been told that our tin was of very poor quality.
So, the Miners' Federation had investigated all of that: what was
needed was a special, more modern machine and a certain amount
of money to buy it. We asked COMIBOL to lend the money to
us—the miners of Siglo XX—so that we could get the machine,
which could create a finer ore that was competitive in the world
market. We already knew where we could buy the machine. So, all
the miners, men and women together, went to La Paz in support of
Siles. We brought our project proposal for tin production with us.
"We have to go and support the government so it will take more
radical measures and solve all this," we said. So we stayed in La Paz
for almost fifteen days, marching through the streets every day,
demanding to be received by Siles Suazo.

However, Siles only controlled the government; he didn't really
have power. That became clear in the end. Not only did Siles not
receive us, but after all those days that we spent in the street, he
ordered the police to tear-gas and beat us. So we had to leave. In
the mines, they stopped supplying us food in the depot. There was
nothing to eat in the mining camp, and they owed us three, four
months' worth of wages.

Siles didn't complete his term. He was forced to resign and call for new elections, which the MNR won with the candidacy of Paz Estenssoro. To implement the new economic policy, Paz chose Sánchez de Lozada as his Minister of Economy. And he, in turn, was advised by Mr. Jeffrey Sachs from the United States.

As a result of this process, Decree 21060 came along. Under the pretext of controlling inflation, they removed six zeros from the Bolivian currency, and the exchange rate was set on par with the dollar. Salaries were frozen. The state-owned mining company COMIBOL was dissolved, and they fired all its workers. But that's not all. The laws were changed. They said that the mines were no longer state-owned and that the workers had been discharged because "the tin era was over"; that employers had the right to freely hire their staff; and that all borders were opened for international free trade. With that decree, the neoliberal model clearly began to be implemented in Bolivia.

That, you see, provoked another crisis. In the mines, they started sending letters of resignation out, first to the most senior workers and then to the others. My partner René received a letter. They told us, "The Era of Tin has passed. So, get out of here. Leave!" Thus, the workers were forced to leave. More than 30,000 miners went through that. Never had such a thing been seen in Bolivia!

So we decided to organize a "March for Life." Thousands and thousands of workers, men and women, marched from Oruro to La Paz to demand that the company remain as it was before. But in the end the army made us stop, with their tanks and planes, and we had to go back.

It was a terrible moment. How could they take away our jobs? And not just the jobs, but the place where we had lived, where we were born, where we had grown up? You see, if you have your own little house and you're fired from work, you go home and look for another job, right? But not us. We had come there from another place. The house was not ours, but rather lent to us by COMIBOL. Still, we had buried our parents and grown old there. It was there that the children had their playmates, and we had our friends and neighbors. That was our life, you know? Suddenly, it was as if our mother had died, and we, the children, didn't know where to go. We looked at each other, wondering when we would meet again, and where our roots were. We didn't know where to go.

Decree 21060 forced us to leave our cities and go to places where we had neither houses, neighbors, nor friends. We ended up in places where we never thought we would live. The government called us "relocated people." In fact, we'd been fired, hadn't we? We'd been sent away from our jobs and our homes. There was a small severance payment, and that was it. We each had to make do as best we could.

To this day we are still trying to settle down in these new places. But many haven't been able to do so. It's difficult to get used to it, because life in the mines is so different from life in the city. The way of thinking is different. Here, we are all separated from one another, and it's not easy to organize.

When we faced "relocation," a new odyssey began for my family. There were no school openings for my children in Cochabamba. They looked at miners with contempt, and no company wanted to employ the men.

Furthermore, upon arriving in Cochabamba, there appeared agencies, supposedly belonging to real estate brokerages, that asked us to deposit our money with the promised of giving us a 6 percent interest rate per month. They were called Orcobol, Finsa, and so on. People were depositing their severance pay in dollars in these houses, and at the end of each month, they would receive 6 percent interest. Let's say a worker received 3,000 dollars; they would deposit it in Orcobol or Finsa, and they would get 180 dollars. What worker earns 180 dollars per month? It was a lot of money! And it wasn't just the miners who were depositing their money in those real estate companies, but also local people. They were selling their property, their cars, and other things to invest the money in those houses and get their interest payments every month.

So it all seemed wonderful! One day, I met a lady who had worked for the company for twenty-five years and had received

3,000 dollars in severance pay. I asked her, "How are you doing? What are we going to do now that we have been fired? We have to insist on getting our jobs back, since they said we've been 'relocated.'" She said, "Me? Why should I? I invested all my little nest egg, my 3,000 dollars in Finsa, and every month I'm getting 180 dollars. When in my life have I ever had 180 dollars to spend? That's more than enough for everything. So, I'm thinking of leaving all the money there. It's been six months since I've been receiving the money."

As things played out, this deal of receiving interest payments involved a bit of deception. It led us all to breathe a sigh of relief, and made us believe that Decree 21060 was a new model. They tried to keep the deal afloat, you see, so that everyone would accept the model and no one would criticize what had been decreed. But then everything collapsed. It didn't even last a year; the companies went bankrupt, and people lost every little bit of their money. Suddenly, all the companies were without money. Some people say that Finsa was created by the MNR government itself, and they themselves took the money. It was as if we had been fired twice. We were defrauded and deceived. Someone should do an investigation of what happened from that time up to today, to see how many people died, how many households were destroyed, how many children were cast out into the streets, how many girls were forced into prostitution, and how many families committed suicide.

When Decree 21060 came out, they told us that this time Bolivia was going to get investments and it would create more job opportunities. They promised 500,000 jobs. On the contrary, however, instead of creating more jobs, they laid off thousands and thousands of workers from the mines, factories, and offices. Now there is no job security, while threats of firing and forced retirement are becoming more and more frequent. What they want is to satisfy people with handouts instead of ensuring employment. Every day, they are forcing people to retire. Whenever they want to, they simply make a company go bankrupt, and then that same company appears in another part of the country or another country. They manipulate everything to get what they want. And there are fewer and fewer people in the workforce because everything is being done by machines.

The thing is, the "big fish" always adapt everything according to their interests and needs, don't they? During the colonial period, for example, when the Spaniards were exploiting our rich Potosí Mountain, they put all the people to work in the mines as enslaved laborers. The did it here and in other places. Then, when there were no more men to work, they went to Africa and they enslaved and brought many people from there, so they could continue working. Today, science has advanced, and they are kicking people out of the workplace, because they now have machines to replace us.

This isn't happening only in Bolivia. I've visited mines in Canada, England, Sweden, Nicaragua, and other countries. There, I could see how big capitalists are replacing human beings with machines. In Canada, I saw places where four hundred workers were once working, but now there are only a pair of skilled laborers. And those workers don't feel the exploitation of the system. One of them told me, "I earn well, I earn ten dollars per hour." But if you think about it, you see that machine is doing the work of four hundred workers who may now be unemployed.

The machine runs on oil and electricity. It doesn't have a wife or children, it doesn't need education or health care services, and it won't unite and organize like us. Somewhere in the world, the boss is quietly getting rich. In effect, the rich no longer need us.

Here, at the same time as they were replacing workers, they took superficial measures to solve our problems. For example, they started bringing things from outside to sell them here. One of them was used clothing from Europe and the United States. We once had our own textile and clothing factories, and so on. We also had our tailors, who were skilled at their jobs. In stores, with 60 pesos, you could buy pants made in Bolivia. Then, all of a sudden, at Thantaqhatu—a store selling used imports—better-quality material started appearing for just 5 pesos, 2 pesos, even one peso. That meant that the entire national industry went bankrupt.

What's sad is that, in the end, people got used to it. Here in Bolivia, it became normal. If before you could buy your daughter pants or shoes from our local factory with x-number of pesos, now you just go to Thantaqhatu. With one peso, you can buy second-hand items, and that solves the problem so that your children don't go barefoot. One comes to accept it, you see.

So it's a collective struggle, a struggle of the entire population, not just the workers. If our national industries are going to advance, there has to be work. That's because when there is work, you have a salary, which means you can buy potatoes from farmers, because they also had the money to plant and sell them. You can build a house for yourself. But when there is no work, there is no money circulating. Without money circulating, who will the factory owners sell their sausages, oil, noodles, or shoes to, for example? Or the farmers: who will they sell their potatoes, lemons, vegetables, and fruit to?

That's why, for us, the main issue is *work*, since even for our national industries to advance, there must be work. Otherwise, we'll end up being beggars. We might get help to go to the hospital, help for childbearing, or help for this or that, but nothing really gets solved.

For those who already have everything, it doesn't matter if what's produced is useful for people, as long as it's good for them. In Brazil, Argentina, or Peru, it's not the poor *campesinos* who are exporting their products, nor is it their production that is being subsidized, just as in Bolivia, it's not the poor *campesinos* who are exporting soybeans. It's the large landowners, mainly foreigners, who are exporting agricultural products from here to other places. In so doing, they are taking work away from small farmers here. For example, if they bring lemons or vegetables from Peru, people can buy those products more cheaply than the ones from here. It's because over there, they do everything with machines, and they use large extensions of land, along with chemicals that make the produce bigger. They even replace the seeds we use with genetically modified ones. All that is also killing off small-scale agriculture here. Because when increasingly sophisticated machines are used, human capital is no longer needed, right?

That's why I was surprised when I heard in Europe that Bolivia was being presented as a "model of adjustment" and "inflation control." Although it may be true that they controlled inflation for a while, it came at the price of thousands and thousands of workers being laid off, especially in state-owned companies, and the sale of our companies to foreign capital. In 1985, the Bolivian peso was on par with the American dollar. By May 2002, we were already at 7.10 bolivianos per American dollar. Argentina is the same as us, but their devaluation is even more rampant. They said we would overcome the crisis. It is being overcome for the rich, but what about us?

Another thing I got wind of in Europe was about the supposed "popular participation" that got going with Decree 21060. Of course, the government pays lip service to it in their documents. But the contradictory thing is that—despite their talk about popular participation—they don't concede it to extant organizations. Instead, they create their own organizations, whose leaders are appointed by the mayors' offices, and these new organizations have their own legal status and everything, to ensure that there's no opposition to the model they're imposing.

They also make new laws—agrarian, electoral, and educational laws—but do so with an irrational logic. For example, in the area of education, they've declared that, since the state has no money, municipalities must take responsibility for education. But what are the municipalities going to do if they're mostly small and poor? In response, they say they're going to allocate money from the national budget to small cities. But where is the money going to come from if all the state-owned enterprises are being privatized?

They sold off the state's resources, but nothing is improving in the country, because the resources from the sales of state-owned enterprises are not generating wealth for Bolivia. In my country, as in so many others, the newspapers are filled with photos of the crooks who are robbing our people's money. And I ask myself, what are they doing in power, if they only know how to steal?

Moreover, they also deceive us by broadcasting trashy news and television programs that don't help at all, like *Laura en América*, for example. Everyone gets hooked on that stuff. It's a disgusting program that callously shows all kinds of situations with substance abusers, sex workers, and crime. But the program doesn't show that these situations are all a result of the economic model. Why don't those people have work? Why do they get drunk? Why are they fighting? Why can't that mother talk to her children but instead has to work, while the children go to the streets and fall into drug addiction and prostitution? The show only shows the problems and says, "What people! What mothers! What youths!" It blames women for everything. And what does the system, the government have to do with all those problems that it shows? Laura Bozzo never talks about that.

Meanwhile other television channels, owned by economically powerful churches, what do they teach us? They tell us that what is happening is because we have sinned, that we have to pray, and we shouldn't get involved in problems. They say nothing about reality, they don't teach people to reason, to analyze the situation, and what it has to do with the government, the economic model, and the system.

I am not saying all this out of resentment, far from it! The facts are there, on the streets, where we have street children, gangs, and so on, and it's not because these people are inherently bad. It's the neoliberal model that gave rise to children involved in delinquency, as a result of their parents' unemployment. Many families were destroyed. Neoliberalism was the most criminal hoax of all, because it meant that a few people enriched themselves at the expense of the poverty of workers and that of the people.

What we have to do is unite all Bolivians, women and men, and fight to assure that there's work, which, in my view, is fundamental. If those who govern us are not capable of guaranteeing work for us, then they should return everything they sold and stole from us. Then we would be able to build better living conditions, create more jobs and generate better working and living conditions for everybody—for the *campesinos* and for all people.

In Bolivia, the neoliberal model was a complete failure because it did not solve our problems. Furthermore, it was what allowed them to rob us, since now we don't own anything. With their "Capitalization Plan,"[2] what they're doing is shamelessly looting the wealth of our country.

The neoliberal model was put in place twenty years ago, and so far it has not improved people's lives. In other countries where this model has been implemented, the problems have not been solved either. Neoliberalism is definitely not in our best interests. You see, it's as if, after so many years of trying to free ourselves from colonizers and oppressors of all kinds, we are now just handing ourselves over on a silver platter to transnational corporations and the IMF.

Now they want to consolidate that model with the FTAA, the Free Trade Area of the Americas.[3] I believe that all the continent's peoples should reject the FTAA, because it's a project that the United States is shamelessly trying to impose on us, to do things in its own way and at its own pace. What the US wants is not "free trade" in the continent, as the name suggests, but rather "control of trade" over the entire region, through which they'll reap huge profits, because they have advanced technology that we can't compete with. Through it, they will be able to continually force us to buy all their products.

In the case of Bolivia, for example, what can we export abroad? The minerals, for instance, are no longer ours; they belong to transnational corporations. The same goes for soybeans: it's not the Bolivian people who export them, but foreigners who settled here, such as the Mennonites. The same goes for garlic, which is produced in large quantities by Japanese communities and exported to Japan, leaving us with completely impoverished land that will no longer be able to produce anything after five years because it's so depleted of nutrients. The same applies to other exports that we might not even know about. So, with this FTAA business, it is already set up so that they will be exporting from themselves to themselves, without us benefiting in any way.

We want an *América Nuestra* [Our America].[4] Over the course of our history, our ancestors, including great figures like José Martí, envisioned a continent that would be ours, and they sought unity among our countries. Their idea was that the wealth that is found here should belong to the whole of a country, not just a small sector of it, but rather to the working people who today are poor and marginalized.

What we seek is well-being for all the peoples of our continent. Instead of the FTAA, what we want is for trade to be truly free, based on fair trade agreements between countries, and without the intermediation of transnational corporations or the imposition of the United States. To achieve that, the solution would be to transform the governments of countries throughout the continent. Governments must represent their people and not the International Monetary Fund.

THE DOMITILA MOBILE SCHOOL

Currently, from my little house in Cochabamba, I am mostly working on the Domitila Mobile School. Where did the idea of that school come from? I think it began to take shape when we were organizing the Housewives' Committee. As a child, I was full of curiosity. I was continually asking my father, when I heard him talking about things, to explain anything I didn't understand to me. That's how you acquire experience and knowledge, isn't it?

From the time I began participating in the trade union movement, I could see that we needed to prepare ourselves, study, and observe things. If you're going to struggle over workers' salaries, for example, then you should at least have a basic understanding of what benefits and harms the worker, don't you think? So, from that time forward, I realized that it was necessary to prepare oneself. But with all the things I had to do—taking care of the house, making my *salteñas*,[5] caring for my husband and children, and also working for the organization—I never had time to devote myself fully to passing on what I had learned.

In the past, among miners, whenever women organized themselves in a group with the aim of learning, of acquiring knowledge, they met with a real lack of understanding. There was an unwillingness to allow women to organize and to prepare and educate themselves. So, you see, the need was there. However, it was mainly after my participation in the Women's Conference in Mexico in 1975 that I started working on education, based on invitations I received, sometimes even outside my country.

In concrete terms, the idea of the school has a lot to do with something that happened during a lecture I gave in August of 1980. I was in England at the time, invited there by coal miners. On August 5th and 6th in Bolivia, a massacre had occurred in the mining camp of Caracoles, where the workers were stripped naked, then shot, and the women were raped. I received a letter that the women of Caracoles had sent to Bishop Manrique, which he distributed. That letter arrived precisely when I was in England. So I had the letter translated and read it at a meeting of coal miners. It was sad, very sad, that letter. It even mentioned that a girl had gone insane as a result of the women being raped. The letter told of how they broke glass on the ground and made the girls lie down naked, while the army marched over their bodies. They first wanted the mothers to tread on them, and when they refused, the army did it. It was also said that there were more than nine hundred people who were disappeared. Everyone who listened was in tears. Suddenly, a lady asked: "And is that army that is doing this to your people an army of white people, of foreigners?"

At that moment, it felt like I'd been punched in the face! I had a mental picture of Bolivian soldiers—the same people as us, with our same faces—marching before me. I had to stand up and say, "No, ma'am, although the orders often come from outside—it's not an army of whites or foreigners, but an army of our own sons, nephews, relatives, friends, and neighbors." "Ah!" she said, "and what education did you mothers give them? How could a brother rape his own sister, kill his own father, and trample on his own brothers. How is it possible that you didn't know how to educate your children, and now you come here sobbing to us?"

Then I began to think: Well, it's also true that we who were confined within the four walls of our homes, how can we know how to guide our children so that when they join the army, they don't listen to their commanders in situations like these? What do we know, if our children enlist as if they were just going to Carnival?" That's when the idea came to me: On returning to Bolivia, I'll converse with women about these issues.

When I was evicted from the Siglo XX mine in 1985, I came here to Cochabamba and met with comrades, including Félix, whom I met during the harvest in Santa Cruz, where he was a union leader for the sugarcane workers and had his union in Montero. I had gone there to give a talk to his group of workers, and that's how we met.

They kept inviting me there. Once, the two of us went with about seven youths from Cochabamba, who were friends of theirs. First, we held a workshop with a group of women, then a group of men, and later on at the university campus. We spent over a month doing that. But it was entirely voluntary work, and it wasn't possible to continue going on that way.

That made us see the importance of creating a team, a school. We started to organize and make plans, thinking about which topics to address. Gradually, the idea of the Mobile School emerged. In a meeting, our comrades decided to name it "Domitila Mobile School." Initially, we were about ten people. However, eventually, because it was hard to make ends meet and everything was done on a voluntary basis, only the two of us remained directly involved. The others still contribute as best they can.

One of our school's first projects was in Quilacollo. For five days, two hours each day, we set up in a school, working with young people who were finishing high school. We dealt with five topics. The first one, our starting point, was: "Why does Bolivia, as a rich country with so few inhabitants, experience such poverty? Can anyone answer me?" Some said it was because we are sinners or because Bolivia is a country of Indigenous and lazy people. Others said it's because we are illiterate. . . . Next, we began to debunk those ideas and then moved on to talk about the country, the external debt, the interest we have to pay, and how all that is the real cause. The next day, we talked about parties, unions, and movements. On the third day, we discussed women and organizing. On the fourth day, we talked about childhood and how we and our children get alienated: how we worship other cultures, other customs, and learn to do so through the media. On the last day, we discussed how young people live in Bolivia and in other countries. We talked about Sweden, Nicaragua, and so on. That's how the week went by. Well, that experience was a kind of starting point for what would happen later.

So far, we have held almost three hundred workshops with the most diverse groups of people and in the most varied places. They are all documented in a small newsletter we named *Imilla*, which in Quechua means young or single woman. Everything is recorded there with text and photos. On Sundays, we hold workshops to train new leaders. At noon, we have a communal lunch where everyone brings something, reviving an old custom from our communities called *ayni*.

This room in my little house is where all the school's documentation is kept. The books, documents, photos, a few videos, and the written reports of all the workshops we've conducted are kept here. We get invitations from schools, church groups, and women's and *campesino* organizations. With the *campesinos*, I speak in Quechua. When I was sick for almost two years and couldn't travel, people would make recordings of my discourses so that I could go on participating that way. Twice a year, a group of US youths comes to visit Bolivia, as part of an exchange program, and their teachers tell them to come here to listen to a talk.

So far, most of the school's work has been voluntary. However, we do get support from a group of friends in the Netherlands, which was formed by a Chilean friend, a contact of ours. The group gets invitations from organizations to perform in the street and in their parties. Once a year, they send us the money they've collected. That helps us to document the workshops, edit our internal newsletter *Imilla*, and also cover some of the transportation and lodging costs when we go to rural areas. We also use it to purchase some medications. Some Swedish friends gave us the computer here. The group from the United States that comes twice a year also pays us for the talks we give to them.

We have friends who have personally helped us, such as the late Pepe Ballón, who made possible some of our publications. Once, a printing house supported us and did a sizeable print run of our first newsletter, which serves as our introduction. Other friends support us by donating books, reference materials, and supplies for the school, such as paper, pencils, and so on. These contributions are significant, although they are small compared to the needs and requirements of the Mobile School. Without them, however, it wouldn't have been possible to do everything we have done so far.

BOLIVIA IN OUR TIME

When I say that our governments should represent us and not represent the IMF, it's because that would completely change the way we take care of and manage the country's resources, and it would also change our approach to the welfare of people in the country.

Bolivia continues to be a very rich country with a poor population, as I mentioned before. I've been able to see this even more clearly, now that I am traveling so widely. For example, the Cochabamba region, where I currently live, and the Chapare region in the Carrasco Province are the most beautiful places you could imagine. All kinds of food are produced in them. There are rivers, lakes, and fish, and there's oil. Beyond the beauty of these places, the climate is neither very cold nor very hot. So it's a paradise, you see! That's why the bourgeoisie settled here in Cochabamba and made their condominiums and neighborhoods where they've got everything—their houses, markets, schools, swimming pools, and sports facilities—whereas the rest of us here have none of those conveniences.

So, the question comes up: "Why is it that, if Bolivia is a rich country, its people suffer from such poverty? Why do the few who are rich become richer, and the poor poorer?" That's Bolivia's key problem: what we have here does not belong to the people. That beautiful airport you see in Cochabamba, the Bolivian airline, the mines, the oil, the timber, and the cultivated lands—the many things you can see in the country—don't belong to us, the people here.

Before, I used to talk more about the situation of the mines, because I was living there and knew about it. Now, living here, I've had the opportunity to see many other things in many different places, and I see that there's the same exploitation there or even worse. That's because, under the neoliberal model, they're selling off the country, giving everything away to foreigners. But the most serious thing is that few people really understand why things are like this.

The fact is that we are getting more and more indebted every day, because they are giving away everything. Those who say they're purchasing something from Bolivia, say a concession for $300-$400 million, often put down almost nothing on signing the contract, not even a cent. They say they will start exploring first, and then make their payments on time. But that's not what happens—it's pure income for them. For example, the mining centers that remained after the decree that broke up the state mining company (the ones that are profitable) now belong to foreign millionaires. The Huanuni mine is one case. It was handed over to a foreign company in England that is managing the mine. Yet since they claim there's a worldwide tin crisis going on, and the price of tin has dropped even further, the owners want to abandon the business. Even so, they don't want to fulfill their agreements, and haven't even given over the money they promised. See how it is?

It's as if I built my own little house and then suddenly someone takes ownership of it, privatizing it in the name of capital. Then they kick me out. If I want to keep living in my own house, they tell me: "Okay, but I am the owner so you have to rent it." Now I have to pay rent on the house, and they increase the rent whenever they feel like it. However, they haven't contributed a single cent, nor have they touched a shovel or pickaxe, or moved a cart of dirt to make the house. If I built this house, it should be mine, right?

I could give numerous examples of this. In remote areas like Beni, the same kind of things happen. There are a lot of people living there in extreme poverty, people who are destitute. Suddenly, a company appears, a timber company, for example, that is logging the wood. People work for them—the company provides jobs—and we can't be looking for ways to get people out of there because they would die, since logging is their work, their livelihood and means of survival. It is difficult to explain to people what is happening, and it is even more difficult to organize people without funds.

If we turn now to farming, it's clear that our people have always been an agricultural people. They knew how to conserve the land and work it according to their needs. In the distant past, we didn't plant more than we needed, nor did we hunt or fish more than necessary. We took only what was needed, because there was the idea that the land belonged to our grandchildren and the grand-children of our grandchildren, that is, to future generations. So, it was always said that it is necessary to preserve the land, that it was to be treasured, and that it was an existential matter. Today that's still true, because if the land does not produce, then even if you have money or gold, what will you eat if there is no food? Will you eat your gold or silver?

So all of humanity should adopt the principle of taking care of nature. However, that's not the case. They bring foreigners here, all kinds of foreigners—like the Mennonites, for example—who get involved in agriculture. They acquire the best lands and grow food, but not so much for their own subsistence, as for commerce.

Take soy, for example. They say that Bolivia exports soy. But it's

not Bolivians who are exporting or profiting from soybean production. It is foreigners for the most part, mainly Mennonites (and
before them Russians who had come here). They grow enough soy
to supply all the oil factories here, and also to export it abroad. But
after so many years under that kind of production, their lands have
become infertile, according to those who've studied the subject. So,
to make those infertile lands produce once again, they're acquiring chemical inputs like fertilizers, and also pesticides to kill the
insects that come along with the plant. They are starting to employ
everything of that sort. So even if all kinds of crops are produced
in Bolivia, it's no longer done in a natural way, but always with
fertilizers and pesticides brought from abroad. So, who benefits
from all this?

Then there is this whole GMO business. I know very little about
it, but I do know that transgenics are foods from plants that are
being made sterile. It's as if they were neutering the plant, you see?
So, they sell those neutered seeds to people, and they plant them.
Of course, the seed yields a larger output. For example, with the
potatoes, they are producing larger ones, but inside they are sickly
and dry, and you can't get seeds from those potatoes. Before, when
you planted your own little potato crop here with your own means,
you had three types of potatoes: the large ones to sell, medium
ones to eat, and smaller ones to plant as seeds. Now they are killing off the potato. There will come a time—if we continue this way
with the type of seed they're providing—when it will be hard to get
our own seeds. That will be terrible, because we'll have to depend
on them to cultivate all our food. They're appropriating everything
with that technology. Why? To be owners. The rich want to own
everything!

And that's not all. They are also appropriating our natural medicines. They use all kinds of organizations and institutions to do
so. They go to all these countries finding out how they cure diseases, for example, in China and India. They came here to Bolivia
to study our *callahuayas*, our community of natural doctors that is
already known worldwide, to see how they heal, how they prepare

their formulas and medicines. Now, in the United States, transnational corporations want to patent those plants and formulas, and then prohibit us from healing ourselves with our own medicines! They are going to take what is ours, and we will have to buy it from them. In other words, they want to own everything, everything that exists on Earth.

Take the example of food. Before, there were no McDonald's here, but now they've brought them. People who know about this have already warned us that, for example, to make their hamburgers the cows are raised with a lot of chemicals. They develop that unnatural meat and are selling it in McDonald's hamburgers all over the world. The meat is stoked up on hormones and everything else that they give them. It's causing diseases in cows and also in humans. Even so, people here are turning to these unnatural foods that all come from the outside. In the case of McDonald's, many people are abandoning the food that we've eaten for centuries and our farmers produce naturally. It's because they lack awareness and information. Food, for example, is meant to alleviate hunger, right? It's for people to nourish themselves. But now it has become a business, to yield profits for those who don't even eat what they make profit on.

All this is called the "global model." That's what they say it is: "globalization." In truth, however, it is a form of globalization that only benefits a few. Poverty is globalized, while nature, Mother Earth, is being destroyed.

All of humanity should respect Mother Earth. If you think about it, what doesn't come from the earth? Everything comes from the earth: food, water to quench thirst, materials to make clothing... One day we were thinking about how even the weapons that the enemy uses to attack us come from the earth, because the bullets, tanks, and chemicals they use against us are made from minerals.

Our people were right to worship Mother Earth, the Pachamama. As they said: "From her, we feed ourselves and make everything." Nowadays, we are witnessing eruptions, earthquakes, and floods that are taking place everywhere. It's because the earth is being destroyed, and the earth, you see, is responding that way.

Now, if you take the example of coca, which is discussed so much internationally, you'll appreciate what is really happening, and it's very different from what the press and government agencies say. The coca-growing region of Bolivia is small compared to the whole country. There are two regions where coca leaves are produced: the Yungas, near La Paz, and the Chapare, in Carrasco province. They don't give much importance to production in the Yungas, saying it is for domestic consumption. But they value the Chapare a lot. Why? Because the Chapare is a beautiful region, very rich in everything. You could say that it's the paradise people have always looked for: it has water, fish, animals, all kinds of food, and everything can be produced there. That's why I believe everyone covets that land. Yet what doesn't exist in the Chapare are roads; people survive there however they can, in extreme poverty.

For a long time, coca leaves have been produced in the Chapare. But it was only when big companies discovered that coca leaves were good for making cocaine that smuggling began and cocaine production started. However, it's not the people employed in stomping[6] on the coca leaves who benefit from it: it's those trafficking cocaine. The press presents it as if everything were being done here in Bolivia, such as when they say: "We found a maceration pit. . . . We found so many millions of dollars. . . . We found this and that." Of course, the powder itself is made here, but many foreigners have also come here to run the cocaine business.

If our government weren't so sold out to the *gringos*, coca could be industrialized for the benefit of the country. For the coca leaf is very useful in medicine: it can be employed to make anesthetics for surgeries and many other valuable things. Local university students, in their laboratories, have made a series of coca-based products: syrups for weight loss and to control diabetes, wines, liquors, biscuits, chewing gum, and so on. They present and sell these items at fairs that are held here. They also sell them at natural medicine stands. They say that a natural insecticide for plants can be made from coca.

The truth is that many oil wells have been found in Chapare's coca-growing region. They found so many wells that they decided to seal them off, most likely so they can carry out the exploration in their own way. However, they justify it by saying that they sealed the wells because narco-traffickers are producing cocaine there. They also allege that that's why they are eradicating the coca crops and threatening to remove people from the area, including many people who were displaced from the mines and found their only way to survive in coca cultivation. To control all of this, the United States has set up three garrisons of the DEA [Drug Enforcement Administration], the US agency that combats drug trafficking, and they have their agents there. These are specialized groups of men and women, supposedly created to "combat drug trafficking." Everyone, including Bolivians working with them, are employees of the North Americans. They've organized all of this to control our oil, under the guise of controlling drug trafficking.

Coca is a sacred plant. It has never been prohibited to cultivate and chew coca leaves. For Indigenous people, coca is as sacred to them as the Eucharist is for Catholics, because the plant accompanies them in life and death. When a child is born, we use it in rituals to rejoice, and when a person dies, we use coca leaves in their wake to bid farewell to the loved one. The same thing happens in the mines. The work is so hard there that they cannot bring in food; the only thing miners can do is chew fresh coca leaves, which gives them more strength and motivation to work. In congresses, to clear the mind, we do the same thing: we chew coca.

It is the rich people of the country and politicians who profit from the cocaine business, not the farmers who cultivate coca. Moreover, a large portion of coca growers are former miners who settled in coca growing lands after the disaster produced by the mass layoffs in the mines. They came to the Yungas and Chapare regions to start their lives anew there. The government, using the pretext of combating drug trafficking, is attacking these people and wants to displace them from these fertile lands, just as they did in the mines. They were never given land or any assistance by the government, so they went there and looked for something they could do to survive. And, of course, coca has a market, doesn't it?

People here are totally against cocaine production, which moreover is very damaging to children and young people. We're not to blame for the fact that foreigners combine certain chemicals with coca and then produce the drug. We know that coca has harmful effects when chemically processed. That's why our gods cursed the white people when they touched the coca leaf. In the legend of coca, Tata Inti and Pacha Mama say: "On that day, they will go mad."

In Bolivia, coca leaves are made into "coca paste," which will later be transformed into cocaine. The paste is refined in Brazil or the United States, where it is most sold and consumed. People should also know that to produce the "coca paste," traffickers need to have chemical products, which come precisely from the industrialized countries. So, who should be condemned and punished? It's not our *campesinos* who bring the chemical products here! Even so, they want to crush the *campesinos*, whereas the industrialized countries are never brought to account. One can even draw a parallel between the producers of cocaine and arms manufacturers. We know bullets are made for killing people, but those who run the arms industry are not brought to trial, are they?

Under the neoliberal model, the same thing plays out with other problems that we've mentioned before: soy, transgenics, hamburgers, timber, and so on. Everything is subordinated to neoliberal globalization. Nothing escapes it. Governments must do whatever they are told by the United States, which now has hegemony over everything through the International Monetary Fund. Even the United Nations can hardly do anything without their approval, don't you think?

Look, for example, at what happened on September 11, 2001, when the Twin Towers, which were a symbol of the US Empire, were burned and destroyed. The United States government took advantage of that situation to convince all the world leaders to allegedly "fight against terrorism."

They say they feel sorry for the people who died in the Twin Towers in New York. We, who have endured invasions, massacres, and torture just for trying to improve our people's living conditions, can understand the pain experienced by those innocent people who died in the attack on the two buildings. That's why, when it happened, we let it be known that we felt pain for those innocent people who worked there and died, and felt their families' pain. It's sad to know that a son, husband, or daughter went to work one day and will never return; that they died there, crushed by the wreckage or burned.

However, if you look around the world, there are so many such attacks that our peoples have experienced: so many deaths and so much suffering that occurs when there's no food or someone loses their job. So, we ask ourselves: who is concerned that people are dying in the streets here, that kids are wandering around or sometimes imprisoned, or that we women lose our children? Who takes notice of all that?

In the case of the Twin Towers, for example, they said they'd already identified the perpetrator, who was Bin Laden. He was their own spoiled child, you see, because they nurtured the man and put him in their service with a view to combating the Soviet Union. Then, he turned against them and attacked the Towers. Allegedly, the Pentagon knew in advance that it was going to happen. So, why didn't they do something to catch Bin Laden, if they have powerful organizations like the CIA, the FBI, and so many others? How could they not capture a single actor? That makes you think.

When we see the crime committed in the Twin Towers attack being so strongly condemned in the press, we agree, sympathize, and feel sorry. We wouldn't want that to happen to anybody. However, when they attack Afghani people themselves, killing them, even innocent children and old people, in a population that's so poor—perhaps even poorer than us—then we say: neither the attack on the Towers, nor the blatant attack they carried out against Afghanistan's entire people is justified.

The United States says it's fighting against terrorism, against the Taliban. I think the main terrorists are the people in the Pentagon and the wealthy who care so little about trampling on almost anyone. We think the real motive behind their attacking Afghanistan is the Middle East's oil, which the US wants to explore, and the interest of those big multinational companies involved in oil. Indeed, Afghanistan's territory is key to their project. That's what they want to control: the route for all the oil they hope to extract from the Arab countries.

It's a pity, but all the world's governments have subjugated themselves to the United States. Although there are protests, as we can see in the media, governments pay no attention to their people and instead support the United States, surrendering to it. And when it comes to imposing their neoliberal policies, they don't care what happens. They believe they can do anything. The whole point is to dominate.

The same can be seen with regard to all that happens to the Palestinian people. It's said that Israel is God's chosen people, and it has always been seen that way. But how is it that the chosen people of God murder so many others? How can they be so unjust toward another people and not give them their own territory to live in? Don't the Palestinians have a right to their own homeland? Israel says the Palestinians kill their people. Yet it was Israel that started the war of invasion many years ago, wasn't it? And hardly anyone talks about that. How many years have the Palestinian people been suffering?—that's forgotten about. Every day we see on television the Palestinians carrying out protests. Yet they don't show us how they were driven out of their own territory, and how an entire people has been exiled and left without a place to live, work, study, and be happy.

With time, the world will come under the hegemony of the United States and the International Monetary Fund, which is who implements these neoliberal policies. The hegemonic group will include those countries that ally with the United States against our peoples. And wherever people begin protesting for work, water, or justice, they will start torturing and massacring them, even doing so with the help of other countries. They will see terrorists everywhere. Here in Bolivia, for example, they used to say we were heretics. Then they said we were communists. Later, they said we were drug traffickers. Now, they'll say we are terrorists. They'll see every person who seeks work, or food and health for their children as a Bin Laden perhaps. That's sad, isn't it?

That's why I say that, in addition to uniting within our country, we need to seek alliances with other countries that are suffering from neoliberal policies and with other peoples who are in solidarity with us.

ORGANIZING AMONG THE PEOPLE

I began to know what it was like to be in an organization when I joined the Siglo XX-Catavi Housewives Committee in 1963. Initially, I thought the struggle was only about social and economic issues, but later I realized it was also political. Then I began asking myself the question: What does it mean to be political?

In my talks, I always say that there are three types of politicians. Some are self-centered and selfish, seeking everything for themselves. Others want everything to be for everyone. And the majority, who are in the middle, say, "I am not political" or "I don't live off politics." However, we are all political, even if we don't think so.

The majority of people are also in the middle and are scared, like in the story where the wolf eats Little Red Riding Hood. They say, "I'm not going to get involved, because politics is only about brazenness and barbarity." Brazenness and barbarity? In fact, it's true what they say, because we don't participate, and we don't even control the votes we cast. That's why politicians do whatever they want. It's because we lack awareness, sufficient knowledge, and an analysis of reality. As it is, we cast our vote because it's obligatory or because the television shows one candidate as likable, another as attractive, or because a husband tells his wife who to vote for.

Now, for example, one month before the mid-2002 elections, we don't even analyze the fact that Sánchez de Lozada is a candidate who went to the United States and agreed to continue selling off our country to them. In other words, our lack of awareness and organization favors a certain type of politics, don't you think?

We have come to realize that as workers, for many years, we deceived ourselves into thinking that through the COB, we would take political power in the country. The COB was the organization that most united our people. The class unity achieved in the union reached such a high level that in 1971, for example, a political thesis was approved affirming that the COB was going to organize workers to seize political power. At that time, the COB was very strong. It even overthrew governments. That happened because it was united, and the political parties also saw its strength. Whenever there was a problem or conflict with the government, they would always ask: What will the COB say? That was its power!

Well, the enemy is aware of these things and surely has investigated them. That's why when the neoliberal model was put in place, the first thing they did was attack the COB's vanguard, which was the Miners' Federation. When the government put out Decree 21060 everything got chaotic. People had to move, thousands and thousands lost their jobs, and we were also left without our organizations. When the Berlin Wall came down—recall that, before then, people used to say that socialism there was good—everyone began to ask themselves, "What's going to happen?" Well, the same thing happened here with Decree 21060. People began asking themselves, "What will happen?"

The situation that the labor movement is going through these days is difficult. Nowadays, workers are simply standing by their tools, waiting to see if they can find work, even if just for a day. Can we resign ourselves to that? No! And we can't tolerate that workers' rights are being lost, that employers have the right to hire freely, and that any worker who wants to organize is dismissed. Those things have to change, don't you think?

Our union was so strong that the unemployed are now rallying behind the COB, despite the pilfering and weakening of the organization. It's no coincidence that the ruling party, even though it claims the COB no longer exists—that it's been destroyed —has devoted funds and sent its agents into it, teaching hundreds of classes with a view to consecrating neoliberalism and privatization. Why do they do that? Because they fear the organization will become strong again. Our goal is precisely to revive the COB's strength and move forward with it.

Additionally, it turns out that the people are so clear-sighted and capable, that—even if those in the COB haven't realized it—other forces and movements have emerged in recent years, alongside the labor movement.

For example, it was a real surprise for me on October 12, 1992 (when we took to the streets in remembrance of what happened five hundred years ago with the arrival of the Spaniards) to see *campesinos* and Indigenous people arriving with their flags, their costumes, and their music, asserting that Bolivia is not only the Bolivia that is known, but is rather the sum of more than thirty nationalities: Quechua, Aymara, Guarani, and others. And they explained why it was necessary to organize an Assembly of Indigenous Peoples, of First Nations.

Another mobilization that impressed me was the "Water War." That was the name that people from Cochabamba neighborhoods gave to the mobilizations to protect their water supply from the Aguas del Tunari company. Most of the population here does not have access to water. The government handed the water utility over to a foreign company, creating a joint venture by the name of Aguas del Tunari, claiming that everyone would have access to water. But, of course, once the water started to come, the rates began to increase. Before, wherever the city water supply reached people, they had formed their own cooperatives, with their own water pumps and pipelines to supply water to their homes. Suddenly, the new company owned all that without having paid anything, not even having replaced a worn-out pipe! Even so, they started charging for it. In the neighborhood where I live, for example, we didn't pay for municipal water, and suddenly we were faced with high water bills. So, the reaction was intense. The entire community rose up over the water issue. And, of course, the police arrived to shoot, beat, and kill. There were two weeks of clashes, all because we were defending our right to water. It was an important mobilization!

That's to say, the new situation has given rise to more and more movements among the people. In a sense, the current situation is better than it was for us before, because in former years, workers like us were alone. Now we're not. Before, workers and *campesinos* were fooled into being divided among ourselves, but now we are uniting more and more every day.

The positive thing, I believe, is that every day our people are realizing that they are no longer passing solutions in our country: that neither marches, nor protests, nor even elections are effective. This is because, for the people, the situation always remains the same. For that reason, there is deeper and deeper integration among us, not only on the level of words, but also through deeds. Our main strategy for saving our country is securing work—which for the *campesinos* also means having land, good seeds, technology, tools, and a market.

That's why we need to try so hard to achieve unity. Because what most weakens popular organization is division, interference, and attempts to break away from the movement. The divisions among movements, despite the passage of time, remain the same as before. If you organize anything, the next day there will be two or three different groups.

The COB is no longer the union it once was. It's heavily infiltrated by political parties and non-governmental organizations, which are also tied to the political parties involved in it. People from the ruling parties—from the AND and MNR—have joined the union and all of them want to be union leaders. The COB's been divided by politicians, both from the right and the left. When they get inside the movement, they approach the social leaders: if the leader comes around and submits, everything is fine. If not, they slander that person and do whatever they can to destroy them.

That also suits the economic model and the wealthy, by keeping people fighting among themselves. The COB has been weakened a great deal in recent years due to the internal divisions created by both left-wing and right-wing parties. For example, when the Movimiento de Izquierda Revolucionaria (MIR) started putting money into it, after government officials were already inside, then the leaders were caught in the middle. Next the Trotskyists appeared, who are never in agreement. In the end, there were four political organizations in charge! Those divisions became evident in the last COB Congress and also in the March for Life. With that way of operating, you see, nobody gets anywhere.

Some churches and NGOs are also contributing to the problem. People who were once committed to organizing the people, who were leaders, are suddenly seized on by a church or an NGO that gets them working on programs dealing only with violence, health, or handicrafts. Inside the NGO they have their workshops, their secretaries, and their employment. At the end of the year, when the funders come back, they render accounts and start all over again. But the health problems of the people are never solved, because they still don't have jobs that would allow them to take care of themselves and get treatment, you see. The same happens with the craft projects; they teach people how to make things and how to sell them abroad. But with this crisis we are in, very little is sold, if anything. Moreover, many of the NGOs don't devote time and resources to help people understand why Bolivians find themselves living in poverty.

For me, an NGO that doesn't teach the people how to organize so that they can take power, on the one hand, distracts them and, on the other, actually holds back those youths and other individuals who were once revolutionaries but are now resigned to what already exists, because they have to make sure that the following year their NGO is approved again, so they can keep their house, car, and secretary, and their good salaries—just by *talking about* health, violence against women, and so on. Yet all those afflictions have a root, they have a parent, which is the system or model that allows them to occur. That root cause must always be clear in everything we do, don't you think?

It's not possible to take power via a union or social movement; what we need is a political organization, a political party that emerges from the people and is not opportunistic. But there is hope that such a party will arise among the organized people. What we need to do to take power is, first, organize our own political party, a party of the people. Second, we need to form a broad front against neoliberalism which, since it is dominating the entire world, requires us to form a front with an international character.

A party would deal with everything at a national level, including what *campesinos*, women, workers, and youth need. In fact, it would address everything that the people need: work, housing, health, transportation, and agriculture. It has to be an organization with a program, a plan, and collective leadership.

The party is different from social movements that are conjunctural or according to social sectors. For example, the women's movement deals with respect for women, violence against women, women's health, and children. There is also the coca growers' movement, which focuses on the coca issue, and the water rights movement, which brought together the entire population of poor people in Cochabamba around the water problem. Again, the Indigenous Pachacuti Movement (MIP) defends the Indigenous cause. The labor movement, likewise, has its own function: addressing the situation of the working class, ensuring employment for men and women, preventing the firing of workers, ensuring fair wages and all of that. The party has to encompass the interests of everyone. That's what its program and its plans do, right?

Previously I thought that the union, the COB, could achieve that. But when the unions entered the elections with the cadre Lechín as our candidate, hardly anyone voted for him.[7] That's because the workers' movement and unions, on the one hand, and the party, on the other, are two very different kinds of things. As workers, we dedicated ourselves to the union struggle and forgot about the party, putting aside all political parties. Yet by doing so,

we handed over democracy—for which we had fought so hard—
on a silver platter to the bourgeoisie, and they always have their
parties. Communist parties were once strong on the left. However,
since the fall of the Berlin Wall, they've ceased to be powerful, and
many leaders were even *disappeared*. Others, turned to the right in
a defeatist way, saying that socialism is no longer feasible.

Working-class people do not have a true party that represents
them. Here in Bolivia we have learned that solving the problems
of hunger and poverty will not be easy. The people themselves
must exercise power, and to take power they need their own party.
And the main issue that can bring us together in a united front is
the issue of work. Work gives dignity to a person. When you have
work—you see—you can have food, housing, and self-esteem.

Therefore, first, the people must unite on all levels, and when I say
"all levels," I mean in the countryside, in factories, and in the social
movements. Even businesspeople have a need and moral obligation
to join the project. Could it be that they aren't suffering too? When
Decree 21060 was enacted, opening our borders for free trade,
for exporting and so that everything could be snuck in, that also
affected our national industries. That's even more true now, because
of the FTAA agreement that they're making, don't you think?

We also need to overcome the many habits that divide us, that
separate workers and *campesinos*, pitting us against each other.
Saying to someone "you are a *Mamani*" or "you are a *cochalo*"
or "you are a *camba*" only divides and distracts us from what is
most important.[8] We have to understand where all these differences come from, who invented them, and how we are going
to overcome them. The people, if united, will be able to change
things. They won't if they're divided. We also have to work with the
churches on this, because there are some churches in the poorest
neighborhoods that serve the interests of the rich by preventing
people from organizing themselves, telling them: "God will solve
our problems. . . ." They also pit people against each other by simply
saying to one, "You keep the Sabbath on Saturday," but to another,
"You observe it on Sunday."

I would like to point out another important thing: we need to remember everything that's been experienced in Latin America, to learn from both our successes and errors. We've made so many attempts at liberation! Here in Bolivia, for example, I always talk about the 1952 revolution because it was a milestone in the Bolivian people's history. It was a revolution that was internationally recognized as an example of how to organize people to bring about change. And it succeeded, even triumphing over the army.

Cuba is another example for us. I have never lived in a socialist country, and I've only been to Cuba for health reasons, when I had cancer surgery. What most impressed me in that country was that, despite the blockade and all the poverty they say exists in Cuba, you don't see abandoned children stealing or beggars on the streets. Children are happy, studying, playing, or walking with their parents. Cuba's advances in medicine are also impressive. Beyond that, there's the issue of how people treat one another and how everyone there works not just for money but because they have something to defend: their country. The freedom of worship in Cuba is also striking. One Sunday, I had a chance to see a large gathering of evangelicals that filled the Plaza de la Revolución with thousands and thousands of people. Fidel was sitting there calmly with his entourage, and the others were singing and saying beautiful things. I couldn't believe it. I thought to myself, "In Bolivia, a country with a government that claims to be democratic and claims to be Christian, how is it possible that they assassinated Father Luis Espinal? But here, in this supposedly atheist, communist country, there is so much freedom?" My thought was: "Luis, you were mistaken, brother, coming from Spain to Bolivia; you should have come to Cuba, and surely you would still be alive at a time when so many people need you." There is much more that could be said. When you think about all the blockades that country has faced for so many years, it truly deserves our admiration.

Cuba also brings "Che" to mind, who left Cuba to come to Bolivia because he wanted to press ahead, working for the whole continent's liberation from the yoke of US imperialism. Although we might question his methods, we can't forget that Che was a great example of dedication to the cause. He was a doctor who could have had his own clinic, made good money, and lived peacefully. Yet he didn't do so. Instead, he devoted his life to pursuing a change that would improve things for everyone. Here in Bolivia, in 1997, in La Higuera in the Vallegrande province, they held a tribute to him at an international gathering, which I attended. When they asked me to speak, I said, "They killed Che thirty years ago, but he lives on. That's because there is more poverty than ever, and as long as there's poverty and misery, Che's utopia will remain alive and active. Che died for the dignity of millions of human beings who in Bolivia and elsewhere in the world have no hope for a decent life. That's why I say, especially to the young people who should take up the banners of freedom for which Che died, the figure of Che should not be used simply as a business or a fashion, but as a commitment to building a new society."

Nor can we forget the Sandinista Revolution in Nicaragua as a great Latin American experiment in the pursuit of change. I went there twice, once in 1979, a few months after the [FSLN] Front's victory, and again in 1984, during the commemoration of the fiftieth anniversary of Sandino's death and the repatriation of Santos López's remains from Cuba, the last combatant of Sandino's General Staff. There were many tributes throughout the country. At that time, I was president of the Bolivian-Nicaraguan Friendship House. In Nicaragua, I was struck by the way young people and women were involved in the revolution. I met and talked with some high school students who had come back from spending three months picking coffee. Along with them were many internationalist youths who had come to learn more about the Nicaraguan revolution and support it. I also met the *comandantes* Mónica Baltodano, Doris Tijerino, and others—women who had faced many challenges as leaders. I was struck that these women were so beautiful, gentle, and delicate, with Doris breastfeeding her baby. I had read about them, but one has this idea that only "Rambos," supermen, and superwomen can do what they did, but that's not true! I also have a great memory of my encounter with Tomás Borge in Nicaragua, which was very important to me and helped me make decisions regarding my own commitment to politics.

People have tried so many things in our countries to overcome the situation we are in! We can't forget all that, can we? It's necessary to recover that history and learn from our past to build our future. All of this is related to the issue of organizing the people that we have been talking about.

Here in Bolivia, as far as political parties are concerned, what we see is that they are generally not organized from within the people but rather spring out of the heads of their leaders. I think that it's based on those movements made up of *campesinos*, students, workers, women, and so on, that we should unite, with an awareness of the need for a national-level leadership capable of bringing them all together. This has to be done by listening: taking into account what people say. Representatives from each sector must be in the party. Women, *campesinos*, workers, youth, and even businesspeople who believe in the country's future—everyone must be there. And then a plan should be built: What will we do? Which path are we going to take? Who is going to lead?

To do this, we have to try to unite the entire people based on our class condition and seek alliances with those who also believe it's necessary to make changes that benefit the entire population and not just a few.

If we are going to take power in the country with a well-organized party involving mindful, honest, and capable people, we'll need to seek alliances and make a continent-wide Anti-Neoliberal Coalition among all the countries suffering from neoliberal aggressions. That's necessary because the whole of bourgeois power has come together in the world with a single objective, a single plan. They control everything: the banks, industry, trade, smuggling, the army, the press—everything is controlled by them. That's how they can subjugate the people.

That's why we also have to build unity among the people, even with those in the United States, where there are so many unemployed people and so many immigrants from other countries. There are a lot of people there who do not agree with what their government is doing. We are not against countries, but against the type of globalization that has been implemented in the world.

If we want to live in freedom in our land, all under the same sky, we have to commit to building unity.

TO CONCLUDE

I would say
that we have to be like great birds . . .
to be able to fly higher and see farther.
Even though
it seems that people have forgotten what
        they were looking for,
their yearnings for justice are still present.
The people remain silent and survive. They see
the "wonders" that come with privatization,
but they know that it only makes the rich richer
and tears apart our nation.
The poor cannot get near those shining attractions
or get anything good out of neoliberalism.
That is why our people
are preparing for another time, which will come.
Not today or immediately. But it will come.
Before I die, what I would like to see
—beyond a shadow of a doubt—is
an anti-neoliberal, anti-imperialist,
        anti-capitalist coalition.
A coalition for a more just society:
With work for the people,
With education and health care for all,
With fair trade among countries,
With respect and solidarity among us

—women and men—children, the youth
    adults, and elders,
Respecting our cultures and languages,
Respecting and caring for the Earth, our Pachamama.
If I could come back from the afterlife . . .
I would continue to fight for Democracy, which
    should always serve the People.
Because my hope for a better world lives on.

—COCHABAMBA, 2002

POSTSCRIPT, 2016
by Moema Viezzer

The last time I saw Domitila was in 2010 when I had the opportunity to participate in the World People's Conference on Climate Change and the Rights of Mother Earth, convened by the Plurinational Government of Bolivia. It took place in Tiquipaya in Cochabamba, following the failure of the 15th United Nations Conference on Climate Change, which had been held months earlier in Copenhagen.

During a break from the conference, I visited Domitila in her home on Derechos Humanos Street in Cochabamba. That's when I was able to give her the Portuguese edition of this expanded version of the book, pass on the royalties to her as usual, and talk with her about these new times.

Among other issues that we discussed in our conversation, she commented in relation to the conference: "I feel sorry that I can't be in that space, which is also my place, along with so many other comrades who are there to defend Mother Earth." Domitila was quite weak; she had just been discharged from the hospital and could barely walk, doing so with support. Speaking about the changes in Bolivia since 2005, she said, after giving some examples of the progress that had been made, "You can't achieve everything at once, but indeed you can already see that quite a difference has been made."

On March 13, 2013, I received several messages in my email with the same news: "Domitila has died." After so much that we had been through together, it was news that could only move me.

So, I searched the print, radio, and television media, which I had access to via the internet, for information about her passing due to lung and kidney cancer, which she had not been able to overcome. She passed away just before turning seventy-five, after having lived a very special life on this earth.

There was widespread recognition of Domitila as a patriotic, democratic, and heroic woman, who belongs in our memory alongside Bartolina Sisa, Juana Azurduy, Gregoria Apaza, and other women who dedicated their lives for the good of Bolivia.

There were several official tributes to her after her death: the government declared three days of official mourning; flags were flown at half-mast at some state offices and departmental and city governments as a sign of mourning; her wake was held in the Cochabamba government's hall of honor, where friends, comrades, and renowned people came to pay their respects. She was buried in the General Cemetery of Cochabamba.

For many years, Domitila and I had shared a dream that we had not been able to realize: the publication of a special edition of the book for Bolivia, aimed at a general readership. With this first expanded edition in Spanish, that dream has come true, and I'm very happy to have helped bring it about.

Comrade Domitila, this new edition of *Let Me Speak!* is yet another proof that, no matter where you are, you continue to bear witness to and nurture the dreams of a society that is based on solidarity and justice for all.

—TOLEDO, BRAZIL
MAY 2016

Notes to "Where Is Domitila?"

1. Luis Arce Gómez, Garcia Meza's Minister of Interior, made this infamous threat. The complete phrase, used not only against Domitila but to threaten all dissidents, was: *"Todos los elementos que contravengan al decreto ley tienen que andar con el testamento bajo el brazo, porque vamos a ser taxativos. No va a haber perdón."* (All those people who break the law have to have their wills in hand, because we are going to be stringent. There will be no pardon.) Translator's note.

2. The Capitalization Plan (*Plan de Capitalización*) was a policy implemented by Gonzalo Sánchez de Losada's government in 1993–96. It promoted privatization with the purported aim of attracting foreign investment. Translator's note.

3. Because of widespread opposition by peoples and leaders of Latin America, the FTAA was never implemented. A turning point occurred at the Summit of the Americas in Mar del Plata in November 2005, when Venezuelan president Hugo Chávez, backed by social movements, unions, and political parties, voiced strong criticism of the treaty and rallied regional leaders to oppose it. Translator's note.

4. Domitila is referring to José Martí's term "Nuestra America," a phrase that refers to the region of Latin America and the Caribbean and carries with it connotations of both unity and self-determination, as well as freedom from US imperialism. Translator's note.

5. A *salteña* is a pastry filled with diced meat, chicken, potatoes, peas, or eggs. Translator's note.

6. Workers stomping on coca leaves is part of preparing the coca paste. Translator's note.

7. In Bolivia's 1980 presidential elections, Juan Lechín ran on the ticket of the Revolutionary Party of the Nationalist Left (PRIN) with the support of the COB. He obtained only 1.2 percent of the vote. Translator's note.

8. Domitila is using colloquial and slang terms for regional and ethnic identities in Bolivia. Translator's note.